COMPUTER
BOOK SERIES
FROM IDG

Access™ 2 For Dummies

W9-BSM-047

Cheat
Sheet

Setting Up a Table

1. Create the database the table goes into.

2. Select the Table tab in the Database window and click on the New button to open the Table Design window.

3. For each field in the table (name, address, and so on), type the field name, pick the data type, adjust the format, and type the description.

4. Open the File menu and select Save.

5. Close the Table Design window.

Planning Your Database

In planning a database, use the following basic principles of database design:

1. A database is a wrapper that goes around tables, forms, reports, and so on.

2. Each table should contain only one kind of data. For example, you should not mix customer data and sales data in the same table.

3. When you need to combine data from different tables, the data must have a common field, such as an account number.

4. Each piece of data should only appear *once* in the database. For example, you shouldn't have one copy of a sales record in a Sales table and another copy in a Customer table. The duplication wastes disk space and can corrupt your data.

5. Do *not* wear a red-and-white polka dot shirt when designing a database. This will not corrupt your data, but it betrays a complete lack of fashion sense.

Access Terms You Need to Know

Database: A wrapper that goes around all the tables, forms, reports, queries, and other things that work together.

Datasheet: A way of displaying table data in a row and column format on the PC's screen.

Data type: The kind of thing a data item is. A data item can be text, a number, a time or date, a memo, and so on.

Dynaset: The answer to a question ("query") you ask Access about your database.

Field: A "slot" in a record that holds an individual data item. Each table is made up of records, and each record is made up of one or more fields.

Form: A way of displaying table data on the PC's screen so that it looks like a paper form, with explanatory text and blanks for each data item.

Fun: What you should be having with Access. If you're not having fun, you're missing the point.

Query: A question you ask about your database. You construct a query in the Access Query window.

Record: All the data items (fields) about a particular thing, such as a person, a sales transaction, or an inventory item. Each record is made up of fields, and each table is made up of records.

Relation: A link between two or more tables that lets you draw information from the tables just as if they were a single table.

Report: A custom-designed printout of your database data. Access lets you create reports in a variety of formats; you can include graphs and calculations if needed.

Table: The basic building block of an Access database. A table is made up of one or more records. Each record has information about an individual thing, such as a person or a sales transaction.

. . .For Dummies: #1 Computer Book Series for Beginners

**COMPUTER
BOOK SERIES
FROM IDG**

Access™ 2 For Dummies®

Cheat Sheet

Basic Survival Skills

Start Access	Double-click on the Access icon in the Windows Program Manager.	Add some data to a table	Open the table or a form that goes with the data. Then type the data in the blanks. Access saves each record as soon as you move to the next record.
Open a database	From the File menu, select Open Database. In the dialog box, double-click on the database name you want.	Undo something	Open the Edit menu and select Undo. You can only undo your *last* entry or operation in Access.
Open a table, form, and so on	At the left side of the Database window, click on one of the tabs: Table, Query, Form, Report Macro, Module. Then double-click on the name of the element you want to open in the Database window.	Get out of a screen window	Double-click on the Control Menu button at the top left corner of the window.
		Quit Access	Press Alt+F4, or select Exit from the File menu.
Create something	To create a new database, open the File menu and select New Database; then type a name in the File Name text box. To create anything else (table, form, and so on), click on the correct tab in the Database window; then click on the New button.	Get an acting job in New York	Work at Zabar's Deli to meet producers; drive a cab; go back to school and finish your B.A. in history; wait tables; get your M.A. in history; drive a cab; get your Ph.D. in history; work at Zabar's; get acting job as a talking potato in off-Broadway show; move back to Cleveland; drive a cab.

Creating Your Database

To create a database, first *plan* the database. Then start Access. Follow these steps:

1. Open the File menu and select "New Database;" alternatively, you can press Alt+N, which is the speed key to create a new database.

2. In the New Database dialog box, select the disk directory into which you want to put the database.

3. Still in the New Database dialog box, enter a name for the database. It must follow the rules for an MS-DOS file name, which means it can't have more than eight letters (though it can also include digits and underscores). Access will automatically add a period and the filename "extension" .MDB, so don't try to add an extension yourself.

4. Still in the New Database dialog box, click on OK.

5. Congratulate yourself on a job well done.

. . .For Dummies: #1 Computer Book Series for Beginners

ACCESS™ 2 FOR DUMMIES®

Hilary D. Shenton
160 Woodland Drive
Portsmouth, RI 02871

by Scott Palmer

Foreword by Frank South
Co-Executive Producer, *Melrose Place*

IDG Books Worldwide, Inc.
An International Data Group Company

Foster City, CA ◆ Chicago, IL ◆ Indianapolis, IN ◆ Braintree, MA ◆ Southlake, TX

Access™ 2 For Dummies®

Published by
IDG Books Worldwide, Inc.
An International Data Group Company
919 E. Hillsdale Blvd.
Suite 400
Foster City, CA 94404

Library of Congress Catalog Card No.: 94-75648

ISBN: 1-56884-090-X

Printed in the United States of America

10 9

1B/SQ/QV/ZW/IN

Distributed in the United States by IDG Books Worldwide, Inc.

Distributed by Macmillan Canada for Canada; by Computer and Technical Books for the Caribbean Basin; by Contemporanea de Ediciones for Venezuela; by Distribuidora Cuspide for Argentina; by CITEC for Brazil; by Ediciones ZETA S.C.R. Ltda. for Peru; by Editorial Limusa SA for Mexico; by Transworld Publishers Limited in the United Kingdom and Europe; by Al-Maiman Publishers & Distributors for Saudi Arabia; by Simron Pty. Ltd. for South Africa; by IDG Communications (HK) Ltd. for Hong Kong; by Toppan Company Ltd. for Japan; by Addison Wesley Publishing Company for Korea; by Longman Singapore Publishers Ltd. for Singapore, Malaysia, Thailand, and Indonesia; by Unalis Corporation for Taiwan; by WS Computer Publishing Company, Inc. for the Philippines; by WoodsLane Pty. Ltd. for Australia; by WoodsLane Enterprises Ltd. for New Zealand.

For general information on IDG Books Worldwide's books in the U.S., please call our Consumer Customer Service department at 800-762-2974. For reseller information, including discounts and premium sales, please call our Reseller Customer Service department at 800-434-3422.

For information on where to purchase IDG Books Worldwide's books outside the U.S., contact IDG Books Worldwide at 415-655-3021 or fax 415-655-3295.

For information on translations, contact Marc Jeffrey Mikulich, Director, Foreign & Subsidiary Rights, at IDG Books Worldwide, 415-655-3018 or fax 415-655-3295.

For sales inquiries and special prices for bulk quantities, write to the address above or call IDG Books Worldwide at 415-655-3200.

For information on using IDG Books Worldwide's books in the classroom, or ordering examination copies, contact the Education Office at 800-434-2086 or fax 817-251-8174.

For authorization to photocopy items for corporate, personal, or educational use, please contact Copyright Clearance Center, 222 Rosewood Drive, Danvers, MA 01923, or fax 508-750-4470.

is a trademark under exclusive license to IDG Books Worldwide, Inc., from International Data Group, Inc.

About the Author

Scott Palmer has more than ten years of experience with database systems, including Access, dBASE, Paradox, XDB, and several others.

In addition to writing, he works as a consultant on database management and computer security. During his free time, he writes popular music and PC game programs.

Welcome to the world of IDG Books Worldwide.

IDG Books Worldwide, Inc., is a subsidiary of International Data Group, the world's largest publisher of computer-related information and the leading global provider of information services on information technology. IDG was founded more than 25 years ago and now employs more than 7,700 people worldwide. IDG publishes more than 250 computer publications in 67 countries (see listing below). More than 70 million people read one or more IDG publications each month.

Launched in 1990, IDG Books Worldwide is today the #1 publisher of best-selling computer books in the United States. We are proud to have received 8 awards from the Computer Press Association in recognition of editorial excellence and three from Computer Currents' First Annual Readers' Choice Awards, and our best-selling ...*For Dummies*® series has more than 19 million copies in print with translations in 28 languages. IDG Books Worldwide, through a joint venture with IDG's Hi-Tech Beijing, became the first U.S. publisher to publish a computer book in the People's Republic of China. In record time, IDG Books Worldwide has become the first choice for millions of readers around the world who want to learn how to better manage their businesses.

Our mission is simple: Every one of our books is designed to bring extra value and skill-building instructions to the reader. Our books are written by experts who understand and care about our readers. The knowledge base of our editorial staff comes from years of experience in publishing, education, and journalism — experience which we use to produce books for the '90s. In short, we care about books, so we attract the best people. We devote special attention to details such as audience, interior design, use of icons, and illustrations. And because we use an efficient process of authoring, editing, and desktop publishing our books electronically, we can spend more time ensuring superior content and spend less time on the technicalities of making books.

You can count on our commitment to deliver high-quality books at competitive prices on topics you want to read about. At IDG Books Worldwide, we continue in the IDG tradition of delivering quality for more than 25 years. You'll find no better book on a subject than one from IDG Books Worldwide.

John J. Kilcullen

John Kilcullen
President and CEO
IDG Books Worldwide, Inc.

Dedication

Dedicated to My,

who makes everything seem possible.

Acknowledgments

Though my name is on the cover, this book was not a solo effort. Several other people helped make it the best book for beginning users of Access.

Most involved on a day-to-day basis was Laurie Smith, my editor at IDG Books, who guided the project at every step with encouragement, constructive criticisms, and an endless supply of good ideas.

The book's technical editor, Beth Slick, was also a joy to work with and made many helpful suggestions. Julie King, the book's main copy editor, actually *improved* on my writing, something which no author ever likes to admit. Shawn MacLaren, Tim Gallan, and Andy Cummings were also invaluable in adding their expertise and helping us to meet our deadline. Also, thanks to the fine souls in IDG's production department.

Janna Custer, acquisitions editor at IDG, took a chance on an untried author and, I hope, is as happy with the result as I am for the privilege of working with her. David Solomon, publisher at IDG, and John Kilcullen, IDG's president, also helped to launch the project, and I owe them both my sincere thanks.

Frank South, co-executive producer of the hit TV series "Melrose Place," took time from his busy schedule to write the foreword. What can I say except that he's a heck of a guy and it's a heck of a show? (Monday nights on Fox, for all you "MP virgins.")

My agent, Connie Clausen of Connie Clausen Associates in New York, handled the business end of the project and continues to give me good advice on just about everything.

My family put up with me all the way, and continues to give me good advice (some of which I even take!) on just about everything.

Publisher's Acknowledgments

We're proud of this book; please send us your comments about it by using the Reader Response Card at the back of the book or by e-mailing us at feedback/dummies@idgbooks.com. Some of the people who helped bring this book to market include the following:

Acquisitions, Development, & Editorial

Project Editor: Laurie Ann Smith

Acquisitions Editor: Tammy Goldfeld

Product Development Manager: Mary Bednarek

Permissions Editor: Joyce Pepple

Copy Editors: Julie King, Shawn MacLaren, Andy Cummings, A. Timothy Gallan, Diane L.Giangrossi

Technical Reviewer: Beth Slick

Editorial Managers: Kristin A. Cocks, Mary Corder

Editorial Assistants: Constance Carlisle, Chris Collins, Kevin Spencer

Production

Project Coordinator: Cindy L. Phipps

Layout and Graphics: Valery Bourke, Mary Breidenbach, J. Tyler Connor, Dominique DeFelice, Cheryl Denski, Sherry Gomoll, Todd Klemme, Jill Lyttle, Drew R. Moore, Gina Scott, Carla Radzikinas

Proofreaders: Kathleen Prata, Melissa D. Buddendeck, Dwight Ramsey, Robert Springer

Indexer: Sharon Hilgenberg

General & Administrative

IDG Books Worldwide, Inc.: John Kilcullen, President & CEO; Steven Berkowitz, COO & Publisher

Dummies, Inc.: Milissa Koloski, Executive Vice President & Publisher

Dummies Technology Press & Dummies Editorial: Diane Graves Steele, Associate Publisher; Judith A. Taylor, Brand Manager; Myra Immell, Editorial Director

Dummies Trade Press: Kathleen A. Welton, Vice President & Publisher; Stacy S. Collins, Brand Manager

IDG Books Production for Dummies Press: Beth Jenkins, Production Director; Cindy L. Phipps, Supervisor of Project Coordination; Kathie S. Schnorr, Supervisor of Page Layout; Shelley Lea, Supervisor of Graphics and Design

Dummies Packaging & Book Design: Erin McDermitt, Packaging Coordinator; Kavish+Kavish, Cover Design

◆

The publisher would like to give special thanks to Patrick J. McGovern, without whom this book would not have been possible.

◆

Contents at a Glance

Cartoons at a Glance
By Rich Tennant

page 7

page 277

page 122

page 253

page 85

page 54

page 163

page 205

page xxiv

page 234

Table of Contents

Foreword

● ●

*O*kay, I had no idea what a database was. As a TV writer and producer, I use my computer mostly for word processing, and almost exclusively for scripts, at that. Occasionally, I play a game or two or log on to a bulletin board, but that's about it. But, when I ran into Scott in CyberSpace, he convinced me to read about Access 2.0.

So, I read. Now I'm cursed. Scott has made it so easy to understand this new software that I'm up nights figuring out ways to create databases for scheduling writers and directors; scheduling home finance payments, dog exercise, fish feeding times, and gutter cleaning; and keeping track of martini recipes.

I recommend his book highly, but I hold him responsible for turning me into the most overly organized and sleepless writer in town.

Frank South
Co-Executive Producer *Melrose Place*
Los Angeles, California

The 5th Wave

By Rich Tennant

"I DON'T GET IT. WE'VE MADE IT SMALLER, FASTER, AND LESS EXPENSIVE, AND IT STILL DOESN'T SELL! JEEZ BOBBY, DON'T LEAN ON THE MOUSE LIKE THAT."

Introduction

● ●

D*o you just *love* computers? When you wake up in the morning, is your first thought about how to frimmitz the programming subroutine to the relational zignab so you can print out reports that nobody but *you* will understand?

If so, then you've got the wrong book.

This book is for people who *have a life* outside of sitting at the computer and want to get their work done as easily, enjoyably, and *quickly* as possible. If you need the answer to a specific question, want to find out how to do something, and *don't* want to waste a lot of time with computer mumbo-jumbo, then this is the book for you.

About This Book

You can read this book in two ways. If you want, you can read it from front to back, just like a novel. With the cover-to-cover method, you'll find that each chapter gives you new Access skills that you can immediately put to use. Unfortunately, this book has much less sex and violence than a novel — but it *does* have lots of nice pictures and cartoons.

If you prefer, you can just dip into this book whenever you need help on a particular topic. Though each chapter builds on the ideas that came before it, the chapters are also self-contained. You can pick and choose what you want to read about. Each chapter begins with a summary of what you need to know to get the most out of the chapter. If you want to pursue things in more depth, you'll find plenty of cross-references to other parts of the book. For example, by going to a particular chapter, in a few minutes you can find out how to:

- Design a database in Access
- Create and print simple reports that are ready in a matter of seconds
- Find any data you need, no matter how big your database
- Create dazzling graphs and bar charts to put in printed reports
- Create and print form letters and mailing labels
- Frimmitz the programming subroutine to the relational zignab — no, wait, that's *one* thing you *won't* find in this book!

How to Use This Book

Using a database package like Access requires both *knowledge* and *skill*. Knowledge, you can get by reading; skill, you can only get by *doing*. You can use this book to meet both those requirements.

To meet the challenges of knowledge and skill, each chapter gives you both *instruction* and *hands-on steps*. The instructional parts cover basic ideas that you need to understand, as well as the basic moves involved in database tasks. You can read these parts on the subway, while doing your laundry, or (depending on your job) while sitting in a getaway car outside the bank.

The hands-on steps assume that you're sitting at your PC and working with Access. These steps show you the specific things you do to set up databases, print reports, and so on. The best part of these steps is that you can use the same steps either with the example database in the book or with your own "real life" database.

If you're already stuck with a problem in Access, you can jump directly to the chapter you need. Just check out the Table of Contents or the Index or use the list of things at the beginning of each chapter to find out what's in that chapter. If you don't need help on a specific problem, you can just browse through the book and read whatever interests you. Or check out the cartoons.

What You're Like (According to Your Mother)

This book assumes that you're a *regular person*. That has nothing to do with a daily serving of bran flakes. It means that you're not a computer expert and, frankly, don't want to be *bothered* with a lot of technical hocus-pocus. You want the facts, plus a little encouragement, and maybe a stupid joke now and then. No 25-syllable words. Just useful information and skills.

It also assumes that you have Microsoft Access on your PC. Though the book is geared for use with Version 2.0 of Access, you can use it with Versions 1.0 or 1.1 as well. Here and there, you'll find notes about parts of the program that are different between Version 1.0/1.1 and Version 2.0.

How This Book Is Organized

This book has five main parts. Each part focuses on giving you specific knowledge and skills. Within each part, the chapters are deliberately kept short so that they're easy to finish without a big time commitment on your part. And inside each chapter, the sections are clearly marked so you can pick and choose the parts you want to read.

Here's the big picture of what's in each part:

Part I: All the DataBasics You Have To Know

If you just want to *get to it* in as short a time as possible, this is the place to go. This part gives you all the basic knowledge and skills you need to get started with Access *right now*. You find out how to plan a database, put information in the database, look at the information when you need it, and get help when you're confused.

Part II: Finding and Playing With Your Data

Although Part I shows you how to view your data, this part shows you several more powerful ways to view and find your data, even if your database is really huge. You find out how to create on-screen forms that catch errors and explain what's in your database, how to do simple searches for information, and how to use logical operators for *really powerful searches*. It's not necessary for you to work out at a gym before doing *really powerful searches,* but it helps.

Part III: Organizing and Printing Your Data

Your data gets even easier to find if you know how to organize it the way you want. This part shows you how to sort the information in your database so that it's in alphabetical or numerical order — for example, by last name, account number, or date. You also find out how to design and print simple reports about your data. Finally, you find out how to divide up your database so that it's totally and completely (timid souls might even say *frighteningly)* efficient.

Part IV: Really Advanced Stuff to Impress Your Friends

This part shows you how to do things that other people only dream about. You find out how to create reports that group your data and do calculations, design and print form letters and mailing labels, and create dazzling 2-D and 3-D graphs to include in your reports.

Part V: The Part of Tens

This part tells you things that you probably never wanted to know, but should. If you really get in trouble on your PC — whether it's with Access or not — this part offers tips on how to fix whatever's gone wrong. It also has secret tricks you can use with Access and explains database words that only a computer nerd could love.

Part VI: Appendixes

This final part covers database data for this book and how to install Access.

Icons Used in This Book

This icon says that something is technical. Not that you absolutely don't *want* to know this stuff — some of it is pretty interesting, in a "nerds go berserk" sort of way — but you don't really *need* to know it to work with Access.

This icon marks a useful tip, inside information, or a shortcut that helps you work with Access more easily.

This icon marks something you should remember, not only because you'll find it useful, but because there'll be a quiz next period.

This icon marks things that can get you into trouble if you aren't careful. Even Access, easy and friendly as it is, has a few time bombs hidden here and there. If you pay attention to the Warnings, you shouldn't have any trouble.

This icon marks interesting background information. You don't strictly need to know it, but it helps you understand Access better.

This icon marks information in other chapters that can help you understand the current chapter.

Where to Go From Here

At this point, you've spent enough time reading the Introduction. It's time to get to it! If you have a specific problem to solve, go ahead and jump to that chapter of the book. If not, start in Part I and learn the basics: just enough to be dangerous. Then get ready to have some fun with Access!

Part I
All the DataBasics You Have to Know

"I STARTED DESIGNING DATABASE SOFTWARE SYSTEMS AFTER SEEING HOW EASY IT WAS TO DESIGN OFFICE FURNITURE."

In this part ...

1 n the early years of database management, people were ignorant. So ignorant, in fact, that many so-called "experts" mistakenly bought automobile repair shops on the theory that they'd be able to use the same tools for both transmissions and databases. A tool is a tool, right?

This part shows you how to use the most basic tools for managing information with Access. It shows you how to plan a database, set up a table, and put in the data. It shows you how to look at your data and, if you need help, how to get on-screen help in Access.

Sadly, this part does *not* show you how to manage an auto repair shop or fix a transmission. Even the embarrassed database experts from the early days don't know stuff like that.

Chapter 1

Database 101 — What the Heck *Is* Access, Anyway?

* * *

In This Chapter

▶ What is Access?

▶ Getting the data you need

▶ Starting Access

▶ Getting Help

▶ Quitting Access

* * *

This chapter gives you an overview of what Access is and how it can make your life easier. *And relax* — we're not going to talk about a lot of abstruse technical stuff that only someone with a pocket protector and a Ph.D. can understand. This chapter explains *just what you need to know* to start Access and have some idea of what you're doing. You find out about specific skills (creating a database, printing a report, monster truck driving) in later chapters. Here, you're just getting your feet wet.

What Is Access?

What is Access, anyway? The answer is simple: It's a database management system. If you don't know what *that* is, don't worry. You've used database management systems all your life. You just haven't *called* them that.

Let's begin with what Access is supposed to manage: data. Data is a bunch of disconnected, disorganized information — just like the receipts you shove into your desk drawer or the contents of the latest trashy novel. And if you've ever tried to find a receipt in that desk drawer — or the "good parts" of a trashy novel — you know that data by itself often doesn't do you much good. After all, how does it help you to have a receipt for that life-saving operation you bought your mother if you can't find it at tax time? We all love our mothers, but let's be serious: A deduction is a deduction.

To make data useful, you need a way to *manage* it — a database management system. You need to organize all the scattered receipts (data) into an orderly form so that you can find what you need when you need it. An organized collection of data is called a *database*.

For your receipts, your database management system might be a set of file folders with a label on each one: "Car expenses," "House payments," "Medical expenses," and so on. Instead of shoving all your receipts into a drawer, you put each receipt into the appropriate file folder. When you need to find a receipt, you no longer have to muddle through a drawer full of wadded-up paper. You just go to the right file folder, look inside, and presto! There's the receipt you wanted. This database is illustrated in Figure 1-1.

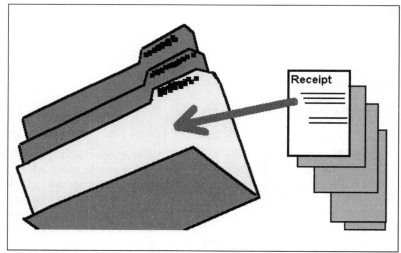

Figure 1-1:
Organizing
receipts
with a
simple
database
management
system.

You can see now that there's nothing at all mysterious about the idea of a database. A database is simply an organized collection of data, and a database management system is what organizes it for you. Some databases are computerized and some aren't.

Ready, set . . . computerize!

If you bought this book, of course, it's a safe bet that you're interested in computerized database management. The big advantage of computerized databases is that all the data is at your fingertips, so you don't need to get up out of your chair (groan!) and make that long trek to the filing cabinet (huff, puff). (Did you ever think of getting more exercise?) And computerized databases offer other advantages as well:

- A computerized database is *fast*. Even if you only have a few hundred file folders, it can take a lot of time to find the file you want. With Access, you can go right to the data you need in a matter of seconds.

- A computerized database is *flexible*. If you need to present your data in a variety of ways, Access does most of the work for you. Need a row-and-column report? Done. Need a summary of sales totals, grouped by region? Done. Need mailing labels? Done. Need 3-D bar and pie graphs? Done. (Hint: Tell the boss you stayed up all night to draw the graphs by hand!)

- A computerized database is *powerful*. Even a jumbo, heavy-duty file folder can't hold a million employee or sales records. But Access can hold as many records as you need — one, a hundred, a million — all on your PC's hard disk.

- A computerized database is *deductible*. Yes, if you use it in your business, Access is fully tax-deductible, so you can use it to offset all those profits you made from offshore oil drilling.

Access gives you a fast, flexible, powerful, deductible, and easy way to make sense out of any data you throw at it.

Create a database to organize your data

One drawback of computerized databases is that they've often been hard to work with — until now. With Access, you don't need to remember a lot of commands. You don't need to be a database expert. You don't even need to be good-looking, though of course, you are. All you need to do is open menus, click on buttons, and follow the instructions that appear on the screen.

When you create the basic building block of a database — in Access, it's called a *table* — the first thing you need to decide is what data should go into it. A customer table, for example, may have each customer's account number, first and last names, address, city, state, zip code, and telephone number. Each of these items goes into its own separate column in the table, as shown in Figure 1-2. Access guides you as you create each column. (I take you step-by-step through the whole process in the next chapter.)

Don't worry about the word "relational"

Sooner or later, you'll hear someone refer to Access as a *relational database management system*. People get into lots of arguments about what that term really means. For practical purposes, it means that you can divide your computerized data into different "file folders" for efficiency but easily combine the data from different file folders when you need to get data from your database. Beyond that, it's just a bunch of pointy-headed computer scientists jabbering at each other. Don't worry about it.

Figure 1-2:
A row-and-
column
table of
customer
data.

Microsoft Access - [Table: Customer Records]						
File **Edit** **View** **Format** **Records** **Window** **Help**						
Cust ID	First Name	Last Name	MrMs	Salutation	Address	C
1	James	WEST	Prof.	Jimbo	Mythic University	Martinsv
2	Harriett	STOWE	Ms.	Ms. Stowe	14 Parakeet Lane	New Yor
3	Jules	TWOMBLY	Mr.	Jules	The ABC Hotel	Las Veg
4	Arnold	HARRIS	Mr.	Arnie	101 Fifth Avenue	Boise
5	Teri	LANE	Ms.	Ms. Lane	5678 15th Street, #	Santa Ba

Smile when you data entry, pardner! Data entry is when you sit down at the PC's keyboard and start putting information into a database. When you do that, Access helps save you from unnecessary typing and also prevents some common kinds of mistakes.

If you have a bunch of records that repeat some of the same data — such as records on people who work for the same company at the same address — you can tell Access to fill in the repeated data for you. You don't have to enter it over and over again. If you're worried about accidentally putting in the *wrong* data — say, a salary of $100,000 for your most junior clerical employee — you can tell Access to refuse any data that looks suspicious. And if someone else is entering the data for you, Access can help prevent mix-ups by displaying an on-screen explanation of what each data item is supposed to be.

Getting the Data You Need

Of course, putting your data into a database is only the beginning. You also have to get the data *out* of the database when you need it. Access not only lets you see multiple records in a row-and-column screen, as in Figure 1-2, but also lets you see one record at a time, as in Figure 1-3.

Tooling around the Access toolbar: On the third line down from the top of your screen is the Access *toolbar*. You can click on the buttons on the toolbar with your mouse to bypass the menus and perform a specific database task quickly and with minimum hassle.

Access displays different toolbar buttons depending on what type of work you're doing at the moment. On the toolbar in Figure 1-3, the second and third buttons from the left let you switch between different ways of looking at your data.

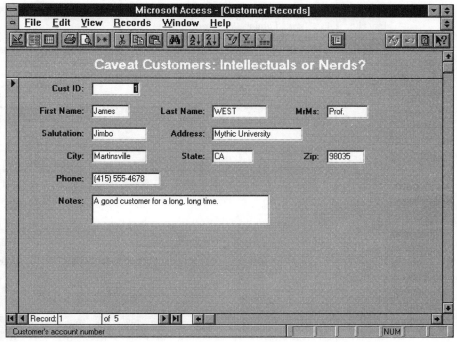

Figure 1-3:
Access lets you see all the details of a single record on the screen.

Print reports about your data

Access does more than just display your data on-screen. You can print out reports in any format you choose: row and column, one record on a page, summaries only, totals and graphs — you name it. If you're ambitious, you can lay out the report yourself. If you're in a hurry, you can let the Access Report Wizard do most of the work for you. Figure 1-4 shows a sample of Access's snazzy report capabilities.

Annoy people with form letters and mailing labels

In addition to using your data in reports, you also can use it to create form letters ("Dear Mr. McMahon: *You may already be a winner . . . !*") and mailing labels. One thing Access can *not* do is write the letters and stamp the envelopes for you. But there's always next year. . . . Figure 1-5 illustrates a form letter and some mailing labels created in Access.

Figure 1-4:
A snazzy
Access
report
(boring
Access
reports sold
separately).

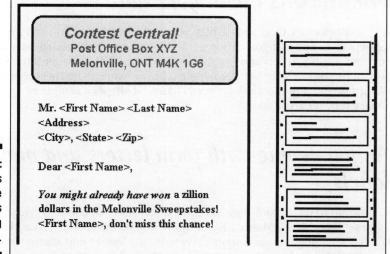

Figure 1-5:
Access lets
you create
form letters
and mailing
labels.

Exchange data with other programs

If you work in an office in which different people use different programs, Access makes it easy to exchange data with your coworkers. Whether they're using Lotus 1-2-3, dBASE, Paradox, FoxPro, or even a simple word processor, Access can import data from and export data to their programs, as shown in Figure 1-6.

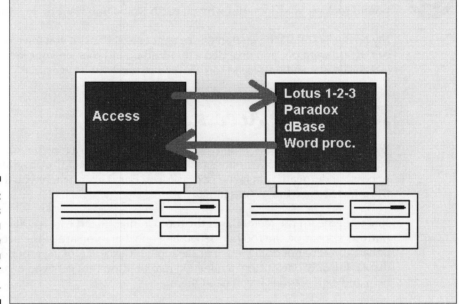

Figure 1-6:
Access lets you exchange data with other programs.

Starting Access

Starting Access is easy — *if* the program is installed on your PC. If it's not installed, follow the instructions in Appendix B to put Access on your hard disk. Don't just copy the Access disks to your hard disk, because the program won't work if you do.

Before you can start Access, of course, you have to *find* it. When you installed Access on your PC, you automatically created an Access "group" in your Windows Program Manager. Open the window for the Access group and double-click on the Access program icon: it has a picture of a key and says "Microsoft Access."

Go ahead and do it now; the next few sections of this chapter take you on a brief tour of the program, and it will be more meaningful if you actually see what happens on-screen when you perform the steps I describe. (If you need help with Windows, a good way to learn is to read IDG Books' *Windows 3.11 For Dummies,* 3rd Edition.)

If you don't use a mouse . . . you're crazy! This book assumes that you're using a mouse or at least some kind of pointing device, such as a trackball. Yes, you can use Windows without a mouse. If you *want* to, you can also drop a hundred-pound rock on your foot. But why on earth would you want to do either?

My advice is simple: If you don't have a mouse, get one. If you have one, use it. And if you went out and dropped a hundred-pound rock on your foot, don't watch "Beavis and Butt-Head" on TV. You're *much* too suggestible.

Reading the Access screen

When Access first starts, you'll see an opening screen. Across the top line of the screen, as always with Windows programs, is the name of the program — Access. Underneath that is the Access Menu Bar. This is where you'll click with the mouse to use the Access menus.

Just underneath the Menu Bar is the toolbar, mentioned earlier. Different buttons appear on the toolbar depending on where you are in the program. Because you're not doing much at the moment except looking around, Access is displaying only one button: a question-mark button that gets you on-screen help and explanations if you need them.

At the bottom of the screen is the status line, which displays helpful information while you're working with Access. It tells you what different menu choices mean, what your next step should be, and so on. Access might also display a "Welcome" box in the middle of the screen. If so, just look around in the Welcome box until you find a button marked "Close." Then click on the button.

Opening a menu

Now that you've started up Access and learned a little bit about the Access screen, I want you to do a few simple things in Access before we wrap up this chapter. For almost everything you will do with Access, you will start by using the File menu to open a database. Try that now. Click on the word *File* in the Menu Bar. The File menu should appear, as shown in Figure 1-7.

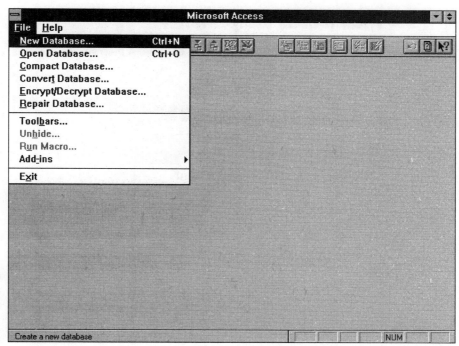

Figure 1-7:
Opening the
File menu.

As you can see, Access gives you menu choices to create new databases, open existing databases, and do other things that you'll learn about as you read later chapters. You'll use the File menu to create a new database in the next chapter; for now, just close the menu by clicking again on File in the Menu Bar.

Getting Help (Not Including Psychiatric Help)

Access is simple to use, but any time you *do* have a problem, you can get help easily. The help system is similar to ones you find in other Windows applications. You can use it to search based on topics or to get help on a specific topic while you're in the middle of something.

The Access Help menu

Click on the Help menu and select Contents. A help screen appears, as shown in Figure 1-8.

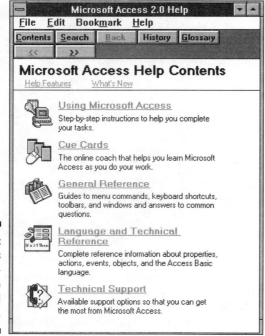

Figure 1-8:
Access provides on-screen help and explanations.

Another easy way to get help is simply to press the F1 function key on your PC's keyboard. This calls up a *context sensitive* help screen: Access will display different information depending on what you're doing at the moment.

Use the buttons at the top of the Help window to find your way around. If you click on Search, you can get help on a specific problem by typing in a name for what you're doing, such as "report." Clicking on the Back button takes you back to the help screen before the current one. And if you're in another help screen, you can return to the Contents screen by clicking on the Contents button.

Cue Cards aren't just for TV stars

There's one other important feature of the Help window: Cue Cards. If you move the mouse pointer over the words "Cue Cards," you'll see the pointer turn into a pointing hand. That means you can activate Cue Cards by clicking the mouse.

Access gives you two kinds of help — Cue Cards and Wizards:

✔ *Cue Cards* are special help screens that guide you step by step through database tasks such as creating form letters and setting up a database. When you need detailed instructions but don't have this book handy, you can let Access coach you by displaying a Cue Card for each step. To use them, you just click on the words "Cue Cards" in the Help window. Access takes you from there. If you're not in a Help window, click on the Cue Cards button in the Tool Bar. That's the second button from the right end of the Tool Bar.

✔ *Wizards* also guide you step by step, but they go beyond Cue Cards in that they do most of the work *for* you. The Help window doesn't say anything about wizards, but any time you start to create something, Access perks up and asks if you want a wizard to do it for you.

Get out of the Access Help window by holding down the Alt key and pressing the F4 function key. Or, if you prefer, just double-click on the Window Control button at the top left corner of the window.

Quitting Access

You've done enough for now, so go ahead and quit Access. Quitting is as easy as starting up. You can do it in three ways:

✔ With the Access window displayed, hold down the Alt key and press the F4 function key.

✔ Double-click on the Window Control button at the top left corner of the Access window.

✔ Click once on the Window Control button to open the Control menu. Then click on Close.

That's it for this chapter! You've discovered the basic ideas of a database management system, as well as the main parts of Access. Congratulate yourself and take a break. Have a cappuccino. Learn a foreign language. Buy a cat. Then, when you're nice and rested, go on to Chapter 2, where you find out how to design and create a database without getting cat hair on your PC.

Chapter 2

Setting Up a Database —
Rule #1 Is Think Ahead!

● ●

In This Chapter

▶ Parts of an Access database

▶ What are data types?

▶ How to plan your database

▶ Creating your first database

● ●

Many things in life don't require you to think ahead. Surprise parties, for example. Bad movies. Unexpected visits from your in-laws. Turning 30. Turning 40. All you need to do is keep breathing, and these things happen automatically.

But when it comes to setting up a database, thinking ahead is an absolute requirement. If you don't do it, you'll end up with a jumbled mess of data that isn't any good to anyone except the computer consultant you hire to fix it for you at a rate of $100 an hour. Plus tips.

This chapter shows you how to think ahead and plan your database — from analyzing your needs (the first step) to setting up the Access database you'll use. You also find out about the basic components of a database and what you can do with each.

The Parts of an Access Database

Most PC database managers create separate disk files for each different thing in the database. For example, if you want to keep customer data, that's one file; if you want to sort the data by each customer's last name, that's another file; and if you want to link the customer data to sales records, that's another file. And so on. About the only thing you can say for this approach is that it keeps you busy trying to remember all the files on your database.

The information on your PC's hard disk is divided into *disk files,* which are like paper file folders in a filing cabinet. Every disk file has a name. The name begins with up to eight letters or digits, followed by a period and an extension of up to three letters or digits. Every disk file is kept in a disk *directory,* which is like one of the drawers in a filing cabinet. Each directory also has a name. If you're not sure that you understand disk files and directories, check out IDG Books' *DOS For Dummies,* 2nd Edition, which explains all that stuff.

Access gives you an easier way to manage your database. In Access, a database is a single big thing that keeps all of your little things together for you. With a click of the mouse, you can see a list of all your database tables, reports, and so on, as shown in Figure 2-1. The database itself is just kind of a "wrapper" that holds them all together.

Before you do anything on the computer, think about what kinds of data you need to manage. Then you can decide how to divide it among the different database tools that Access provides — tables, forms, reports, and so on.

To make those decisions, of course, you need to know what data management tools Access gives you and what each tool does. You use each tool to design a particular part of your database.

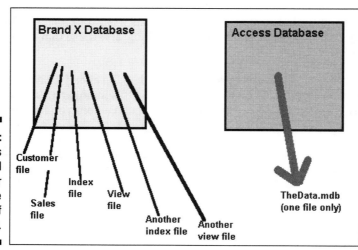

Figure 2-1: Access keeps all your database stuff together.

Use Tables to Hold Your Data

Inside the database "wrapper," the starting point of an Access database is called a *table*. A table holds all the data records of a particular type. A table may hold all your customer records, for example, all your inventory records, or all your sales records. A table shouldn't hold more than one type of records. If you try to keep all your customer and sales data in a single table, you can plan on spending at least two or three fun weekends trying to figure out what's wrong with your database. Then, it's time to visit the bank machine and get that $100 an hour for the guy in the pin-striped suit.

All records in a table should hold basically the same type and amount of data. If some records need to hold a lot more data than others, you need to redesign your database.

Each record in a table contains all the information about a single thing. A customer record, for example, may hold a customer's account number, name, address, phone number, and date of first purchase. A sales record may hold the account number of the customer who bought the item (more on that later!) and the item's inventory number, description, and price.

The first step in designing an Access database is deciding which tables you should have. You shouldn't — and don't need to — put all your data in one table, because Access lets you put put different kinds of data in separate tables. Any time you need to combine data from separate tables, you can do so easily. You don't need to cram all your customer, sales, and inventory data into a single table.

Rows and Columns and Bears (Oh, My!)

The easiest way to think of table data is, well, as a table. Figure 2-2 shows a row-and-column table of data in Access. There are no bears. I was only kidding about the bears. Honest.

Notice how the table is set up. When a table is displayed in this way, Access calls it a *Datasheet View*.

The names of the columns appear at the top of the table. Columns, in database jargon, are called *fields*. Each field holds a single piece of information.

Cust ID	First Name	Last Name	MrMs	Salutation	Address	City
1	James	WEST	Prof.	Jimbo	Mythic University	Martinsville
2	Harriett	STOWE	Ms.	Ms. Stowe	14 Parakeet Lane	New York
3	Jules	TWOMBLY	Mr.	Jules	The ABC Hotel	Las Vegas
4	Arnold	HARRIS	Mr.	Arnie	101 Fifth Avenue	Boise
5	Teri	LANE	Ms.	Ms. Lane	5678 15th Street, #5-A	Santa Barbara

Figure 2-2: How Access stores data in a row-and-column table.

The rows are called *records.* Every record has the same fields, and the fields are the same size in each record. Thus, a First Name field that is 15 letters long in one record won't be 35 letters long in another.

The flip side of a table is a *form,* which you learn about in a minute. In the meantime, bear with me. (No, that's *not* a bear with me. There are no bears. Just be patient.)

Use queries to find your data

After you put data into a database, you sometimes need to search for specific pieces of data. Suppose that you're manning the phones one Sunday night (you *do* work on Sunday nights, don't you?), and a customer calls to make sure that you sent an order to the right address.

You can handle the situation in three ways. The first, and easiest, is to put the customer on hold until he or she hangs up in disgust. If you ever called a business on Sunday night, you know how popular this method has become.

Data types for different types

One thing you can't see in Figure 2-2 is that columns in an Access table often contain different *data types.* Just as it's more efficient for people to divide the world into solid objects, liquids, gases, and cream pies, database managers divide up *data* into different data types. Data types help Access zip through your data more quickly and accurately to get the information you need. Typically, database managers have data types for text, number, date, and yes/no fields. Access also has types for currency (dollars), free-form memos, and other things. You learn how to use data types in Chapter 3.

The second method is to scan down the customer data table, row by row, until you get to the customer record you want. If you have more than a few dozen records in your table, this option, too, will cause customers to hang up in disgust unless their lives are really boring.

The best choice, however, is to use a simple query to find the record you need. A *query* is a question that you ask Access, such as, "What records have the zip code 90210?" or "How many customers bought books on bungee-jumping?" or "Wouldn't you really rather be a toaster?"

When you create a query, you tell Access which field you want to look at — say, "Last Name" — and what you want to search for — say, the name "Wilds." Then, as in Figure 2-3, you just click on a button with the mouse, and Access immediately shows you the record you need. (Unfortunately, the caller's name was "West," so he hung up, anyway.)

Use forms to enter your data

Forms are another important Access tool. When you fill out a paper form, you write the data in blanks on a page. When you fill out an Access form, you type the data in blanks on the screen, as shown in Figure 2-4.

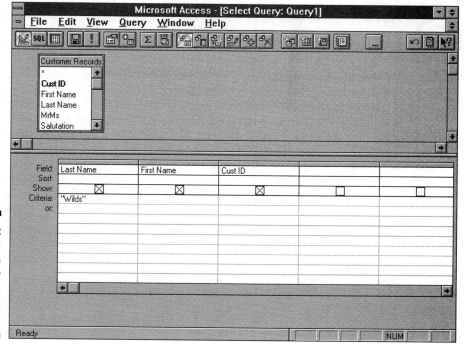

Figure 2-3:
Using a query to search for the wrong name in the database.

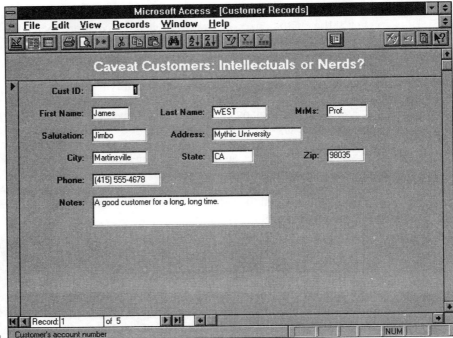

Figure 2-4:
Filling in the
blanks of an
on-screen
form.

When you enter data into your own database, it's easy to remember what data should go where. But if other people will be entering data for you, forms can be a big help.

When designing a form, always assume that it will be used by someone who knows nothing about your data and your database. In Access, you can include statements in your form that explain what type of data is supposed to go into a particular blank; be sure to take advantage of this feature. That way, if a data-entry person doesn't know, for example, what kind of data to put into the "MrMs" blank, help is available right on the form.

Access forms offer a great deal of other terrific features that make data entry easier and more accurate. You can put radio buttons and check boxes on a form, for example. You find out how to use many of these features in this book.

Use reports to print your data

You can create reports in a variety of formats in Access. You can create complete reports that include all the data in your database; summary reports that give you totals and calculations; or specialized reports that contain only one or two fields.

As far as layout goes, you can create a row-and-column report, a one-record-at-a-time report, form letters, or mailing labels. Figure 2-5 shows an example of a one-record-at-a-time report.

Planning Your Database

Now that you know what tools Access has to offer, it's time to plan your database. You need to ask yourself two main questions:

✔ What data do you need to manage?

✔ What do you need to do with the data?

Let's look at an example. The database we're going to create in this book is for a fictitious used-book store called *Caveat Emptor,* which is Latin for "Let the buyer beware." The proprietor of this bookstore is a fellow who refers to himself, suspiciously enough, as "Honest Janis."

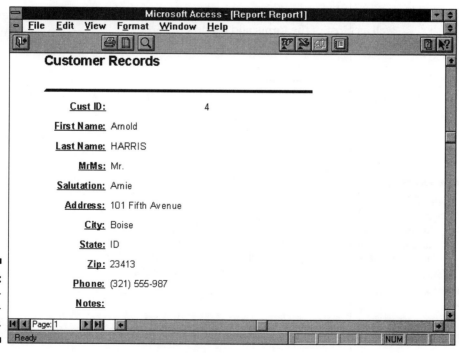

Figure 2-5: A one-record-at-a-time report.

Caveat Emptor has a large number of regular customers, many of whom have accounts at the store. In addition, the store has a vast inventory of used and rare books — including, of course, several copies of the book you're now reading. That adds up to three main groups of data:

- Customer names, addresses, and phone numbers
- Current books in stock
- Sales transactions

In Access, each of these groups of data will get its own table. Whenever necessary, you can combine the data from different tables to create consolidated forms or reports.

Janis needs to do several things with the data in his database, as shown in Figure 2-6. First, he needs to be able to locate the data for an individual customer by searching for the customer's account number or last name. Second, he needs to print form letters and mailing labels to keep customers up to date on the latest used-book acquisitions. Third, he needs to have Access update the inventory database and print reports.

These requirements dictate how Janis sets up each table in the database, as well as most of the forms and reports.

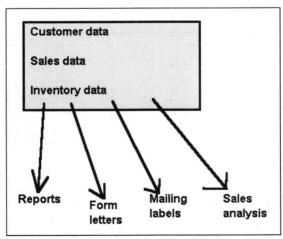

Figure 2-6:
Requirements
for the
Caveat
Emptor
database.

Creating Your First Database

Now that you know what data you need to manage and what you want to do with it, let's get to the main event of this chapter: creating an Access database. After all that buildup, the actual process of creating the database may be something of an anticlimax because it's very easy.

If you aren't already running Access, start it up by double-clicking on the Access icon in the Windows Program Manager. Access should have its own program "group," and that's where you'll find the icon.

When the Access opening screen appears, click on File at the top left of the screen and select New Database from the menu. The New Database dialog box appears, as shown in Figure 2-7.

A dialog box provides an easy way for you to communicate with Access. Rectangular buttons that are labeled with words like "OK" are called *push buttons.* They tell Access to do something. When the dialog box has a blank, Access often fills in the blank for you with a "dummy" name such as *db1.mdb.* You can change the information in the blank to whatever you want as long as it's a valid disk file name.

If you need more help understanding dialog boxes, check out *Windows 3.11 For Dummies,* 3rd Edition, by Andy Rathbone.

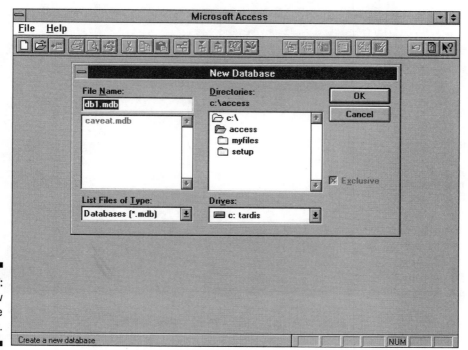

Figure 2-7:
The New
Database
dialog box.

At the top left of the dialog box, you can see that the File Name blank is highlighted. The highlight means that if you just start typing, you can enter the name you prefer into the blank. Any time you see the highlight in a dialog box, you know that Access will send whatever information you enter to the highlighted location.

Because the name of the store is Caveat Emptor, type **Caveat** into the File Name blank. Then use the mouse to click once on the OK button at the top right. Access creates the new database for you, as shown in Figure 2-8.

Notice that along the left edge of the Caveat database window, Access displays push buttons for each of the tools discussed earlier in this chapter: tables, queries, forms, and reports. You learn how to use each of these database tools in chapters to come.

For now, that's it! Access automatically saved your database to your PC's hard disk, so shut down Access and take a break. Whenever you set up a database, remember to analyze the data you need to manage, figure out what you need to do with the data, and use Access to create the database. And please, don't feed the bear. Bears are just like cats: Give them a bowl of milk (or a side of beef) and you'll *never* get rid of them.

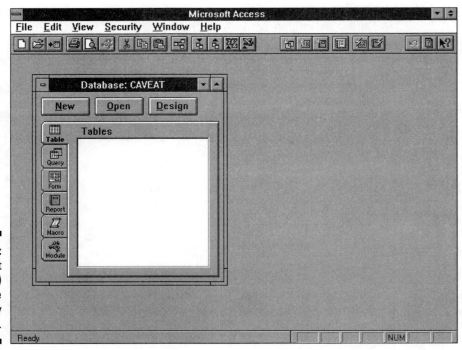

Figure 2-8:
A new (but empty!) database created by Access.

Chapter 3

Creating a Table for Your Data

● ●

In This Chapter

▶ Planning the structure of a table

▶ Creating a table

▶ Defining fields

▶ Understanding data types

▶ Saving a table

● ●

*I*n Chapter 2, you create a sample Access *database* — a kind of "wrapper" that holds all your different data management tools together. In this chapter, you create your first *table,* which is the basic building block of your database.

Each table holds data about a particular kind of thing. In this chapter, you create a table called *Customer Records* to hold all the customer data collected by Janis, our imaginary bookstore owner from Chapter 2.

When you design a table, you should be guided by one consideration: What do you need to accomplish with your database? Because Access is so simple to use, it's a lot easier to focus on *what* you're doing than *how* you're doing it.

Planning the Structure of Your Table

When database people talk about the *structure* of a table, it sounds kind of mysterious. But all it really means is what fields the table contains. When you create a table, the first step is to figure out what fields you need, what kinds of fields they should be, and how big they should be. And those decisions, of course, are determined by what you need to do with the table.

A field is just an item of information about something or someone in the database, such as a first name, street address, part number, or list price.

Assume that you have three main goals for your sample Customer Records table. You want to be able to do the following:

- ✔ Keep track of customer names and addresses
- ✔ Print reports of customer data
- ✔ Print form letters and mailing labels

To keep track of customer names and addresses, you might establish the following fields:

> Account Number
>
> Name
>
> Address
>
> City, State, Zip

If you were keeping track of your customer information on paper, this three-field setup would be fine. (Actually, if you were writing the information on paper, you wouldn't even *worry* about things like fields. You'd only worry about whether people could read your handwriting!)

But Access has a lot of power that you can't use if you limit yourself to these three fields. Suppose that you wanted to put customer records in order by zip code or to print the first and last names in a different order than they appear in the Name field. You'd be out of luck! With a computer database, you can do all those things, as long as you separate the different items of information into different fields. If you don't, you might as well stick with paper.

If you want to take full advantage of Access, you need to put separate parts of the name and address data in separate fields, as follows:

> Account Number
>
> First Name
>
> Last Name
>
> Address
>
> City
>
> State
>
> Zip

That's a lot better. Indeed, this setup does a terrific job of taking care of the first two goals of the sample table: keeping track of customer names and addresses and printing reports. The table even contains an Account Number field in case two customers have the same first and last names. (This field will also be helpful later on, when you create a sample Sales table and want to combine its data with the data from your Customer Records table.)

But what about the third goal of the sample table: to print form letters and mailing labels? In a form letter, you need to print *Mr., Ms.,* or something like it before the person's name in the address. And, in the case of Honest Janis, many of the customers are personal friends. He'd never address his pal Jim West as "Mr. West," even in a form letter. So you also need a field that indicates what name to use where the letter says, *Dear so-and-so.*

After adding the Mr/Ms and Salutation fields to the mix, the final field list looks like this:

Account Number

First Name

Last Name

MrMs

Salutation

Address

City

State

Zip

These fields do everything necessary. Notice that nothing we've done so far is the least bit technical. It's all common sense and thinking ahead. If you have common sense and can think ahead, you can be a database expert with Access! If you don't have these qualities, you can be a very successful politician.

Creating the Table

After you know what fields you need in your table, it's time to begin creating your table in Access. Before you get into the specific, hands-on part of creating an example table for this book, you should know the basic steps in creating any Access table:

1. Decide on the fields you need. You just did that.

2. Open the Table Design window. Each field in the table is one line in the top part of the Table Design window. For simple stuff, the top part of the window is all you need to use.

3. In the top part of the Table Design window, enter each field's name, data type, and description. If needed, you can also use the bottom part of the window to specify field length, format, and so on.

4. It's optional, but if you want to have one field as a unique identifier for each record, you can designate that field as the table's primary key.

5. Finally, you save the table design and exit from the Table Design window.

If you jumped right into this chapter after you finished Chapter 2 and you're still looking at the screen with the Caveat database, you can blink now and rest your eyes for a second. If you took a break after the last chapter, follow these steps to get back into the Caveat database:

1. **Start Access by double-clicking on the Access icon in the Windows Program Manager. If the Access Welcome box displays, close it by clicking on the Window Control button at the top left corner of the box.**

2. **After you're in Access, click once on File in the menu bar at the top left corner of the screen.**

   Clicking on File opens up the File menu and makes your mother very, very proud.

3. **Click on the file name CAVEAT.MDB in the File menu.**

   This file is the sample database you created in Chapter 2. It should appear at the bottom of the File menu.

If the CAVEAT.MDB database is not listed at the bottom of the File menu, select Open Database from the menu. In the Open Database dialog box, you should see the CAVEAT.MDB database on the left side. To open the database, double-click on it with the mouse.

Playing with push buttons

The Database window has two groups of buttons:

- The left side of the window has push buttons (or tabs, if you prefer) with the names of the different database tools — Table, Query, Form, and Report. You can depress only one of these buttons at any time. The button stays depressed until you click on one of the other three buttons. At the moment, the Table button should be depressed. That means that anything you do applies to tables. If the Table button *isn't* depressed, click on it once with the mouse.

- At the top of the window are the New, Open, and Design buttons. Clicking on the New button tells Access that you want to create a new table (if the Table button is pressed).

Go ahead and click on the New button now to create a new table. The New Table dialog box will appear, as shown in Figure 3-1.

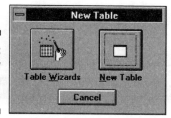

Figure 3-1:
The New
Table dialog
box.

A dialog box is an easy way for you to tell Access what to do. Dialog boxes contain buttons that make Access do different things. When you click on one of the buttons, the dialog box relays your wishes to Access — and you're on your way. In this case, just click on the New Table button, as shown in Figure 3-1.

As soon as you click on the button, the Table Design window appears. Make the window fill the whole screen by clicking on the Maximize button in the top right corner of the window. This button looks like a little triangle pointing up. Your screen should look like Figure 3-2.

Take a second to notice that the Access screen is changed. Before the Table Design window opened, the top three lines were different, as shown in Figure 3-3.

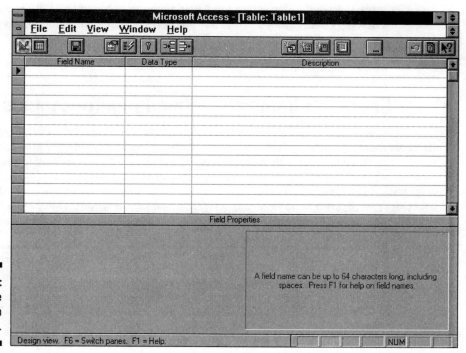

Figure 3-2:
The Table
Design
window.

Figure 3-3:
What the top three lines looked like before the Table Design window.

The top line of the screen always shows the name of the current window. The second line, the *menu bar,* always contains menus that are appropriate for whatever task you're doing at the moment. And the third line is the *toolbar.* You can click on buttons on the toolbar to speed up your work in Access. The toolbar offers different choices of buttons depending on what you're doing in Access.

Creating the table's fields

For each field in the table, you always need to specify a field name, data type, and field description. Unlike the name of the database itself, which can't be more than eight characters long, field names can be up to 64 characters long. The only characters you *can't* use are periods (.), exclamation marks (!), and square brackets ([ ]).

Character limits and other dangerous topics

The reason that database names can't be longer than eight characters (letters, digits, and underscores) has nothing to do with Access. It's because MS-DOS, the PC's operating system, keeps track of disk files and limits their names to eight characters, a period, and a three-character extension. Access puts the extension .MDB on all database files, so that leaves only eight characters for you to play with. If you're confused by MS-DOS, then congratulations! It means you're paying attention. Reading IDG's *DOS For Dummies* is a good way to feel less confused. (Of course, so is hitting yourself on the head with a steel pipe, but reading *DOS For Dummies* isn't injurious.)

The Table Design window is divided into two main parts. In the top part, you can specify the name, type, and description of each field. You can tell that Access is ready for you to specify the first field when you see the little triangle at the left end of the first line as well as the blinking cursor in the first column of the first line. In the bottom part of the window, you specify various properties of each field. I'll get to that in a minute.

To specify the first field of the sample table, type **Cust ID** in the first column of the first line and press the Tab key. Access creates a field named *Cust ID*. Notice that as soon as you press Tab, the second column seems to come to life. The word *Text* appears, along with a little button at the right side of the blank. In addition, Access displays several blanks at the bottom part of the screen.

The little down-arrow button is called a *list-box button*. If you click on it, Access displays a list from which you can select the field's data type. Any time you see a little button like this at the right side of a blank, it's for opening a list box.

Click on the button at the right side of the blank. Access shows you a list of the data types you can assign to this field. For the sample table, assume that you want to make the Cust ID field a counter field. Click on Counter in the list. After you make your selection, the list box closes automatically.

You're seeing some new terms here, such as *data type* and *counter field*. Fear not, Grasshopper: all things (except the federal budget) will become clear to you. Take it on faith for the moment. If that doesn't work, try two quick shots of tequila: that *always* does the trick.

Now press Tab again. The cursor moves to the Description column. Type **Customer's account number** for the description. *Don't* press Tab again. You have one more thing to do with this field.

You may have wondered why I told you to call the field *Cust ID* instead of *Account Number*. The reason is that *Cust ID* is shorter and will fit more easily when the data is displayed in a row-and-column table.

Designating the table's primary key

The final thing to do with the Cust ID field is to designate it as the table's *primary key*. The primary key field is the one field that helps Access keep all the table's records in order, find them more quickly, and link the Customer Records table to other tables for consolidated reports. Please take it on faith for the moment: I promise that I'll get to all this good stuff later.

One thing you *do* need to know now is that every record must have a different value in the primary key field. For example, you don't want Bob Jones, Bob Smith, and Bob Bob to have the account numbers in their records' Cust ID fields.

This rule won't be a problem in the sample table, because the primary key field is a counter field. With counter fields, Access automatically assigns a new value for each record. The first record gets 1, the second record gets 2, and so on.

To make Cust ID the primary key field, follow these steps:

1. **Make sure that the cursor is in the row with the Cust ID field.**

2. **Click on the little key button at the top center of the screen.**

    A picture of a key appears at the left end of the Cust ID row, showing that the field is designated as the primary key field.

Choosing the right data type

You may wonder why Access goes to the trouble of having different data types for fields. The reason is simple: The data type tells Access how to treat the field's data. For example, when you select Number as the data type, Access knows that it can do mathematical operations with the data in that field — something it can't do if you select Text as the field type. In Access, you can specify any of the following data types:

Text: Use this data type for — well, *text*. Sometimes, you may also want to use it for numbers when you don't need to perform any calculations with them. For example, you *could* add up all the telephone numbers or zip codes of bookstore customers, but it would be utterly stupid. Put numbers like these in a text field.

Memo: Use memo fields for *free form* text. Most Access fields hold a specific amount of information, but a memo field can hold up to 32,000 characters — about eight typed, single-spaced pages' worth of text. You might use a field like this to keep miscellaneous notes about each customer: family birthdays, book preferences, a log of telephone calls, and so on. (In fact, you add a memo field to the sample Customer Records table when you get to Chapter 9.)

Number: Specify this data type when you need to perform mathematical operations on the data. You can use a field like this to keep track of how many orders a customer places, for example.

Currency: A currency field is a special kind of number field that's designed to handle money values. Later in the book, when you design the Sales table for the sample database, you use this data type on the field that holds the price of each book.

Date/Time: If you don't know what this field is for, you should seek immediate medical help. Oh, all right — a Date/Time field is for holding dates and times, such as the date of a customer's last order.

Counter: A counter field is another special kind of field. When you specify that a field is to be a counter field, Access automatically assigns a unique *counter* number to each record. Access puts the value 1 in the counter field of the first record, the value 9 in the ninth record, and so on.

Yes/No: This type of field keeps track of yes/no situations, such as "Is this customer's payment overdue?"

OLE Object: This one is probably the most exciting field type, but it's pretty advanced stuff. With this data type, you can put almost anything in a field: a picture, a graph, a sound recording, an Excel worksheet — you name it.

Adding another field

After you finish defining the first field in your table, press Tab. The cursor automatically moves down to the first column of the second row. You then can define your second field.

For the sample table, call the second field First Name. Type **First Name** in the first column and then press Tab to move to the Data Type column.

For this record, accept the suggested data type — Text. You don't need to open the list box this time. But now, you have another problem: The First Name field is too big.

Limited field size

One drawback of computerized database management — even with Access — is that fields are limited to a specific size. You can't have one record with a 10-character First Name field and another record with a 1,000-character First Name field. (You can *change* the size of the field, but then the fields are limited to the *new* size.) The exception is when you use a memo field. A memo field is stored in a special way that lets it hold a variable amount of data.

Changing a field's size

If you look at the bottom left part of the screen, you can see that Access has assigned a field size of 50 to the First Name field. That's too long: Not even Engelbert Humperdinck has a 50-letter first name! Usually, 10 characters is enough for a First Name field.

You can get down to the Field Size blank in two ways. You can click on the blank with the mouse or press the F6 function key. Then, to change the field size, take the following steps:

1. **If the field size is highlighted in reverse video (white letters on a black background), simply type in the new value.**

   Access automatically deletes the original value.

2. **If the field size isn't highlighted, press Delete or Backspace.**

   Access erases the current value, and you then can type in the new value.

3. **Press F6 or click on the field's Data Type blank.**

   Access returns you to the top part of the window, and you can finish defining the field.

Go ahead and change the First Name field size to 10 in your sample table. Then press Tab. The cursor should move to the Description column. Type **Customer's first name** for the description.

Defining the Rest of the Fields

Press Tab again. The cursor moves down to the first column of the next line. You can tell that Access is ready to have you enter data for another field because the little triangle is now at the left end of the second line. Define the rest of the fields in your sample table as follows:

Field Name	Data Type	Size	Description
Last Name	Text	15	Customer's last name
MrMs	Text	5	Honorific (don't ask!)
Salutation	Text	15	Dear . . .
Address	Text	25	Street address
City	Text	15	City
State	Text	5	State or province
Zip	Text	10	Postal code

Remember that you should use the Number data type only when you will be performing mathematical operations on the data in the field. That's why the Zip field is specified as a Text data type, even though it contains numbers. Another advantage to making the Zip field a Text data type is that you can use it for customers who live in countries that use letters in their postal codes.

Saving the Table Definition

After you define all your fields, you have just one more thing to do — but it's a biggie. You need to save your table definition.

To save the table definition, click on File in the menu bar at the top left of the screen and select Save from the menu. The Save As dialog box appears, as shown in Figure 3-4.

Figure 3-4:
The Save As
dialog box.

Unless you tell it to do otherwise, Access saves your database in the same directory in which you put the Access program (normally C:\ACCESS). That's fine, but if you know how to create a disk directory, it's a good idea to create a separate database subdirectory, which you might call C:\ACCESS\MYFILES. That way, if you eventually create several databases, all will be in their own directory, separate from the Access program files.

To create a new directory under the Access directory, open the Windows File Manager. Then highlight the Access directory. From the File menu, select Create directory and type the name of database directory in the dialog box. Then click on OK. For more about directories in Windows, see *Windows For Dummies.*

In case you don't feel like straining your gray matter to think of a name for your saved table, Access suggests *Table1* as a possibility. That suggestion presents two problems. First, it doesn't tell you what's in the table, and second, it's *boring.* So when you save the sample table, type **Customer Records** where it says *Table1.* Then click on the OK button at the right side of the dialog box.

And that's it! You've defined your first database table in Access. Close the Table Design window by double-clicking on the Window Control button in the top left corner of the window, shown in Figure 3-5. Be sure that you double-click on the button for the Table Design window, not for the Access main window.

When the Table Design window closes, you see the Database window again. But now, the Customer Records table is listed in the window.

Time for a break! Get up, stretch your legs, and have a steaming cup of darned good coffee.

Click on this button, not the one above it

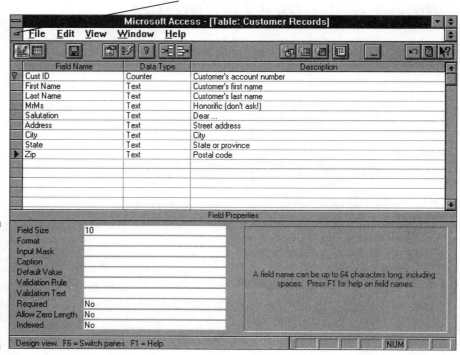

Figure 3-5:
Click on the
Table
Design
window's
control
button.

Chapter 4

Let Table Wizard Create a Table *for* You

. . . .

In This Chapter

▶ What is the Table Wizard?

▶ Designing a table with the Table Wizard

▶ Modifying a table design

. . . .

*I*t's easy to design and create tables in Access. All you need to do is fill in field names, choose each field's data types, fiddle with each field's format, write some descriptions, and you're done. Then you name the table and save it.

In fact, there are only two ways to make it any easier to create a table in Access. The first is to persuade your boss that someone else should do the job. The second is to use the Access Table Wizard and let it create the table *for* you.

It's true that having someone else do the work is just about the simplest way to handle any task. But the Table Wizard can make your life *almost* as easy. And your boss never has to know.

A Quick Review

In case you came in late, here are the basic concepts used in this chapter:

✔ *Table*: the basic building block of an Access database. A table contains information such as customer, sales, or animal control records.

✔ *Record:* the basic building block of an Access table. Each record contains all the database information about one thing, such as one customer, one sales transaction, one giraffe, and so on.

✔ *Field:* the basic building block of an Access record. Each field contains a single item of information about the thing described in the current record, such as one customer's account number, the amount of one sale, or which tiger ate the giraffe.

✔ *Database:* the big wrapper that goes around all the tables that work together. For example, a database might contain tables for customer names and addresses, sales made to those customers, and zoo animals owned by individual customers.

Calling the Table Wizard . . .

In this chapter, you find out how to create another copy of the Customer Records table, this time using the Table Wizard. Don't worry too much if you have a typo here or there in this second sample table, because at the end of the chapter, you delete the table. Try not to get too attached to it.

Start Access and open the Caveat database. (If you haven't created the Caveat database, select New Database from the File menu and type **Caveat** in the dialog box.) Make sure that the Tables tab is on top at the left side of the database window and that the Customer Records table is listed. Your screen should look like the one shown in Figure 4-1. If the Table tab isn't on top, click on it with the mouse. If you didn't previously create the Customer Records table, don't worry about it.

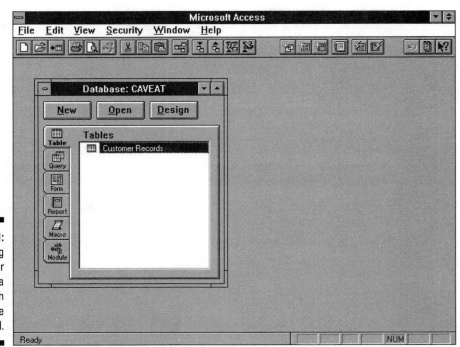

Figure 4-1:
The starting screen for creating a table with the Table Wizard.

See the buttons in the toolbar across the top of the screen? If you move the mouse cursor over one of the buttons and leave it there for a second, Access displays a little box that contains an explanation of what the button does.

Click on the New button at the top of the Database window to create a new table. The New Table dialog box appears, as shown in Figure 4-2. Click on the big Table Wizards button. (Some of the wizards are *indeed* big; the Report Wizard is six-foot-seven.)

Figure 4-2:
The New
Table dialog
box.

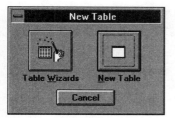

Take a moment to examine the Table Wizard dialog box, shown in Figure 4-3. Here are the things to notice:

- ✔ On the left side of the dialog box is a list of sample tables that are available. Each sample table has fields that would commonly be used for that type of table.

- ✔ Just below the list of sample tables are two radio buttons, Business and Personal. If you click on the Personal radio button, the list of sample tables changes. Instead of displaying sample tables such as Customers and Orders, it shows tables such as Friends and Household Inventory. Access offers you 26 sample tables for business and 19 sample tables for personal use.

- ✔ In the middle of the dialog box, Access shows you a list of fields available for the currently highlighted sample table. If you switch back to the list of Business tables and click on the Customers table, you can see that the Sample Fields list includes many of the same fields you included in your Customer Records table in Chapter 3.

- ✔ On the right side of the dialog box, Access shows whatever fields you select from the Sample Fields list. The Table Wizard puts these fields in the table it creates for you. The list is labeled, appropriately enough, *Fields in my new table*.

Selecting fields in Table Wizard

Normally, your first step is to select a table from the Sample Tables list. This table should be as similar as possible to the new table you want to create.

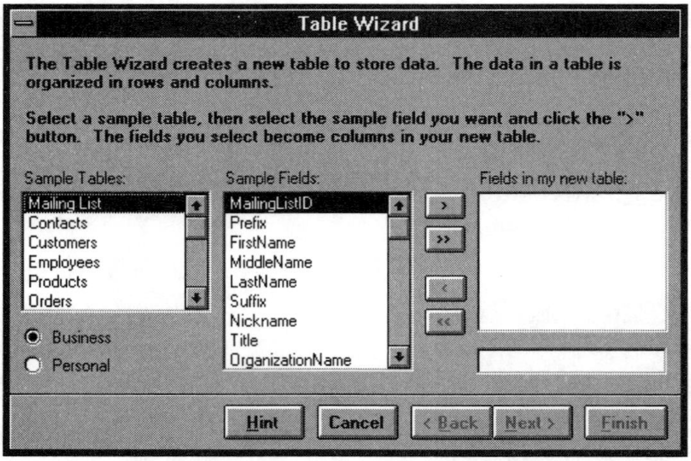

Figure 4-3:
The Table
Wizard
dialog box.

After selecting the sample table you want, you need to tell Access which of the sample table's fields you want to use in your new table. To select a field for the new table, you just double-click on the field's name in the Sample Fields list. This automatically adds the field to the Fields in my new table list. If you change your mind once you've selected a field, you can deselect it by double-clicking on its name in the Fields in my new table list.

The four buttons between the two lists give you another way to select and deselect fields for the new table. What each button does is shown in the table below.

Table 4-1	The Field Selection Buttons
Use This Button . . .	*To Do This.*
>	The top button, which has a single arrow pointing right, selects the currently highlighted field from the Sample Fields list and displays it in the new table field list. You can do the same thing by double-clicking on a field name in the Sample Fields list.
>>	The second button, marked with a double arrow pointing right, selects *all* fields in the Sample Fields list and displays them in the new table field list.
<	The third button, marked with a single arrow pointing left, removes the currently highlighted field from the new table field list and removes it from the list. You can do the same thing by double-clicking on a field name in the new table field list.
<<	The bottom button, marked with a double arrow pointing left, removes *all* fields in the new table field list and leaves the list empty.

Creating the Table in the Table Wizard

To create this chapter's example table by using the Table Wizard, first make sure that the Business radio button is selected so that the correct sample tables appear in the list. Then follow these steps:

1. **In the Sample Tables list at the left, click on Customers to select the Customers sample table.**

   Notice that the Sample Fields list changes to show fields available in the Customers table.

2. **In the Sample Fields list, double-click on the Customer ID field.**

   It should appear in the new table field list on the right.

Now, add the rest of the fields for the new table:

3. **In the Sample Fields list, click on FirstName to highlight it.**

   Then click on the single right-arrow button to add the field to the new table field list.

4. **In the Sample Fields list, double-click on LastName, Address, City, State, Region, and Postal Code.**

5. **Remove the Region field from the list.**

   Oops! You shouldn't have believed me when I told you to double-click on the Region field in Step 4. (Didn't your mother tell you not to trust computer-book authors?) Now you have to remove it. In the new table field list, double-click on Region. The field disappears from the list.

After you add fields to the new table field list, your screen should look like the one shown in Figure 4-4.

Repeated fields

If you look carefully at the field lists for the sample tables, you may notice something a little odd. Some fields appear in more than one table. For example, both the Customers and Orders tables have a CustomerID field; both the Employees and Time Billed tables have an EmployeeID field; and so on. The reason for these common fields is that they let you link together two or more tables and use multiple tables at the same time.

Later on, you create reports that combine information from both your sample Customer Records table and a Sales table. Having a field common to both tables comes in handy at that point.

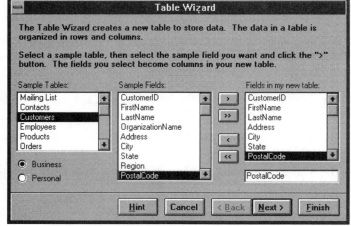

Figure 4-4:
Access
displays
your
selected
fields in the
new table
field list.

Naming the table

After you're sure that the right fields are in the new table field list, click on the Next button. Access displays a dialog box and asks what you want to name your new table.

In this dialog box, you name the table and select a field as the table's primary key. To name the table, just click in the blank at the top of the dialog box and type the table name.

Give your sample table the name *More Customer Records.* Just click in the blank under What do you want to name your table? and delete the word *Customers.* Then type **More Customer Records.** Your screen should look like the one in Figure 4-5.

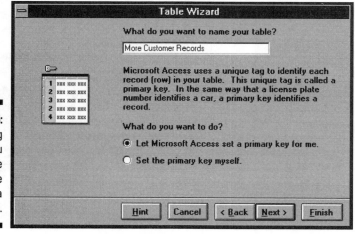

Figure 4-5:
This dialog
box lets you
name the
new table
and select a
primary key.

Selecting the primary key

The last thing you need to do to finish your second sample table — or any table you create with the Table Wizard — is to specify the primary key. A *primary key* is a field that Access uses to determine the order in which records are displayed and to speed things up when you search for a record; you can find more details in Chapter 3. A primary key is also necessary when you link tables together, like when your grandparents and all the other relatives show up for Thanksgiving, and you can't get them all at a single table, and Grandpa and Uncle Frank get into a big fight and . . . uh, what was I talking about?

Oh, yes, primary keys. Actually, for the moment, I want you to take the easy way out and let Access pick the primary key for you. The program does that automatically unless you tell it otherwise, so just click on the Next button. Access selects the CustomerID field as the primary key — which, as it happens, is a good choice.

Access then displays a new dialog box, shown in Figure 4-6, and asks whether the new table is related to any other tables in the database. In plain English, it's just asking whether you want to link the new table to any tables you already created. In the case of the sample table, you don't, so click on the Next button to move ahead.

Believe it or not, that's just about all you need to do to create your second sample Customer Records table. Access displays the "checkered flag" dialog box, shown in Figure 4-7, and says that it has enough information to create the table. However, the table you get from the Table Wizard usually needs a few adjustments. If you look at the dialog box, you can see that a radio button is already selected so that you can modify the table design. If the button isn't selected, click in the little circle next to Modify the table design.

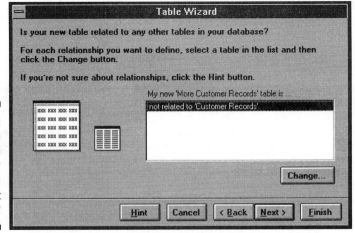

Figure 4-6:
Is the table related to any others? If so, will the table admit it?

Figure 4-7:
The
checkered
flag dialog
box.

Sometimes, you may want to use Cue Cards when you modify the Table Wizard's design. (If you recall from Chapter 1, Cue Cards are special help screens that Access displays to help you through certain tasks.) If you do, just click in the Open Cue Cards check box near the bottom of the dialog box. Access then displays Cue Cards for modifying a table design on the right side of the screen as you work.

If you don't want to use the Cue Cards (for this example, you don't need them), just click on the Finish button.

Modifying a table design

After you click on the Finish button, Access displays a screen that's a bit more familiar — it's the same screen you saw if you designed the example table in Chapter 3. You can use this screen not only to design a table for the first time, but also to *re*design a table when you want to change something.

Basic steps in modifying a table design

The basic steps in modifying the Wizard's table design apply to modifying *any* table design. In general, here's what you do:

✔ To modify a field name, just move the cursor into the blank where the field name currently appears. Delete the current field name and type the new name.

✔ To modify a field's data type, click in the Data Type column in the field's row. Then open the list box and select a new data type from the list.

✔ To change a field size, click in the Field Size blank in the bottom part of the screen. Then delete the current field size and type the new field size.

✔ To insert a new field, click in the row *above* where you want to insert the new field. Then press the Insert key on your keyboard or select Insert Row from the Edit menu. Finally, define the new field's name, data type, and so on in the usual way.

✔ To delete a field, click in the row for the field you want to delete. Then select Delete Row from the Edit menu.

Modifying the Wizard's table design

If you've been following along and creating the sample table with the Table Wizard, you can see on your screen that, apart from the field names, the table design is almost exactly like the one you create "by hand" in Chapter 3. Access even picked the CustomerID field as the primary key!

If you want this table to be like the one you create in Chapter 3, it needs a few changes. The field names aren't quite right, and, as you'll see in a moment, the field sizes are *way* too big.

Changing the CustomerID field

The first change is pretty trivial. You need to change the name of the CustomerID field to *Cust ID*. The CustomerID field is already highlighted in the table design screen, so just type **Cust ID**. Access automatically replaces the old field name. (If CustomerID isn't highlighted, you have to delete it manually by using the Delete or Backspace key on your keyboard.)

Just as when you design a table for the first time, Access automatically saves the new field definition as soon as you move out of the current row of the table. So now, click in the second line or tap your keyboard's down-arrow key once. The highlight should move down to the FirstName field.

Changing the FirstName Field

Like the CustomerID field, the FirstName field in the sample table needs a slight change. You need to put a space between *First* and *Name*. In addition, however, the Table Wizard set the field size at 50, which is much larger than needed. In general, the Table Wizard plays it safe by making each field big enough to hold the longest entry you might ever put in it. So when you use the Table Wizard, you'll probably need to adjust the field lengths.

Change the FirstName field by following these steps:

1. **With the highlight in the Field Name column of the First Name row, press the F2 function key.**

   This removes the highlight from FirstName and moves the cursor so that it's at the right end of the field name.

2. **Press the left-arrow key four times, so that the cursor is between the *t* in First and the *N* in Name.**

3. **Press the spacebar once to insert a space between *First* and *Name*.**

4. **Click in the Field Size blank in the bottom half of the screen.**

   That's in the gray part of the screen marked *Field Properties*.

5. **Delete the 50 and type 10, which is the field size you want.**

6. **Click in the LastName row in the top part of the screen.**

   If you prefer, you can simply press the F6 key on your keyboard and then press the down-arrow key once. Access automatically saves your new field definition.

Now make the same moves to change the LastName field so that its name is *Last Name* and the field length is 15.

Inserting the MrMs and Salutation fields

The next change to the sample table is to insert the MrMs and Salutation fields into the table design. This process may seem difficult at first, but it's actually easy.

First, move the cursor to the Address field row by clicking in that row. Then open the Edit menu.

Down toward the bottom of the Edit menu is the choice Insert Row. Click once on that menu choice. Notice that a new, blank row opens up above the Address row.

Here's a different way to do the same thing. Instead of using the Edit menu, just press the Insert key on your keyboard. Again, a new, blank row opens up just above your current cursor position.

The rest is a cakewalk. Click in the first new row under Last Name and enter **MrMs** as the field name, Text as the data type, and **5** as the length. In the second new row, enter **Salutation** as the field name, Text as the data type, and **15** as the length.

Finishing the table modification

Now, all you need to do is change the remaining fields so that they're like the fields in the original Customer Records table. In the same way that you changed the FirstName and LastName fields, make the following changes in the remaining fields:

Old Field Name/Old Length	*New Field Name/New Length*
Address/255	Address/25
City/50	City/15
State/50	State/5
PostalCode/20	Zip/10

After you finish, save the changes you made by opening the File menu and clicking on Save.

Finally, close the table design window by double-clicking on its Window Control button at the top left corner. As usual, be sure that you click on the button for the table design window, not the button for Access!

Deleting the Practice Table

The fruit fly has a life span of just a few days; the average political campaign promise, just a few minutes. So it is with the practice table you created in this chapter. Because you're not going to use it again, you can delete it from the database.

Don't delete the wrong table! But if you do, don't panic, either. If you catch your mistake immediately after making it, Access lets you undo the deletion. Just select Undo Delete from the Edit menu, and your deleted table will reappear in the Database window.

To delete the More Customer Records table from the Caveat database, follow these steps. You can use the same method to delete any table from any database:

1. **In the Database window, click on the table name to highlight it.**

   To delete the sample table, click on More Customer Records.

2. **Open the Edit menu.**

3. **Select Delete to delete the table.**

   Access displays a dialog box asking whether you really want to delete the table. Click on OK, and Access deletes the table.

If you prefer to use the keyboard to delete the table, you can simply press the Delete key instead of using the Edit menu.

The 5th Wave By Rich Tennant

System Integration at Disney World

"LOOK, I HAVE NO PROBLEM RUNNING MICKEY-MICROS AND PLUTO-PCs THROUGH A TINKERBELL BUS, BUT WE'RE NEVER GOING TO HAVE A HUEY-DEWEY-LOUIE-LAN ON A MINNIE-MINI WITHOUT SERIOUSLY UP-GRADING ALL OF OUR GOOFY SOFTWARE."

Chapter 5

Putting Data in Your Table

. . . .

In This Chapter

▶ Opening the Datasheet window

▶ Entering customer data

▶ Editing records and fixing mistakes

▶ Moving around in the Datasheet window

. . . .

*I*f you've been reading the chapters in sequence, you've already seen how to plan a database, design a table, and set up the table's fields. What you *haven't* seen is how to put data in the table. (You also haven't seen the pile of candy bar wrappers under Honest Janis's desk, but that's another story.)

What you need to do now is put some customer data into your table. It's not hard — in fact, compared to entering data in old-style database managers, it's incredibly easy — but there are a few tricks to learn on the way.

To understand the ideas in this chapter, you should know the basic concepts of a database (Chapter 2) and a table (Chapter 3). To do the example exercise, you need to have created the Caveat database (Chapter 2) and the Customer Records table (Chapter 3).

If you're putting data into your own "real life" table, just read this chapter to get the basic ideas. Then follow the steps with your own table instead of the one in the book.

Opening the Datasheet Window

If you quit Access after finishing Chapter 4, start it up again and open CAVEAT.MDB. In the Database window, the Customer Records table should be listed. (If it isn't, click on the Table tab.) Double-click on Customer Records, and the Datasheet window opens up. Click on the Maximize button at the top right corner of the Datasheet window so that it fills the entire screen.

The Datasheet window is where you put data into the database. You can also use it to view and search for your data. Figure 5-1 shows the features that are available in the Datasheet window.

Across the top of the window are the names of the fields in the Customer Records table. Each field gets its own column in the datasheet. In the first row, you can see the little triangle at the left, indicating that Access will put anything you type into that first line. The inverse-video highlight is in the Cust ID column because that's where the cursor is when you first open the window.

At the bottom left corner of the window, Access displays the number of the current record (or row). And you can use the buttons on either side of the "Record" blank to move around in the datasheet.

Datasheet View in Access is the same thing as *Table View* in other database programs.

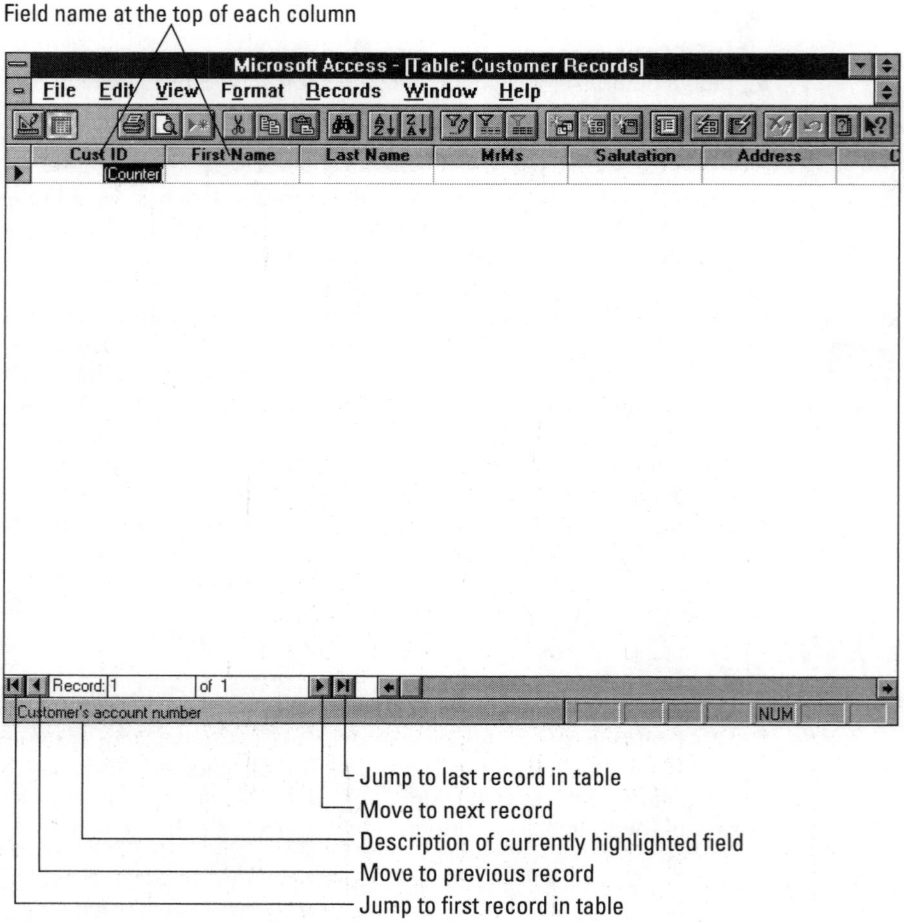

Field name at the top of each column

Cust ID	First Name	Last Name	MrMs	Salutation	Address	
(Counter)						

Microsoft Access - [Table: Customer Records]

File   Edit   View   Format   Records   Window   Help

Record: 1   of 1

Customer's account number

NUM

Jump to last record in table
Move to next record
Description of currently highlighted field
Move to previous record
Jump to first record in table

Figure 5-1:
Important features of the Datasheet window.

Entering Customer Data

The best way to learn how to work in the Datasheet window is to actually enter some data. So this section walks you through the steps of entering data for the Caveat database.

Right now, the highlight is in the Cust ID column. Because that's a counter field, Access fills it in automatically for you. To get to the next field, press Enter or Tab. The cursor moves into the First Name column. To enter the customer's first name, type **James** and press Enter. The cursor automatically moves to the next column.

Whoa! Something else happened as soon as you typed the *J* in *James.* As shown in Figure 5-2, a little pencil icon appeared at the left end of the line, and the *Counter* text moved down to the next line.

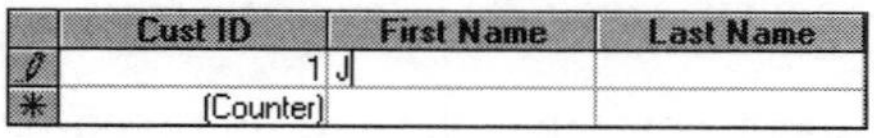

Figure 5-2:
A pencil icon
appears
when you
start entering
data.

Cust ID	First Name	Last Name
1 J		
(Counter)		

Every time you *finish* entering a record — that is, when you complete a row in the datasheet and move down to the next row — Access saves the record to your PC's hard disk. That way, even if the electricity goes off and your computer shuts down, the only data you can lose is from the record you're entering at the moment. The pencil icon appears at the left end of the line until the record is saved.

Go ahead and enter the rest of the data for this record. (If you make any mistakes typing, don't worry about them right now. You learn how to correct mistakes a little later.)

There's one more little surprise waiting for you. (Would I tell you? It'd spoil the surprise!) To enter the last name, type **West** and press Enter. For MrMs, type **Prof.;** for Salutation, type **Jimbo;** and for Address, type **Mythic University.**

When you click the mouse or press a key, Access sends the result of your action to the place on the screen that has the *focus.* This concept sounds pretty technical, but it's easy in practice. Usually, the place that has the focus is highlighted or has a blinking cursor in it. In this case, the focus is in the current cell of the datasheet. If you start typing, Access places your text in that cell.

When you pressed Enter after typing *Mythic University,* the window automatically moved to the right over the datasheet, bringing the next column (City) into view. When you move past the edge of the current screen, Access automatically moves the window so that you can see more of the datasheet. The same thing happens if you fill up more rows than can fit on the screen: The Datasheet window moves down.

To complete the sample record, enter the following data: for City, type **Martinsville;** for State, **CA;** and for Zip, **98035.**

After you type the zip code and press Enter, Access does exactly as you would expect: moves you down (and left) to the first column in the next row. Access is now ready for you to enter more records. Did you hear a little whir inside your PC? That whir was the sound of Access saving the record you just entered to the PC's hard disk. If you look at the left end of the row that contains James West's record, you can see that the pencil icon has disappeared, indicating that the record has been saved.

Notice that although Access is ready for you to enter a second record, it hasn't yet displayed the pencil icon in the second row. That's because you haven't entered any data yet, so there's no unsaved data to worry about.

To continue building the datasheet, enter the following four records:

This database has 15 records, which are all listed in Appendix A. You can enter as many or as few as you want, but for now, just enter the four listed below. In Chapter 10, you change the structure of this database, and it will require a little extra typing for the records you've already entered.

You don't need to type any data into the Cust ID field. It's a counter field, and Access fills it in automatically.

First Name:	Harriett
Last Name:	Stowe
MrMs:	Ms.
Salutation:	Ms. Stowe
Address:	14 Parakeet Lane
City:	New York
State:	NY
Zip:	10087

First Name:	Jules
Last Name:	Twombly
MrMs:	Mr.
Salutation:	Jules
Address:	The AB Hotel
City:	Las Vegas
State:	NV
Zip:	34567

First Name:	Arnold
Last Name:	Harris
MrMs:	Mr.
Salutation:	Arnie
Address:	101 Fifth Avenue
City:	Boise
State:	ID
Zip:	23413

First Name:	Teri
Last Name:	Lane
MrMs:	Ms.
Salutation:	Ms. Lane
Address:	5678 15th St., #5-A
City:	Santa Barbara
State:	CA
Zip:	93101

You may have gotten a little surprise when you entered the street address for Teri Lane. Because the address is slightly longer than will fit in the on-screen column, the text moved to the left as you typed the last couple of letters. That happens because the length of the address is limited by the *field length* that you specified when you designed the table, not by the width of the column in the datasheet. Even though you can't see it right now, all your data is safe and sound. Later on, you find out how to change the width of datasheet columns.

After you finish entering the data, your screen should look exactly like the one shown in Figure 5-3 — only bigger.

Moving Around in the Datasheet

In your sample datasheet, the highlight is currently in the first column of row six. Experiment a little bit by moving around in your datasheet. Try the following:

✔ Move to the first record by clicking on the First Record button at the bottom left corner of the screen.

✔ Move to the last record by clicking on the Last Record button. Although Access displays six rows on-screen, the highlight moves to row five because it's the last "real" record in the sample table.

✔ Move to the fourth record by clicking on the Previous Record button. Notice that the record number (displayed at the bottom-left corner of the screen) changes.

✔ Move to record number three by pressing the up-arrow key on your keyboard.

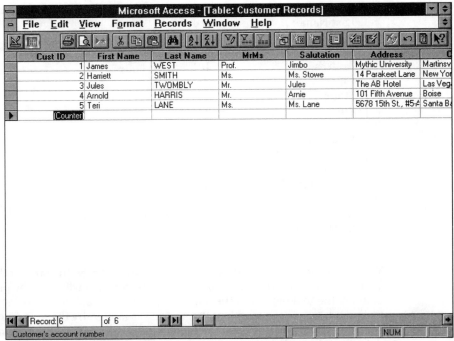

Figure 5-3:
The
Customer
Records
datasheet
after
entering five
records.

✔ Move to the First Name column by pressing the right-arrow key.

✔ Move to the Zip column by pressing the End key.

✔ Move to the Cust ID column by pressing the Home key.

✔ Move to the Last Name column by clicking in it with the mouse.

Table 5-1 summarizes the tricks for moving around the Datasheet window.

Table 5-1 How to Move Around in the Datasheet Window

To Move to This Position	Do This
First record in table	Click on the First Record button at the bottom left corner of the Datasheet window.
Last record in table	Click on the Last Record button.
First column in table	Press the Home key.
Last column in table	Press the End key.
Next column to the right	Press the right-arrow key, or Enter, or Tab.

To Move to This Position	Do This
Next column to the left	Press the left-arrow key or hold down the Shift key and press Tab.
Up a row	Press the up-arrow key.
Down a row	Press the down-arrow key.
Up 26 rows	Press the PgUp key.
Down 26 rows	Press the PgDn key.
Top left corner of the datasheet	Hold down the Ctrl key and press the Home key.
Lower right corner of the datasheet	Hold down the Ctrl key and press the End key.

In database and spreadsheet jargon, the little box formed by the intersection of a row and a column is called a *cell.*

Did you notice a difference when you used the mouse to make the final move to the Last Name column? Previously, when you moved to a different cell in the datasheet, Access highlighted the cell's contents in reverse video. This time, it displayed a blinking cursor in the cell at the point where you clicked the mouse. The blinking cursor means that you can edit the field contents. If you start typing in a cell where the contents are highlighted, what you type replaces whatever was there before.

And *that* brings us to the very important topic of editing data in a table. To prepare for the next section, press Ctrl+Home to move to the top left corner of the datasheet. Then sit up straight (poor posture is a leading cause of computer backaches!) and get ready to have some fun.

If you were using any other database package, this would be the point at which you'd save your work. But with Access, you don't need to worry: It's already been done *for* you!

Editing Data and Fixing Mistakes

As it happens, you made a couple of mistakes when you entered the data in your sample table. Oh, all right, you entered everything just as you were supposed to, but Honest Janis is going to get mad at somebody about the errors, and I'm putting the blame on you. (I can't afford to lose this job; I've got two cats and five credit cards to support. You understand.)

Replacing text completely

In the second record of the sample table, Harriett's last name should be *Stowe,* not *Smith.* To correct it, follow these steps:

1. **Press the down-arrow key once.**

2. **Press the right-arrow key twice.**

   The word *Smith* should be displayed in reverse video.

3. **Type Stowe.**

   The new text automatically replaces the old cell contents.

Editing text without replacing it

If you want to edit the data in a cell without replacing it completely, you can do it in two ways. First, you can click in the cell with the mouse; this automatically opens the cell for editing. Or you can use the arrow keys to move to the cell and then press the F2 function key to open the cell for editing. Either way, Access saves the changes you make as soon as you move out of the current row in the datasheet.

To see how the editing process works, suppose that the address you entered for Jules Twombly in the third record is wrong. He doesn't live at the AB Hotel in Las Vegas — that's a nice enough hotel, but it's frequented by gangsters, computer book writers, and Wayne Newton impersonators. Instead, Jules lives at the ABC Hotel, a $2,500-a-night place on the Las Vegas Strip.

To edit the Address cell, follow these steps:

1. **Press the down-arrow key once.**

   Notice that Access saves the new version of Harriett Stowe's record.

2. **Press the right-arrow key three times.**

   The entire contents of the Address cell should be highlighted. If you were to start typing at this point, Access would delete the current text in the cell and replace it with whatever you typed.

3. **Press the F2 function key.**

   Access opens the cell for editing. Notice that the cursor is at the end of the text in the cell, just to the right of the *l* in *Hotel.*

4. Press the left-arrow key six times.

The cursor should be just to the right of the *B* in *AB*.

5. Type C and press the down-arrow key once.

The highlight moves down to the next row, and Access saves the changed version of Jules's record.

Editing keys in Access

What? Edit *keys*? How do you do that?

No, you misunderstand. I don't mean that you edit keys in Access — I mean that Access provides you with editing keys. You can use these keys to edit text and other data in datasheet cells.

After you open a cell for editing, you can move around the cell and edit its contents using any of the key combinations in Table 5-2.

Table 5-2	Access Editing Keys
To Do This	*Press These Keys*
Edit data in a field	F2 function key
Move to the beginning of a field	Home
Move to the end of a field	End
Move left one space	Left arrow
Move right one space	Right arrow
Move right one word	Ctrl+Right arrow (hold down the Control key and press the right-arrow key)
Move left one word	Ctrl+Left arrow
Copy highlighted data to the Windows clipboard	Ctrl+Insert
Paste data from the Windows clipboard to the current cell	Shift+Insert
Undo the last editing change	Alt+Backspace (or select Undo from the Edit menu)

Access provides a few other editing keys that apply to special situations. You have a chance to use those further along in the book.

Closing the Customer Table

Now that you've finished entering and editing your customer data, it's time to close the table and take a break. To close the table, double-click on the Window Control button at the top left of the table's window. (Be sure *not* to click on the Access main window button unless you want to close Access, too!) If you're not a good double-clicker, you can also close the window by selecting Close from the File menu.

If you have trouble double-clicking the mouse fast enough, you may want to tell Windows to let you double-click it more slowly. You can do that by opening up the Windows Control Panel (that's in the Main program group) and selecting the Mouse icon. For full details about this, see *Windows 3.11 For Dummies,* 3rd Edition, from IDG Books.

Chapter 6
Get Help Whenever You Need It

• •

In This Chapter

▶ How to use Context-sensitive Help

▶ Using the Help Table of Contents and hypertext

▶ How to search for a Help topic

▶ How to use Cue Cards

• •

*T*here's an old saying: If you teach someone how to fish, then . . . no, wait, that's not it. If you give someone a fish, pack it in dry ice . . . no, that's not it, either. Anyway, the point is, this book teaches you how to use the most important features of Access. But what if you forget something and don't have the book handy or used the pages to wrap fish? What do you do then?

That's when the powerful Access Help System comes in handy. It enables you to *teach yourself* new skills as you need them. In Access, you can:

✔ Browse through Help topics at random by using the Table of Contents.

✔ Use the Context-sensitive Help feature to get help with whatever you're working on at the moment.

✔ Click on Search to get help on any topic you can name.

✔ Use Cue Cards to get step-by-step instructions for database tasks *as you're doing them*.

✔ Use Wizards and let Access do most of the work *for* you.

In the spirit of teaching you how to fish — or at least how to find out things for yourself — this chapter takes you step by step through the Access Help System. Wizards are covered in separate chapters.

Getting Help in Access

The most obvious place to look for help is on the Help menu, which is always at the upper right of the top-line menu bar.

The first item on the menu is Contents. If you select this menu choice, Access displays a screen that lists all the major topics in the Help System, as shown in Figure 6-1.

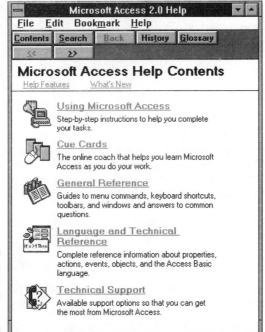

Figure 6-1:
The Help
Table of
Contents.

Using hypertext links

Virtually every screen in the Access Help System has *hypertext*. No, the term doesn't refer to very, very nervous text. What it means is that when you see a topic you want to read about, you just click on the topic, and Access takes you directly to a Help screen about that topic. The new Help screen has more hypertext, which lets you jump to other screens, and so on.

Access remembers the location and size of the Help window from the last time it was displayed. If you want the Help window to appear in a certain location or be a certain size, you can drag it around the screen and resize it with the mouse. Access displays the window in its new size and/or location until you change the window again.

The following steps put the Table of Contents and hypertext through their paces to show you how they work. If you quit Access after the last chapter, start it up again and open the Caveat database you created in earlier chapters. Then do the following:

1. Open the Help menu and click on Contents.

The Table of Contents window opens, as in Figure 6-1.

2. Notice the mouse cursor.

The cursor, which is usually an arrow, turns into a little pointing hand when it's over some of the text in the window. When the cursor turns into a hand, it's pointing at hypertext.

3. Click on the hypertext *Using Microsoft Access.*

Access immediately takes you to a window that lists the most important help topics, as shown in Figure 6-2.

Any time you see the cursor turn into a pointing hand, you know that it's over a hypertext item. To see more about the item, just click the left mouse button.

Try clicking on hypertext items a few more times to jump from one Help screen to another. Don't worry. Access leaves a trail of bread crumbs so that you can find your way back to the starting screen if you need to!

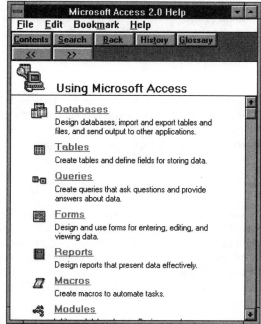

Figure 6-2:
Hypertext links take you from one Help screen to another.

Using the Help buttons

Take a closer look at the buttons that appear at the top of every Help screen: Contents, Search, Back, History, and two buttons marked with double arrows. Figure 6-3 shows these buttons.

Figure 6-3:
Help screen
buttons.

The Contents button

If you move from the Help Table of Contents screen to another screen (as you just did by using hypertext links), clicking on this button takes you back to the Contents screen.

The Search button

You can use this button to search for the Help topic you need. You learn how to use it in the next section.

The Back button

If you move from your starting Help screen to another screen, clicking on this button retraces your steps. It takes you back the way you came, one Help screen at a time.

The History button

If you click on this button, Access displays a little window that lists the previous 40 Help topics you've seen. You can use the scroll bar on the right side of the window to move down through the list if all the items aren't visible in the window. It's a great way to locate a Help topic that you looked at once and can't find again.

The arrow buttons

If you click on the arrow button marked >>, Access displays the next Help screen in a series of related screens. The arrow button marked << takes you to the preceding Help screen in a series. If you're at the last screen in a series, there isn't any next screen, so the >> button doesn't do anything if you click on it. The same thing applies if you're at the first screen in a series: There isn't any preceding screen, so clicking on the << button doesn't do anything.

Normally, the label on a button or menu choice is displayed in solid black type. Sometimes, however, the text is displayed in gray letters that are a little hard to read. This means that the button or menu choice doesn't apply to what you're doing at the moment, so it's "grayed out" and isn't available at the moment.

Using the Help menus

Just like most windows, Access Help windows have a menu bar at the top. The menus give you several extra tricks you can use to get help faster.

Creating bookmarks

Did you ever use a bookmark? It's a little slip of paper, or an index card, or a mackerel that you put between the pages of a book so that you can instantly find your place again. Well, you can do the same thing with Access, except that you can't use the mackerel.

The following steps take you through the process of setting a bookmark and returning to it. If you're not currently at the Microsoft Access Help Contents screen, click on the Contents button to return to it.

Now suppose that you want to find out how to add records to a table. Do the following:

1. **Click on the hypertext *Using Microsoft Access* on the left side of the Help window.**

   The Using Microsoft Access window appears.

2. **Click on the hypertext *Tables*.**

   A window appears that lists the help topics available for tables.

3. **Click on the hypertext *Adding and Editing Data*.**

   A window appears for this topic.

4. **On the first hypertext line of the window, click on the hypertext *Adding a Record Using a Form or Datasheet*.**

   A new window appears that shows information about this topic.

5. **Click on Bookmark in the menu bar to open the Bookmark menu.**

6. **Click on Define in the Bookmark menu.**

   The Bookmark Define dialog box appears, as shown in Figure 6-4.

7. **To create the bookmark, just click on the OK button in the dialog box — and it's done!**

   There are just three more steps in this demonstration (originally, there were *Thirty-Nine Steps,* but that got us into trouble for copyright infringement).

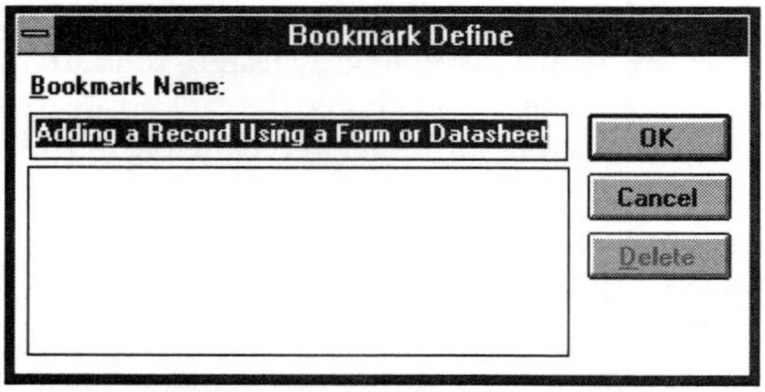

Figure 6-4:
The
Bookmark
Define
dialog box.

Bookmark Define

Bookmark Name:

Adding a Record Using a Form or Datasheet

OK

Cancel

Delete

8. **Click on the Contents button to return to the Help Table of Contents screen.**

9. **Click on Bookmark in the menu bar to open the Bookmark menu.**

   The menu is different this time. Instead of offering only one menu choice, Define, it now has a second menu choice: 1 Adding a Record Using a Form or Datasheet.

10. **Click on the second menu choice.**

   Access takes you directly back to the screen where you placed the bookmark. Stay right there: You're going to do something else that's really incredible.

Annotating Help screens

Another impressive feature of the Access Help System is that you can attach little notes to Help topics. You can record your thoughts on a Help topic — either as a reminder to yourself or as a suggestion for other people who may be entering data on your PC.

To see how this feature works, add a note to the current Help topic. Follow these steps:

1. **From the Edit menu, select Annotate.**

   The Annotate dialog box appears.

2. **Enter your note.**

   The cursor is already in the correct part of the dialog box for you to enter text. So type the following: **It's better to use forms when you're entering data, but using datasheets is okay.**

3. **Click on the Save button in the top right corner of the dialog box.**

As soon as you save the annotation, a little paper clip icon appears in the top left corner of the Help window. Whenever you see the paper clip, you know that a note is attached to the current Help screen. Click on it, and your note appears. To close the note window, just click on the Cancel button on the right side of the window. Then click on the Contents button to return to the Help Contents screen.

TIP

Underlined letters in the menu

Any time you see a menu choice that has a letter underlined, such as Print Topic, the underlined letter is the speed key for that menu choice. To activate the menu choice without having to open the menu, press the Alt key plus the underlined letter.

Getting help about the Help System

It probably won't surprise you, but the Help System gives you information about *every* feature in Access — even the Help System itself!

To get "Help on Help," you need to be in a Help window already. Then just click on Help. A menu appears. The options on the menu are

- **How to use Help:** This information explains how to use each different Help feature, just as I'm doing in this chapter.

- **Always on Top:** This option tells Access to keep the Help window displayed on-screen at all times.

- **About Help:** Select this option, and Access displays a screen that shows the current version of the Help System. You can ignore this menu choice.

Printing Help screens

If you want a paper copy of a particular Help topic, you can print one by selecting Print Topic from the Help window's File menu. Make sure that (a) you *have* a printer and (b) the printer is turned on and ready to print.

Using Context-Sensitive Help

Context-sensitive Help is at once Access's easiest and most powerful Help feature. *Context sensitive* means that Access gives you help on whatever you're doing at the moment. If you're in the Database window, Access displays a Help screen about setting up a database. If you're designing a table, you get help on that task — and so on.

To use Context-sensitive Help, just press the F1 function key. That's all you need to do. Access displays a Help screen that it thinks is relevant to what you're doing. If you need a different Help screen, you can still use the buttons and hypertext links to get there.

If you click on the question-mark button that's always on the right end of the toolbar, the mouse pointer turns into an arrow with a question mark. Then you can just click on the part of the screen where you need help.

Searching for a Topic

Access also enables you to search for a Help topic, which is another easy-to-use but powerful feature. You can get to the Search dialog box (shown in Figure 6-5) in two ways:

✔ If you're not already in the Help System, select Search from the Help menu.

✔ If you *are* already in the Help System, click on the Search button in the top of the window.

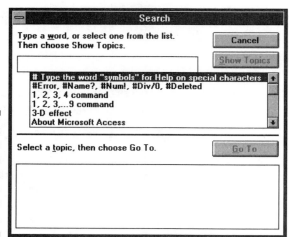

Figure 6-5:
Use the
Search
dialog box
to find the
Help topics
you need.

Suppose that you are setting up a table and aren't sure which data type to use for a particular field. You can search for help on data types by following these steps:

1. Open the Search dialog box.

The cursor is automatically positioned in the blank where you type the topic you want to search for.

2. Enter the search topic.

For this example, type **data types.** As you type, the list box underneath the blank automatically moves to the topics that relate to data.

3. Select a subtopic.

In the box, double-click on the topic data types: field. In the next list box down, Access displays all topics relevant to that subtopic, as shown in Figure 6-6.

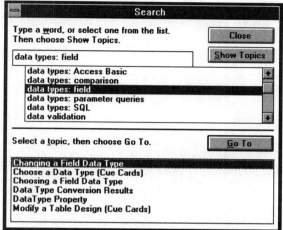

Figure 6-6:
The Search dialog box displays relevant Help topics.

4. Double-click on the Help topic you want to see.

For the purposes of this example, double-click on Choosing a Field Data Type. Access takes you to a Help screen with advice on that topic.

You can search for any Help topic in exactly the same way.

Using Cue Cards and Wizards

Cue Cards and Wizards are the final stop on your tour through the Access Help System. These features go beyond just giving you general information; they take you step by step through whatever it is you need to get done.

The main difference between Cue Cards and Wizards is that Cue Cards give you step-by-step instructions on what to do, while Wizards actually do most of the work *for* you. Each important Wizard has its own chapter in this book, so in this chapter, I'll just tell you briefly how to use Cue Cards.

All you really need to do is select Cue Cards from the Help menu. The main Cue Cards window appears, as shown in Figure 6-7.

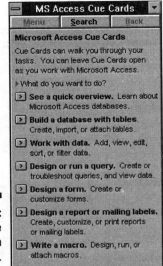

Figure 6-7:
The Cue
Cards main
window.

Suppose that you want to add a table to the sample Caveat database. In the Cue Cards main window, click on the button for Build a Database with Tables. Access automatically displays a series of Cue Cards on the right side of the screen, with your work area still showing on the left side of the screen. As you go along creating the new table, you just click on the appropriate button in the Cue Cards window to get instructions on what you should do next.

If you don't need the Cue Cards anymore, you can get rid of them by closing the Cue Cards window. You do this in exactly the same way as you'd close any other window: by double-clicking on the Window Control button at the top left corner of the window.

Play with the Access Help System until you get a feel for it. Then you can use it any time you need to get *instant information* about Access!

Chapter 7
Looking at Your Data

• •

• •

Creating tables, playing footsie with Access Wizards, and browsing help screens are all fine ways to spend a few hours. But at some point, you've got to be able to *see* the data in your database. Otherwise, it does you about as much good as an accordion in a rap group. In this chapter, you learn to change a table's datasheet so that you can see everything you need at a glance.

Changing the Look of Your Datasheet

If you want to make your datasheet easier to read — or you just don't like the way it looks — you can easily do a datasheet "makeover." You can change the width of columns, make rows taller or shorter, and even change the order of columns. To get some practice at changing your datasheet layout, open the Caveat database you created in earlier chapters (or follow along with your own database). Double-click on Customer Records to display the table's datasheet, shown in Figure 7-1.

You can do a number of things to improve this datasheet. In particular:

✔ Several of the columns (Cust ID, First Name, Last Name, MrMs, Salutation, State, and Zip) are much wider than they need to be.

✔ The datasheet may be easier to read if the rows were double-spaced.

✔ The datasheet would make more sense if the MrMs column came before the First Name and Last Name columns.

You could make some other changes as well, but these are a good start.

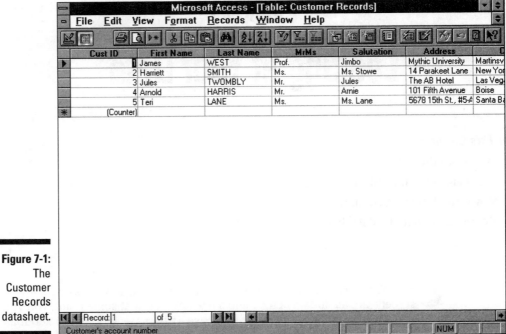

Figure 7-1:
The
Customer
Records
datasheet.

Changing Column Width

You can change a column's width in two ways. The first is quick and easy but not very precise, while the second is precise but involves a couple more steps.

Changing column width using the mouse

The first method is simply to drag a column's right border with the mouse. To do this, move the mouse cursor into the gray row where the column labels appear, at the top of the datasheet. Notice that the mouse cursor changes shape. Depending on where it is, the mouse cursor can be either:

- ✓ A down-pointing arrow, which means that you can select the current column, or
- ✓ A double left-and-right pointing arrow, which means that you can drag a column border to resize the column.

To try this method out, do the following:

1. **Position the cursor on the vertical line that serves as the right border of the Cust ID column.**

2. **Move the cursor up the border until it's in the gray row between the column captions *Cust ID* and *First Name*.**

   Notice that the mouse cursor changes into a double left-and-right pointing arrow.

3. **Hold down the left mouse button and slowly roll the mouse to the left.**

   As you do, the column border moves to the left, causing the column to become narrower. Stop when the mouse cursor touches the *D* in *Cust ID*.

4. **Release the left mouse button.**

   The column has narrowed, and the caption is centered in the new column width, as shown in Figure 7-2.

The problem with using this method is that it's very hard to get exact column widths. The following two sections describe a more precise way to resize columns. This second method also offers another advantage: You can use it to resize more than one column at a time.

Figure 7-2:
The new,
narrower
Cust ID
column.

Cust ID	First Name	Last Name	MrMs	Salutation
1	James	WEST	Prof.	Jimbo
2	Harriett	SMITH	Ms.	Ms. Stowe
3	Jules	TWOMBLY	Mr.	Jules
4	Arnold	HARRIS	Mr.	Arnie
5	Teri	LANE	Ms.	Ms. Lane

Selecting single or multiple columns

Before you can use the second method to resize a column, you must first *select* the column. First, move the mouse into the gray area at the top of the column. When the mouse cursor turns into a little downward-pointing arrow, it means that you can select the column. Click on the left mouse button. Access displays the column name in reverse video, as shown in Figure 7-3. The highlight indicates that the column is selected. Any changes you make now affect the selected column.

Go ahead and try selecting the First Name column in the sample datasheet. Your screen looks like the one in Figure 7-3.

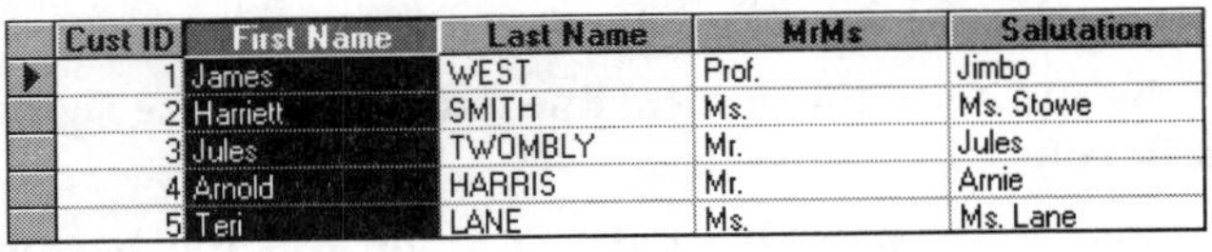

Figure 7-3:
The First
Name column
is selected.

If you want to select more than one column at a time, just select one column and hold down the Shift key. Tap the Right Arrow or Left Arrow key. Each time you tap the key, an additional column will be selected.

Hold down the Shift key on your keyboard and successively click in the gray areas at the top of the Last Name, MrMs, and Salutation columns. Then release the Shift key and let go of the mouse. All four columns should be highlighted, as shown in Figure 7-4. This means that all the columns are selected.

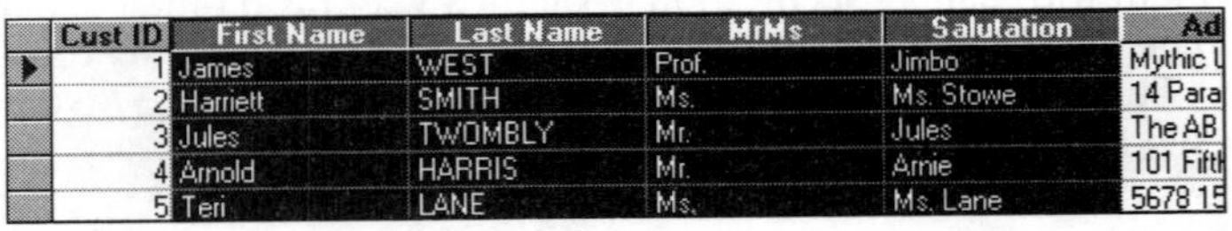

Figure 7-4:
All four
columns are
selected.

Resizing multiple columns

You can resize all selected columns at one time. To do so, select the columns you want to resize, and then open the Format menu and select Column Width. The Column Width dialog box appears, as shown in Figure 7-5. The width of the selected column appears in the Column Width blank. The width of the columns in the sample datasheet is 18.8 characters, as shown in the figure. If the selected columns are different widths, the width blank will be empty, but it won't affect your ability to resize all the columns

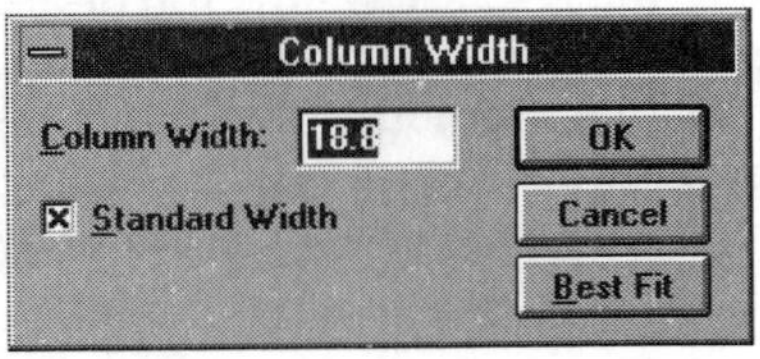

Figure 7-5:
The Column
Width dialog
box.

You can change the width of the selected columns in two ways. If you know precisely how wide you want the columns to be, you can enter a number in the Column Width blank to replace the current value. Otherwise, you can click on the Best Fit button to let Access choose a new width that's just big enough for the column heading.

The column width in the datasheet has no effect on the field length in the table. Making a column narrower doesn't reduce the amount of data you can put in a field, and making it wider doesn't increase the amount of data you can enter. The only reason to change column widths (and row heights) is to make the datasheet easier to read.

In the sample datasheet, the column headings are plenty wide enough to accommodate the data, so just click on the Best Fit button.

After you specify a column size, click anywhere in the datasheet to remove the reverse-video highlight and deselect the columns. Access automatically resizes the columns for you, as shown in Figure 7-6.

Figure 7-6:
Access
automatically
resizes the
selected
columns.

Cust ID	First Name	Last Name	MrMs	Salutation	Address
1	James	WEST	Prof.	Jimbo	Mythic University
2	Harriett	SMITH	Ms.	Ms. Stowe	14 Parakeet Lane
3	Jules	TWOMBLY	Mr.	Jules	The AB Hotel
4	Arnold	HARRIS	Mr.	Arnie	101 Fifth Avenue
5	Teri	LANE	Ms.	Ms. Lane	5678 15th St., #5-A

You now are able to see more of the data from your sample datasheet on-screen. The Address, City, and State columns are all there. Only the Zip column is still cut off by the right edge of the screen. To fix the problem, use either of the two methods you just learned to make the State field narrower so that all the columns will be visible on-screen.

Widening a column

You can widen a column with the same methods you use to narrow a column: either drag the right border or use the column width dialog box. In the example datasheet, the address column is slightly too narrow to display all of Teri Lane's address. Using the mouse, drag the right border of the Address column to the right until all of Teri Lane's address is visible.

Changing Row Height

If you look at the sample datasheet on your screen, you can see that changing the column widths made the datasheet a lot more readable. But the records are still jammed together vertically. The datasheet would be even easier to read if the rows had more height — or were "double-spaced," if you like.

You can change row height in almost exactly the same way that you change column width. At the left edge of the datasheet is a vertical gray area. If you move the cursor into this area, it turns into either:

- ✔ A right-pointing arrow, indicating that you can use it to select the current row, or

- ✔ A double up-and-down arrow, indicating that you can use it to resize rows in the datasheet.

Note that there is one important difference between resizing rows and columns, however. Columns in the datasheet can be different widths, so you can resize just one column at a time. But rows in a datasheet must all be the same height. If you resize one row, you resize all the others at the same time. You don't *need* to select multiple rows as you do to resize multiple columns.

To make the rows taller, just move the mouse cursor into the gray area at the left until it looks like a double up-and-down arrow. Then hold down the left mouse button and slowly drag the horizontal bottom edge of the row downward. As you do, you can see the row height increasing. Release the mouse button when the rows are the size you want them to be.

For practice, make the rows in the sample datasheet taller. When the rows look as if they're about double-spaced, release the left mouse button. Access resizes all the rows in the datasheet, as shown in Figure 7-7.

Figure 7-7:
All the rows
have been
resized.

Cust ID	First Name	Last Name	MrMs	Salutation	Address	City	State	Zip
1	James	WEST	Prof.	Jimbo	Mythic University	Martinsville	CA	98035
2	Harriett	SMITH	Ms.	Ms. Stowe	14 Parakeet Lane	New York	NY	10087
3	Jules	TWOMBLY	Mr.	Jules	The AB Hotel	Las Vegas	NV	34567
4	Arnold	HARRIS	Mr.	Arnie	101 Fifth Avenue	Boise	ID	23413
5	Teri	LANE	Ms.	Ms. Lane	5678 15th St., #5-A	Santa Barbara	CA	93101

As you may have guessed, you can also resize rows by selecting Row Height from the Format menu. Except for the fact that all rows are resized at once, this method works exactly the same as resizing columns through the Format menu.

Moving Columns

You may want to make one other change to the sample datasheet layout. (Or you may not, but this is America, and database diversity is guaranteed by the Constitution. I think.) The MrMs column may work better placed to the left of the First Name column.

Just as resizing columns (and rows) has no effect on the size of the fields in the underlying table, moving columns has no effect on the order of fields in the table. Moving a column only changes the placement of the column in the datasheet.

To move a column, move the mouse cursor into the gray area at the top of the column until the cursor changes into a down-pointing arrow. Then click the left mouse button once. Access highlights the column, as shown in Figure 7-8.

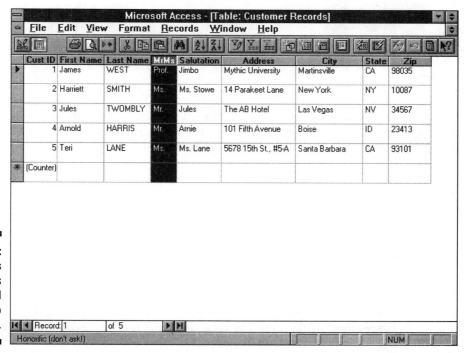

Figure 7-8:
The MrMs
column is
highlighted
and ready to
move.

Now, with the mouse cursor in the top (formerly gray) row of the highlighted area, hold down the left mouse button. The mouse cursor changes shape again, indicating that Access is ready to move the column. Holding the left mouse button down, drag the mouse slowly until the cursor is in the middle of the column that's *just to the right of where you want the new column to be.* When you release the mouse button, Access places the highlighted column on the left of the column where you had the mouse cursor.

That may sound a little confusing, but after you see how the process works, it's not. Try it yourself by moving the MrMs column in the sample datasheet to the left of the First Name column, as shown in Figure 7-9.

Figure 7-9:
The MrMs
column now
appears on
the left of the
First Name
column.

Cust ID	MrMs	First Name	Last Name	Salutation	Address	City	State
1	Prof.	James	WEST	Jimbo	Mythic University	Martinsville	CA
2	Ms.	Harriett	SMITH	Ms. Stowe	14 Parakeet Lane	New York	NY
3	Mr.	Jules	TWOMBLY	Jules	The AB Hotel	Las Vegas	NV
4	Mr.	Arnold	HARRIS	Arnie	101 Fifth Avenue	Boise	ID
5	Ms.	Teri	LANE	Ms. Lane	5678 15th St., #5-A	Santa Barbara	CA

Wondering how to change the labels at the tops of the datasheet columns? You can't do it in the datasheet window which is where you are right now. You can only do it through *field properties* when you design or modify a table.

Freezing Columns

Because the sample table is a small one, you can see all its columns on-screen at once. But suppose you had a table with 25 fields? You may want the MrMs, First Name, and Last Name columns to stay put at the left side of the screen as you move right to view columns not visible on the screen.

That's when Access's ability to freeze columns comes in handy. If you've used a spreadsheet package such as Lotus 1-2-3 or Microsoft Excel, you may already be familiar with this trick.

To see how it works, start by making all the columns in the sample datasheet wider so that Access can't display them all on-screen at once. Follow these steps:

1. **Move the mouse cursor into the gray area at the top of the First Name column.**

   The cursor turns into a down-pointing arrow. Click once with the left mouse button to highlight the column.

2. **Hold down the Shift key and click in the gray areas of the columns to the right of the First Name column until they're all highlighted.**

3. **Open the F̲ormat menu and select C̲olumn Width.**

4. **In the C̲olumn Width dialog box, type 23 as the new value. Then click on OK.**

5. **Click anywhere in the datasheet to remove the highlight.**

   Your screen should look like the one shown in Figure 7-10.

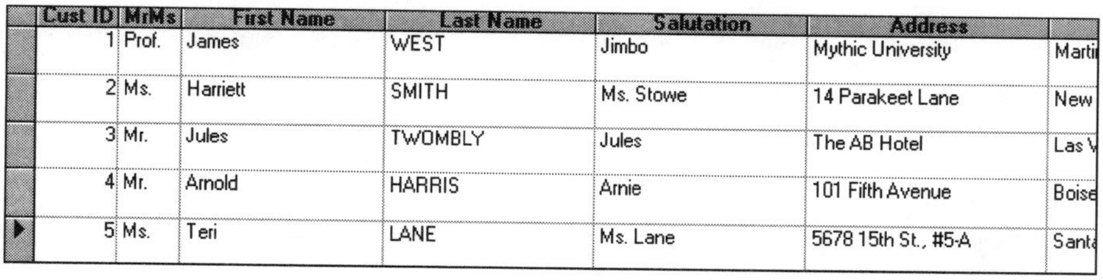

Figure 7-10:
The columns
are wider,
and some
columns can't
be seen.

Cust ID	MrMs	First Name	Last Name	Salutation	Address	
1	Prof.	James	WEST	Jimbo	Mythic University	Marti
2	Ms.	Harriett	SMITH	Ms. Stowe	14 Parakeet Lane	New
3	Mr.	Jules	TWOMBLY	Jules	The AB Hotel	Las V
4	Mr.	Arnold	HARRIS	Arnie	101 Fifth Avenue	Boise
5	Ms.	Teri	LANE	Ms. Lane	5678 15th St., #5-A	Santa

Now select the Cust ID, MrMs, First Name, and Last Name columns. (If you need help remembering how to select columns, refer back to the section "Selecting single or multiple columns," earlier in this chapter.)

In the F̲ormat menu, select Free̲ze Columns. The highlighted columns freeze, just like your apartment when the heat goes off in the dead of winter.

So what? The columns look just the same. You'll see the difference, though, when you scroll to the right. Remember the little buttons at the bottom of the datasheet? You use the single right-arrow button, shown in Figure 7-11, to move to the right if all the columns aren't visible. Likewise, you use the single left-arrow button to move to the left.

Click on the single right-arrow button, and you move to the right in the datasheet. (If you prefer, the datasheet can move to the left while you sit still: That's probably better if you're prone to motion sickness.) Notice that the frozen columns don't disappear off the left side of the screen as they normally do when you scroll. Instead, they stay put, as shown in Figure 7-12. That's what it means to freeze the columns.

U̲nfreezing columns is just as easy. Simply open the F̲ormat menu and select Unfreeze All Columns. Go ahead and unfreeze the columns in your sample datasheet now.

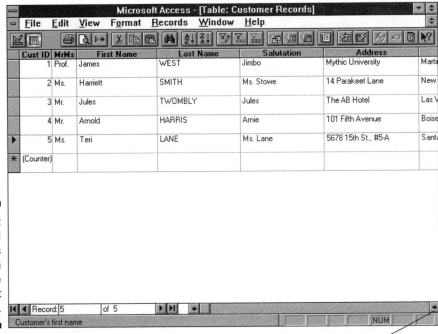

Figure 7-11:
The scroll right button is at the bottom of the Datasheet window.

The scroll right button

Figure 7-12:
Frozen columns stay put while the rest of the datasheet moves left.

Cust ID	MrMs	First Name	Last Name	City	State	Zip
1	Prof.	James	WEST	Martinsville	CA	98035
2	Ms.	Harriett	SMITH	New York	NY	10087
3	Mr.	Jules	TWOMBLY	Las Vegas	NV	34567
4	Mr.	Arnold	HARRIS	Boise	ID	23413
5	Ms.	Teri	LANE	Santa Barbara	CA	93101

Save Your Changes

Access automatically saves some things, such as the data in a record when you move to the next record. But changes in the layout of a datasheet are *not* saved automatically.

To save the datasheet layout, simply open the File menu and click on Save Table. So that all your hard work on the sample datasheet layout doesn't go for naught, save it now.

If you want to take a break, shut down Access and plop down on the couch. There's a good rerun of "Gilligan's Island" starting right about now. Otherwise, turn the page and head for the next chapter. (The Skipper would be proud of you, little buddy.)

Part II
Finding and Playing With Your Data

The 5th Wave By Rich Tennant

PORTRAIT OF A CYBERHOLIC

HEY, MISTER! WHEN I SAY PUT YOUR HANDS UP, I MEAN BOTH OF THEM!

In this part ...

Basic skills are important. If you didn't know how to make change, balance a budget, or write your name, you'd have few career options except to run for Congress.

But basic skills, which are covered in Part I, can only take you so far. This part shows you more advanced stuff you can do with Access. You find out how to change a table design, create on-screen forms that explain your database and catch errors, and search for data.

And if you *still* want to run for Congress, well, that option is always open for you.

Chapter 8

Redesigning Your Table

*H*ardly anything is perfect on the first try. Mozart supposedly could knock out a perfect string quartet in an afternoon, but music historians now believe that the story was concocted by his publicist. Other than Mozart's perfect string quartets, there's only chocolate-almond ice cream, the Los Angeles Lakers, and Blossom Russo.

It's next to impossible to set up the perfect table on your first try. Just when you think you've set up the Customer Records table perfectly, your boss walks in and requests some changes. He knows that you're a whiz and is sure that you can make the changes quickly and easily. And guess what? With Access, you *are* and you *can*.

To help you understand and work with the concepts in this chapter, you should read Chapter 3 first.

What Changes Can You Make?

What can you change about your table? In a word, *anything you want.* (Okay, so that's three words; sue me.) You can change the definition of fields you created, add fields, move fields, delete fields, and Marshall Fields. In this chapter, you learn how to do all these things because your boss has suddenly got *lots* of good ideas that he wants you to put in the database design.

If you need to redesign a database, don't beat yourself up about it (unless you just *like* doing that sort of thing). In most cases, changes aren't needed because of anything you did wrong, but because your database users either: (a) change their minds about what they want; (b) get an idea for a new feature they want you to add; or (c) didn't explain what they really need in the first place.

In fact, (c) is the worst cause of database design changes, because it's the most avoidable. When you're designing a database for anyone other than yourself, make sure that you make *them* be clear about what they want. If they refuse — well, this book doesn't sanction violence, but . . .

Changing Fields (or, Fooling with Field Formats)

As with other database-creation tasks, the best way to learn how to change the fields in your database is to work through a few examples. With that in mind, the following sections show you how to make changes to the sample Caveat database you've been working on since Chapter 2.

 If you haven't already done so, start up Access and open the Caveat database. In the Database window, click on the Design button at the top right. The table design window appears, as shown in Figure 8-1. Maximize the table design window so that it fills the entire screen.

Turning on automatic uppercase

Suppose that you are asked to change the Last Name field in the Customer Records table so that it automatically converts the customer's last name to all uppercase letters. This change will save the data-entry person some work. It will also ensure that no matter who enters a customer record, the last name will always be in uppercase.

Field Name	Data Type	Description	
⑧▶ Cust ID	Counter	Customer's account number	▲
First Name	Text	Customer's first name	
Last Name	Text	Customer's last name	
MrMs	Text	Honorific (don't ask!)	
Salutation	Text	Dear ...	
Address	Text	Street address	
City	Text	City	
State	Text	State or province	
Zip	Text	Postal code	▼

Table: Customer Records

Field Properties

Format	
Caption	
Indexed	Yes (No Duplicates)

A field name can be up to 64 characters long, including spaces. Press F1 for help on field names.

Figure 8-1: The table design window.

In order to make the Last Name field automatically change letters to uppercase, you need to fool around with the field properties at the bottom of the screen.

This is nothing scary: You already set the length property for each field when you designed the table. To set this other property, just follow these steps:

1. **Click in the Data Type column in the row that contains the Last Name field.**

   The Field Properties pane (in the bottom half of the screen) displays more choices, as shown in Figure 8-2.

2. **Click in the Format blank in the Field Properties pane.**

3. **Type a right-pointing angle bracket (>) in the blank.**

4. **Click in the Last Name row in the top part of the screen.**

5. **Save the changes in the table design by selecting Save from the File menu.**

Figure 8-2:
Field
properties
available for
text fields.

Field Properties	
Field Size	15
Format	
Input Mask	
Caption	
Default Value	
Validation Rule	
Validation Text	
Required	No
Allow Zero Length	No
Indexed	No

A field name can be up to 64 characters long, including spaces. Press F1 for help on field names.

And that's it! The next time someone enters a customer record, Access will automatically convert the customer's last name to uppercase letters. No more using the Caps Lock key and then forgetting to turn it off.

You can also use the Format property to put *boilerplate text* into a field. Suppose that you wanted the Cust ID field of every record to include the text *Acct. #* followed by the customer's ID number, which Access assigns automatically. In the Format blank for the Cust ID field, you'd type **"Acct. # " 0000** (including the quote marks). When you looked at the datasheet, every Cust ID field would include that text followed by the ID number, padded out to the left with zeroes, such as *Acct. # 0005.*

Understand that the boilerplate text is simply part of how the account number is shown in the datasheet. It's not actually part of the data in the Cust ID field.

Setting field properties

What you did in the preceding section was assign a *field property* to the Last Name field. Making Access change letters to uppercase is only one of the things you can do in the Field Properties pane. You use another field property (Input

Mask) later in this chapter, when you add a phone number field to the Customer Records table. But here's a summary of what the field properties are and what they do:

Field Size: The Field Size property tells Access how many characters (letters, digits, punctuation marks, and stuff like that) can be put into a field. A text field can be as many as 255 characters. Unless you specify otherwise, Access gives all text fields a size of 50 characters. (Other types of fields also have a field size, but you don't need to worry about them because Access handles their size for you.) Remember that the field size is *different* from the size of a field's column in the datasheet.

Format: This property enables you to control how some types of data are entered and displayed. For example, you can use it to convert letters typed in a field to uppercase. You also can use it to control the number of decimal places in a number; to specify the way in which dates and Yes/No values are displayed; and to insert boilerplate text in a field.

Input Mask: The Input Mask property enables you to do two things. First, you can restrict what type of data can be put into specific slots of a field. Second, when all the values in a field will have the same format, you can put boilerplate formatting characters into the field. In the next section, you use this property to jazz up a phone number field.

Caption: This property lets you specify the caption at the top of the datasheet column for the currently selected field in the top part of the screen. If you don't fill in this property, Access simply uses the field name.

Default Value: A default value is a value that you want Access to automatically enter into a field unless you specify otherwise. Typical examples of default values would be $1,000 for your monthly phone bill, *Rex* for a dog's name, and 0 for the number of boys who are good enough for your daughter.

Validation Rule: This property tells Access what data is and is not acceptable in a particular field. For example, if you're creating a database for a bookstore that doesn't carry books that sell for less than $10, you can make $10 the minimum value in a price field for an inventory table.

Validation Text: Validation Text is a message that appears on-screen if the user tries to enter a value that's prohibited by a field's validation rule. Access allows you to use profanity in these messages, but it's generally not a good idea unless you're an experienced database user (@#$%^!!!).

Required: If you set this property to Yes for a field, Access does not allow the user to save a record unless data is entered in the field.

Allow Zero Length: This property applies to text fields. If you set it to Yes, you can enter two quote marks to indicate that the field doesn't apply to the current record. (In computer lingo, this is known as entering a *zero-length string*.) For example, a blank fax number field might mean that you don't know the customer's fax number. But if you enter two quotes, it shows that the field is empty because the customer does not have a fax number.

Indexed: This property speeds up things when you search for records based on the data in the field. It's entirely optional and, for small databases (a thousand records or less), won't make any difference. Indexes are explained in Chapter 15.

If you already have records in your table, you can lose data when you change a field, especially if you're changing its size or data type. Before making any changes in your table design, it's a good idea to copy your database file to another directory as a backup and make your changes to the original.

Adding Fields

Adding new fields is even easier than changing fields. The following examples show you how to add a field to your sample table and also how to use the Input Mask property.

Adding a field to a table design *doesn't* add any data in the new field. If the table already contains records, you need to go back and add the data into the new field for those records.

Adding a field at the end of the table

Suppose that Honest Janis — the imaginary bookstore owner for whom you've been creating the sample database — wants to add a phone number field to the table. It's a good idea because the bookstore sometimes needs customer phone numbers.

If you've been following along and working on the sample database in this chapter, you should still be at the table design window. The easiest place to add the field is at the end of the table, underneath the line for the Zip field. Easy is good, so let's do it that way. To add the phone number field, follow these steps:

1. **Open the Table Design window for the Customer Records table and click in the line under the Zip field.**

   A black triangle appears at the left end of the line, indicating that you're in the right place.

2. **Enter the field name.**

   Type **Phone Number** and then press Tab or click in the Data Type column of the same row.

3. **Specify a data type.**

   What data type should you use? Remember that even though the field will contain phone numbers, you aren't going to do any arithmetic with the numbers. Therefore, just accept the default data type of Text.

4. **In the Field Properties pane in the bottom part of the screen, click in the blank next to Input Mask.**

5. **In the Input Mask blank, type (999) 999-9999.**

   Be sure to include a space between the closing parenthesis and the next 9, and *don't* include the period at the end. For now, don't worry about what an Input Mask does; you learn all about it shortly.

6. **Click in the Description column of the Phone Number line in the top part of the screen.**

   Type **Customer's phone number** to enter the description. Your screen should look like the one in Figure 8-3.

7. **Save the changes in the table design.**

   Just click on the Save button at the top of the screen. The Save button is a toolbar shorcut for opening the File menu and selecting Save.

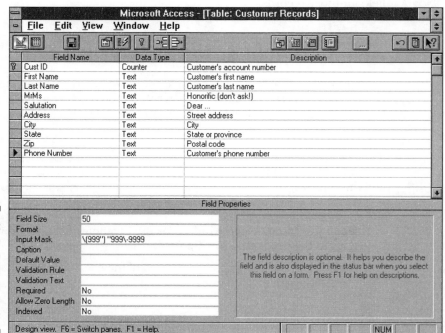

Figure 8-3:
Adding the
phone
number field
to the
sample
table.

Understanding input masks

The first thing to understand about *input masks* is that they're different from masks used by superheroes, bank robbers, and the uncle who, according to your parents, is a little funny in the head. You use input masks to control and format the data in a field.

In the preceding section, you did two things when you specified the mask for the Phone Number field:

> ✔ You put some formatting characters in the field: parentheses to enclose the area code and a hyphen to separate the parts of the phone number.
>
> ✔ By filling the rest of the field with 9s, you told Access that only digits or spaces can be put in the field. No letters or other characters are allowed.

There's more to input masks, but that's plenty for now. The main thing to remember is that if you need to (a) format data that has the same structure in every record or (b) restrict data to digits or spaces, you can use an input mask to do it.

Inserting a field in the middle of the table

You insert a field in the middle of the table by making yet another revision to the infamous Customer Records table. The field you insert will hold the date of the customer's first purchase.

The basic technique is this: Click in the line for the field that's *just below* where you want to insert the new field. Then select Insert Row from the Edit menu. An empty row opens up above the field where your cursor was located. After that, you simply define the field in the normal way.

To insert and define the new field in the sample table, follow these steps:

1. **Click in the line for the Phone Number field.**

    You're going to insert the new field above the Phone Number field.

2. **Open the Edit menu and select Insert Row.**

    A blank row should open up above the Phone Number field.

3. **Enter the field name.**

    Type **First Purchase Date** and then press Tab to move to the Data Type column.

4. **Choose a data type.**

    Click on the list-box arrow on the right side of the blank. In the list that appears, select Date/Time by clicking on it.

5. **Click in the Format blank in the Field Properties pane at the bottom of the screen.**

6. **Select the format.**

   Click on the list-box arrow on the right end of the blank. From the list of available Date/Time formats, click on Short Date to select it.

7. **Enter the field description.**

   In the top part of the screen, click in the Description blank for the new field. For the description, type **Date of customer's first purchase.**

8. **Save the new table design.**

   Click on the Save button in the toolbar. Your screen should look like the one in Figure 8-4.

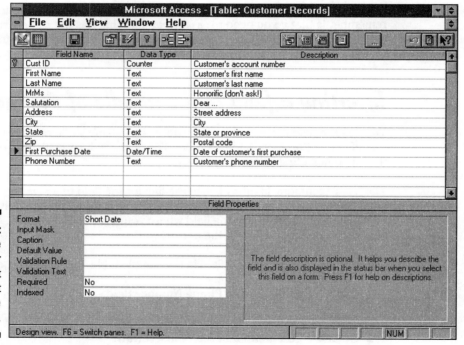

Figure 8-4:
The sample table after you insert the First Purchase Date field.

Moving Fields

In general, the order of fields in a table isn't that important. As I explain in Chapter 7, you can rearrange the order of columns in the datasheet. However, the table's field order does control the order in which fields are *normally* displayed in datasheets, forms, reports, and so on. At times, you may want to change the order by moving a field.

The general technique is as follows:

1. **Select the row for the field you want to move.**

2. **Drag the field until the mouse pointer is pointing at the row that's *just below* where you want to place the field.**

3. **Release the mouse button.**

To see how it's done, move the First Purchase Date field in the sample table so that it comes just after the Cust ID field and just before the First Name field. Follow these steps:

1. **Click in the gray area (the *row selector*) at the left end of the line for the First Purchase Date field.**

   Access displays the row in reverse video to indicate that the row is selected.

2. **Move the mouse pointer so that its tip is directly over the white triangle in the row selector part of the line.**

   The mouse pointer should look like a single arrow. If it changes to a double up-and-down arrow, it's not in the right position.

3. **Hold down the left mouse button and drag the row up until the tip of the mouse pointer is over the First Name row.**

4. **Release the mouse button.**

   The First Purchase Date row should now be above the First Name row.

Remember that you can always rearrange the order of the columns in the datasheet. Doing so has no effect on the order of fields in the table.

Deleting Fields

Imagine that shortly after you finish moving the First Purchase Date field to its new location, Honest Janis changes his mind. He decides that the table doesn't need a First Purchase Date field after all, so you need to delete the field from the table. But you're not frustrated: Janis has promised that if the database is ready on schedule, he'll buy you a first edition of this book. (Come to think of it, you already *have* a first edition of this book, so why are you working so hard?)

Sweet and generous person that you are, you decide to delete the field anyway. And it's the easiest thing you've done yet.

To delete a field, just follow these steps:

1. **Click in the row selector area of the field you want to delete.**

   For the sample table, click in the row selector area of the First Purchase Date field. Access displays the selected row in reverse video.

2. **Either open the Edit menu and select Delete or just press the Delete key on your keyboard.**

   Access displays a dialog box and asks whether you really want to delete the row.

3. **Click on OK.**

   Access deletes the field, and the field disappears from the field list window.

4. **Click on the Save button in the toolbar.**

   Access saves your modified table design.

Filling in Phone Numbers

As a final housekeeping detail, open the Customer Records table in the sample database and fill in the Phone Number fields for the five records you previously entered. Notice that as soon as you click in the Phone Number field, the input mask appears, as shown in Figure 8-5.

Figure 8-5:
The input mask appears in the Phone Number field

	Salutation	Address	City	State	Zip	Phone Number
	Jimbo	Mythic University	Martinsville	CA	98035	( ) -
	Ms. Stowe	14 Parakeet Lane	New York	NY	10087	
	Jules	The AB Hotel	Las Vegas	NV	34567	
	Arnie	101 Fifth Avenue	Boise	ID	23413	
	Ms. Lane	5678 15th St., #5-A	Santa Barbara	CA	93101	

When you type the phone numbers, don't worry about typing the parentheses and the hyphen: Access already put them in the field for you. Type *only* the numbers:

James West	415 555 4678
Harriett Stowe	212 555 2345
Jules Twombly	201 555 6213
Arnold Harris	321 555 9876
Teri Lane	805 555 1234

You don't have to worry about creating the perfect database on your first attempt because Access makes it so easy for you to make revisions. Now that you've redesigned the sample table to Honest Janis's liking, shut down Access and enjoy his good mood.

Chapter 9
Adding and Using Memo Fields

· ·

In This Chapter

▶ Adding a memo field

▶ Entering a memo

▶ Viewing and editing a memo

· ·

Memo fields are powerful but controversial. They're so controversial, in fact, that until now, you could only learn about them at certain monasteries in Asia where they shave your head and feed you steamed rice and make you sing "The Brady Bunch" in Chinese. Most Access books don't cover memo fields. The authors are afraid.

However, the proprietor of the bookstore (your boss Janis) spent some time in one of those monasteries — don't worry, his hair grew back — so in this chapter, you learn how to create and put data in memo fields. Don't tell anyone that you have this information: The other Kung Fu masters would punish Janis severely for revealing it.

Adding a Memo Field

All fields *except* memo fields must be the same size in every record of a table. For example, you can't set up a text field to hold 10 characters in one record and 200 in another.

Memo fields are different from other fields in two ways:

- ✔ They can vary in size. Memo fields are designed so that they can hold different amounts of data in different records.

- ✔ They can be a lot bigger. Text fields can hold a maximum of 255 characters (letters, digits, and so on). A memo field can hold up to *32,000* characters. That's about eight single-spaced pages of text.

Even though memo fields are different from other fields, you add them to a table in the same way you do any other type of field. To prove it to yourself, add a memo field to the Customer Records table in the sample Caveat database. Open the database, get into the table design window (with the Customer Records table highlighted in the Database window, click on the Design button), and follow these steps:

1. **Click in the row at the bottom of the table design, right under the Phone Number field.**

2. **For the Field Name, type Notes.**

3. **For the Data Type, select Memo.**

4. **For the Description, type Miscellaneous notes, including phone calls.**

5. **Save the table design by clicking on the Save button in the toolbar.**

6. **Close the table design window and return to the Database window.**

Memo fields can vary in size and hold so much data because Access stores their contents separately from the rest of the table data. Instead of trying to cram an unknown but possibly huge amount of text into the table, Access places a *pointer* in the memo field that tells it where it stored the text. When you open a memo field, Access follows the pointer, retrieves the data, and displays it on-screen.

Entering a Memo

The great thing about memo fields — apart from their sentimental association with "The Brady Bunch" song — is that you don't really need to put anything in them. You can store many notes in the memo fields of some records and not put any at all in others.

To practice entering some notes in a memo field, open the Customer Records datasheet. Using the Tab key or the right-arrow key, move over to the last column in the datasheet, marked *Notes*. Type the following in the Notes field for the first row (the record for James West): **A good customer for many years.**

Notice that as you type, the text scrolls off to the left. You could continue typing text, entering as many as 32,000 characters. Of course, you could only see a few words of text at a time, which would be a real drag. Fortunately, Access offers a way to display more of your memo text on-screen at a time.

To see how it works, press the down-arrow key twice to move to the Notes field for Jules Twombly. This time, you're going to enter a longer memo. The method you used to enter the memo for James West won't do. Instead, press Shift+F2 (hold down the Shift key and press the F2 function key). The Zoom box appears, as shown in Figure 9-1.

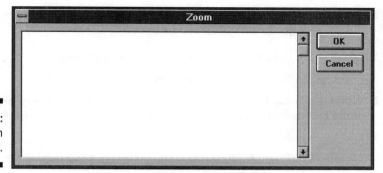

Figure 9-1:
The Zoom
box.

In the blank space in the middle of the box, type the following:

Jules is a heck of a guy. Always pays his bills on time and has excellent taste in books. Not at all afraid of those Kung Fu masters. Wife: Becky. Two daughters: Lori and Sarah.

When you finish typing, click on the OK button in the Zoom box. Press the down-arrow key to move out of the current row, and Access saves the memo data automatically.

If you change your mind while you're entering text in the Zoom box and don't want to save the text, you can either click on the Cancel button or just press the Esc key.

Viewing and Editing a Memo

In the datasheet, you can see the first few words in the memo field, as shown in Figure 9-2. But that's obviously not enough to be practical.

You can open the memo field for viewing or editing in exactly the same way as you did when you entered the memo text in the first place. Just position the cursor so that it's in the memo field and then press Shift+F2 to open the Zoom box.

Figure 9-2:
The first few
words of a
memo field
are shown
in the
datasheet.

City	State	Zip	Phone Number	Notes
Martinsville	CA	98035	(415) 555-4678	A good customer fc
New York	NY	10087	(212) 555-2345	
Las Vegas	NV	34567	(201) 555-6213	Jules is a heck of a
Boise	ID	23413	(321) 555-9876	
Santa Barbara	CA	93101	(805) 555-1234	

Try it with the memo field in the first row of the sample table — the record for James West. Follow these steps:

1. **Position the cursor in the Notes field of the first row.**

2. **Press Shift+F2 to open the Zoom box.**

3. **When the Zoom box opens, the cursor should be at the very beginning of the memo text. Using the mouse, click just to the left of the *g* in *good*.**

4. **Edit the memo.**

   Type **really.** The note should now read: *A really good customer for many years.*

5. **Holding down the Ctrl key, press the right-arrow key three times.**

   The cursor should be on the first letter of the word *many.*

6. **Press the Delete key to erase the text *many years.***

   In its place, type **a long, long time.**

7. **Save the changes.**

   Click on OK and then press the down-arrow key to move out of the row.

To select text for deletion in the Zoom box, position the mouse at the beginning of the text that you want to select. Then, holding down the left mouse button, drag the mouse until all the text that you want to delete is highlighted. If you're a keyboard whiz, you can also select text one word at a time by holding down *both* the Shift and Ctrl keys and then pressing the right- or left-arrow key.

That's all there is to creating, entering, and editing memo fields! Close the datasheet and take a break. Get ready to learn about forms in the next chapter. And watch out for those Kung Fu masters.

Chapter 10
Creating Forms with Form Wizards

● ●

In This Chapter

▶ Forms! What are they good for? Absolutely . . . lots!

▶ Using Form Wizards

▶ Types of forms you can create

▶ Selecting a form's style

▶ Moving around in your table with a form

● ●

*F*orms are a part of modern life. There's the *brilliant, graceful* form your best friend's daughter exhibits in her ballet recital (deny it at your own risk!); the form that the "earth was without, and void" you hear about in church; the Tai Chi forms that your spouse is always practicing in the back room; and, of course, the dreaded IRS Form 1040.

None of these forms has anything to do with Access forms. Access forms, in fact, are much more useful than any of them, except maybe the one about the earth having form, which is *really* useful because it keeps us from flying off into space. In Access, *forms* give you another way — a very *powerful* way — to enter and view the stuff in your database.

What Are Forms Good For?

Saying that "forms are powerful," that they "get your wash 44 percent brighter," or that they perform other miracles doesn't tell you all that much. That's TV-commercial talk, which means that it says nothing. So what are forms and what good are they?

So far, you've learned that you can use the Access datasheet to enter and view all records in a table.

But although the datasheet is good for viewing lots of records at the same time in a row-and- column format, it does have some important disadvantages:

✔ You can view many records at a time, but you normally can't view *all* the data in each record because some of the columns disappear off the right side of the screen.

✔ Apart from the column captions, you can't put text on the datasheet to explain the meaning of each field. If new employees are entering data, they may be confused. In a simple table like the one you created for the book-store customers, this limitation isn't much of a problem. In more complex databases, it can be a *serious* problem.

✔ It's just not as *easy* to enter records using a datasheet as it would be if the screen looked more like a paper form.

Forms let you overcome all these disadvantages. Usually, you'll create forms that display all fields for one record on-screen at the same time, include explanatory text; and look very much like paper forms. If you're an absolute genius (which you *will* be by the time you finish this book), you can put *list boxes* and other *control*s on a form to make it even easier to use. You also can include photos, graphics, and even sound recordings.

Calling Up a Form Wizard

Like most things in Access, creating a form is easy. In this section, you learn just how easy it is by creating a sample form for the Caveat database. If you took a break after the preceding chapter, start up Access again and load the database.

Up to now, everything you've done in the database centered around tables, so you never really used the other tabs in the Database window. Now, however, you're going to create a form. The first step is to click on the Form tab at the left side of the Database window, as shown in Figure 10-1.

When you click on the Form tab, the Database window is empty because you haven't created any forms yet. To create a form, click on the New button at the top of the Database window. The New Form dialog box appears, as shown in Figure 10-2.

The buttons at the top of the Database window (New, Open, and Design) work with whatever element is selected at the moment. In earlier chapters, clicking on New enabled you to begin creating a new table, because the Table tab was selected. Access displays the currently selected tab at the top of the list — it's the one without a vertical border on its right side. In Figure 10-1, the Table tab was selected. Now, the Form tab should be selected.

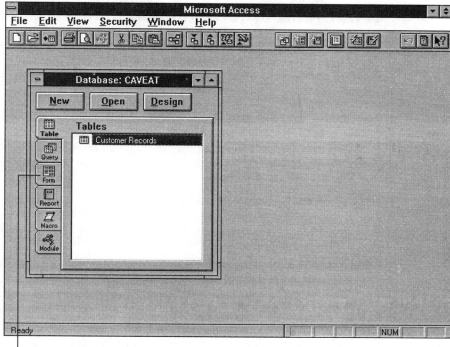

Figure 10-1:
Click on the
Form tab in
the
Database
window.

└ Click here to create a new form

Figure 10-2:
The New
Form dialog
box.

Because a database can have more than one table, you need to tell Access
which table you want to use with the form. At the right end of the Select a
Table/Query blank, you see a down-arrow button, indicating that a list box is
associated with the blank. Click on the button, and Access displays a list of
tables in the database. The sample database has only one table — Customer
Records. Click once on that table to select it.

What kind of form do you want?

After you select a table, click on the Form Wizards button. Access displays a dialog box, shown in Figure 10-3, and asks which Wizard you want to use. What it's really asking, however, is what kind of *form* you want. You can create five basic kinds of forms with Wizards:

- **Single-Column:** A Single-Column form displays the fields on successive lines of the screen. If you were creating a Single-Column form from the Customer Records table, for example, line 1 would be the Cust ID field, line 2 would be the First Name field, and so on. You're going to create a Single-Column form in this chapter.

- **Tabular:** A tabular form displays the fields in rows and columns — which is exactly the same layout as a datasheet. You probably won't use this type of form very often because its only advantages are related to the more heavy-duty features of Access (some of which you learn in Chapter 24.)

- **Graph:** This kind of form includes a graph. To create a graph form, you must select a table that contains some numeric values that Access can chart on a graph, such as sales figures. The Customer Records table doesn't have data like that, but the Sales table, which you create later, does.

- **Main/Subform:** This kind of form combines data from more than one table in the database. It enables you to see (and change) the data in both tables at once.

- **AutoForm:** As its name implies, this form is one that Access creates for you automatically. It includes every field in the table and uses a standard layout. For many situations, it's all you need. An AutoForm form is laid out exactly like a Single-Column form.

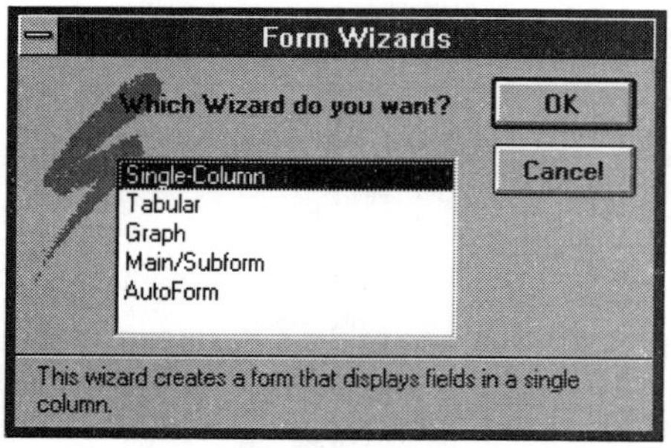

Figure 10-3:
You can
choose from
five types of
forms.

As I said earlier, the sample form you create in this chapter is a Single-Column form. Single-Column should be highlighted in the dialog box; just click on OK to select that choice. If Single-Column *isn't* selected, double-click on it. The field selection dialog box appears, as shown in Figure 10-4.

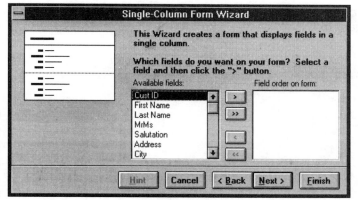

Figure 10-4:
The field
selection
dialog box.

This dialog box looks a lot like the Table Wizard dialog box I discuss in Chapter 4. In the lower right portion of the dialog box, Access displays two list boxes. The one on the left lists all fields in the Customer Records table. The one on the right, which is currently empty, shows all fields that are selected to appear on the form.

A form doesn't have to include *all* the fields in a table. You can include as many or as few fields as you want. For entering new records, though, it's best to create a form that includes all fields in the table.

Selecting fields for the form

The next step is to pick the fields that you want to appear on the form. You select fields by using the buttons between the available fields and selected fields lists. These buttons work the same as they do in the Table Wizard dialog box:

- The top button — a.k.a. the "select one" button — selects the currently highlighted field in the available fields list and adds it to the selected fields list.

- The second button, marked with two right-pointing arrows, selects all fields in the available fields list and adds them to the selected fields list.

- The third button, marked with a left-pointing arrow, removes the currently highlighted field from the selected fields list.

- The bottom button removes *all* fields from the selected fields list.

For the sample form, you want to include all fields, so click on the "select all" (second from the top) button. Access displays all the fields in the selected fields list.

Now click on the <u>N</u>ext button. Access displays a form style dialog box, as shown in Figure 10-5.

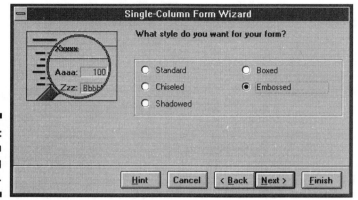

Figure 10-5:
The form
style dialog
box.

If you're in a hurry, you can simply select <u>F</u>inish after selecting the fields and let Access finish the form for you. You don't get to choose the style of the form's on-screen display, but everything else will be the same as if you created the form yourself. You *do* have to select the fields; otherwise, Access creates a blank form. It would have made more sense if Access automatically included all available fields on the form, but nobody's perfect (except you and your boss).

Selecting the form's style

The *style* of the form determines how it will look on-screen. There really isn't a lot of difference between the styles, except that the Boxed style looks kind of interesting. At the moment, though, you're just cruising through the Wizard's woods, so click on <u>N</u>ext to accept the Embossed style. Access displays another dialog box and asks you to give the form a title, as shown in Figure 10-6.

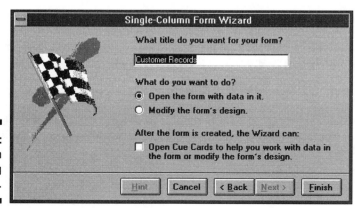

Figure 10-6:
The form
title dialog
box.

Access suggests that you give the form the same title as the table on which it's based. That's fine but rather dull. So in the title blank, type **Caveat Customers: Intellectuals or Nerds?**

At this point, everything is the way you want it (except for the federal deficit and lots of other things you can't control), so click on Finish. Access creates the form, shown in Figure 10-7.

Saving the form design

The final step is to name and save the form design. To do that, open the File menu and select Save Form. The Save As dialog box opens, as shown in Figure 10-8.

In the Form Name blank, type **Caveat Customers** and then click on OK. The next time you look at the Database window with the Forms tab selected, Access will list this form.

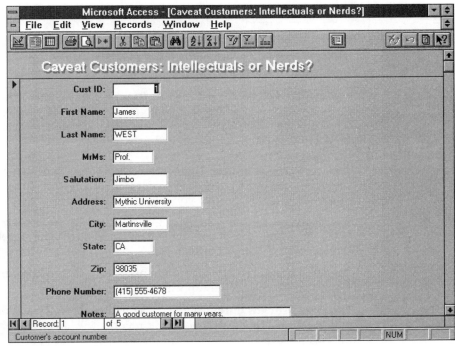

Figure 10-7:
The finished
Access
form for
intellectuals
and nerds.

Figure 10-8:
The Save As
dialog box.

Changes in the Toolbar

Before going on, take a look at the toolbar, shown in Figure 10-9. It's got a lot of new stuff on it. You use many of these buttons in the upcoming chapters.

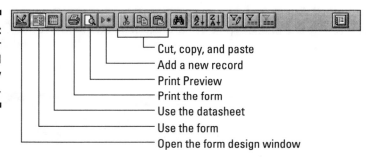

Figure 10-9:
New toolbar
buttons and
what they
do.

At the moment, you're looking at the new form as it will appear when you view or enter customer records. The second button from the left (the Form View button) is "pushed" because it's the one you select to view the form. From left to right, the other buttons identified in the figure are

The Form Design button: This button opens the form design window, where you can make changes in an existing form layout. You use this window in Chapter 13 when you modify the sample form you just created.

The Datasheet button: The Datasheet button switches from the form view to the datasheet view of your table. To get back to the form, you simply click on the Form View button again.

The Print button: Use this button to print records from the current table in the same format as they appear on-screen.

The Print Preview button: If you click on this button, Access displays a preview screen that shows how your records will look when printed with the current form.

The New Record button: Use this button to move to the end of the table, where you can add a new customer record.

The Cut, Copy, and Paste buttons: These let you cut, copy, and paste data from your form to other Windows programs.

The other new buttons on the toolbar aren't important in this chapter. But just in case you're curious, the Binoculars button lets you search for things (such as a customer's name); the A...Z and Z...A buttons let you sort customer records in ascending (A to Z) or descending (Z to A) order; and the two funnel buttons let you apply filters that hide some of the data.

You can tell which toolbar button is selected because the selected button looks as if it has been "pressed."

Moving around in the Table

In this section, you learn about moving around *in* the Customer Records table in the Form window. That's different from moving around *under* a table, which is sometimes good for picking up loose change or the odd contact lens.

But rest easy: Moving around your table with a form is very similar to moving around it with a datasheet. Here are the moves to make (see Figure 10-10 for the buttons to click):

✔ **To move to the first record:** Click on the First Record button or press Ctrl+Home on your keyboard (hold down the Ctrl key and press the Home key).

✔ **To move to the last record:** Click on the Last Record button or press Ctrl+End (hold down the Ctrl key and press the End key).

✔ **To move to the next record:** Click on the Next Record button or press the PgDn (Page Down) key.

✔ **To move to the previous record:** Click on the Previous Record button or press the PgUp (Page Up) key.

✔ **To move to a specific record number:** Click in the Record Number box and delete the record number that's currently in the box. Type the number of the record you want to see and press Enter.

Play around with the buttons and key combinations a few times just to get the feel of them. It's easier than you probably expected.

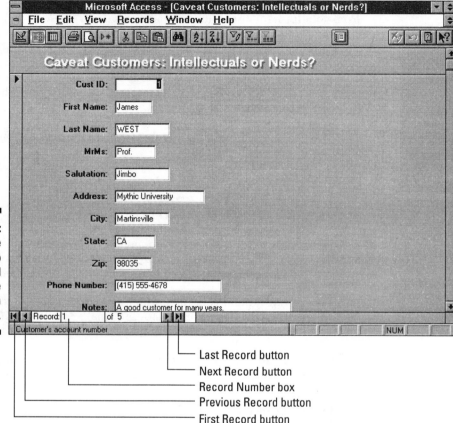

Figure 10-10:
Use these buttons to move around in the table while using a form.

Last Record button
Next Record button
Record Number box
Previous Record button
First Record button

Entering Data With a Form

Entering data with a form is just as easy as entering data with a datasheet. To enter data using a form, you follow these steps:

1. **In the Database window, select the Form tab by clicking on it with the mouse.**

   The Database window will list all the forms you've created for the current database.

2. **Double-click on the name of the form you want to use.**

   The Form window will appear. This is where you can enter new records using the form.

3. **When the form appears, open the <u>R</u>ecords menu. Select <u>G</u>o to, and when the submenu appears, select <u>N</u>ew.**

   Access creates a new, blank record after the current last record in the table. The new record is displayed in the form. All of its fields are blank, because you haven't yet entered any data. The cursor will be in the first field.

4. **Enter data in the first field.**

   Type the appropriate data in the first field. If it's a counter field (as in the book's example Customer Records table), you don't need to type anything. Just press Tab to go to the next field. Access will automatically fill in a value for the first field.

5. **Enter data in each field of the new record. When you get to the last field, just press Tab one more time.**

   The new record will automatically be saved to disk.

6. **Close the Form window (double-click on its Window Control button).**

   Access returns you to the Database window. If you want to verify that the data you entered is in the table, you can display the table's datasheet.

Now that you've acquired yet another valuable Access skill — creating and using forms — get up and stretch your legs. Better yet, make those legs walk you down to the nearest ice cream store and indulge in some chocolate almond. Consider it a "form" of reward for your hard work.

Chapter 11
Finding Stuff Fast with Find

• •

• •

*F*inding things is a problem for everyone. You can't find your car keys, or your checkbook, or your mother-in-law's sense of humor. You can't find the nerve to ask your boss for a raise. You can't find your youthful idealism. And you can't find any good TV shows on Sunday night.

One thing you *can* find — you hope — is the information in your database. And with Access, it's as quick and easy as you could imagine. If the information that you need is something simple, such as the data on all customers who have the last name *Trump,* you can use the Find command. You just click on the Find button, type the word *Trump,* and get your answer. If what your looking for is more complicated, Access helps you create a *query* to find whatever you need. For example:

✔ With Find, you could display the records for all customers who live in California.

✔ With Find, you also could display the records for all customers who have the letters *an* anywhere in their record.

✔ With a simple query, you could display only the first and last name fields of the records for customers whose zip code is 90210.

✔ With a more complex query, you could display the records for all customers whose names contain the letters *an,* or have the zip code 90210, *and* are professors at California University. And, so that you don't have to redo the query every time you need the information, you can save it to reuse later, just like fast-food hamburgers you pop into the freezer (but without the cholesterol).

Both ways of finding information have their pluses and minuses. Using Find is fast and easy, but you can look for only one thing at a time: a last name, a string of letters, or a zip code, for example. Using a query is a bit more involved (although still easy), but you can look for combinations of things, display only the fields you want, and save the query to use again later. With queries, you can also *change* the data in your table.

This chapter covers everything you need to know about using the Find command. I cover queries in the next chapter.

The Magical Find Button

 The easiest way to find stuff in your database is to use the Find command. Normally, you just activate the command by clicking on the Find button on the toolbar — it's the button with the binoculars icon. You also can select the Find command from the Edit menu or press Ctrl+F (hold down the Ctrl key and press F, which is the Find speed key).

 Remember that the toolbar changes depending on what you're doing at the moment. Unless you have a datasheet or form open, the Find button (with the binoculars) won't be on the toolbar.

To experiment with the Find command, try using it in the sample Caveat database that you created in earlier chapters. Suppose that you want to find the records of all customers who live in California. To do so, follow these steps:

1. **Make sure that the Caveat database is loaded in Access and that the Database window is showing on the screen.**

2. **Click on the Form tab in the left side of the Database window and open the Caveat Customers form.**

   If you didn't work through Chapter 10 and create the form, you can follow along in this chapter by clicking on the Table tab and opening the datasheet. It won't be as much fun but you'll get the idea.

3. **Maximize the Form window.**

   To do so, click on the button in the top right corner of the window.

4. **In the form, click in the blank for the State field.**

   Access moves your cursor to that field. (If you're using the datasheet instead of the form, click in the State column.)

5. **Click on the Find button in the toolbar.**

   The Find dialog box appears, as shown in Figure 11-1.

   The dialog box contains several options, but right now, you're only interested in finding the records of customers who live in California.

Figure 11-1:
The Find
dialog box.

6. **Reposition the Find dialog box.**

   Using the mouse, drag the dialog box down and to the right so that you can see the blanks for the customer's account number, first name, and last name.

7. **Enter the state abbreviation in the Find What blank.**

   Type **CA** in the blank. Remember that if the cursor isn't in the blank, all you have to do is click in the blank.

8. **Click on the Find First button.**

   Access instantly displays the record for Prof. James West in Martinsville, California.

9. **Click on the Find Next button.**

   Access displays the record for Teri Lane, who lives in Santa Barbara, home of movie stars, superb quiche, and the best darned coffee and cigarettes you can drink.

10. **Click one more time on the Find Next button.**

    Access displays a message box and asks whether you want to continue searching from the top of the table. It does this because when you clicked the Find Next button, you were in the middle of the table, and Access doesn't remember that you started at the top of the table.

11. **Click on No.**

    Access displays another message box, shown in Figure 11-2. Notice that Access has reached the end of the table. There are no more records of people living in California. Really. Access wouldn't lie to you about something like that. About how good your hair looks, maybe, but not about matching records. Never.

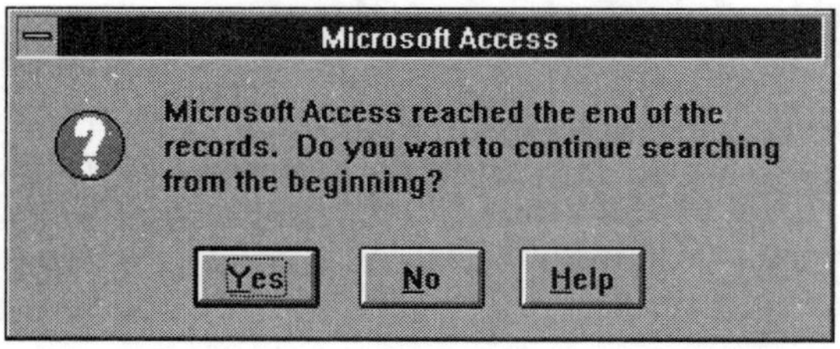

Figure 11-2:
End of the
table dialog
box.

12. **Click on OK**

13. **Close the find dialog box by clicking on close.**

Before you click on the Find button, move the cursor to the field you want to search. Unless you tell Access to do otherwise (more about that in a minute), it only looks in the field where the cursor is when you start the search.

Finding Stuff in All the Fields

To become even better acquainted with the Find command, try another Find operation. Move to the first record in the Customer Records table by clicking on the First Record button or pressing Ctrl+Home. Then click in the Cust ID field so that the cursor is in that field.

Even though a form is displayed on-screen, the data is still stored in the Customer Records table. The Form is just one way of looking at the data in the table.

Suppose that you've been working for three nights straight and, in your semicomatose state, you vaguely remember a customer whose record has two *R*s in it somewhere. The word may be the customer's name, or the city, or the sound he makes when he drinks a soda too fast — you're just not sure.

Bleary-eyed, hands trembling, you click on the Find button to open the Find dialog box, shown again in Figure 11-3. Do that now. If you can't make your hands tremble, the situation will lack drama, but the search will work just as well.

Figure 11-3:
The Find
dialog box.
Focus your
eyes. Yes,
that's it. The
Find dialog
box.

Find in field: 'State'	
Fi**n**d What: CA	**Find First**
Where: Match Whole Field ⬍ Direction	**Find Next**
Search In ○ **U**p	
◉ Cu**r**rent Field ○ A**ll** Fields ◉ **D**own	**Close**
☐ Match **C**ase ☐ Search Fields as F**o**rmatted	

Looking at the Find dialog box

Notice that the *CA* is still in the Fi**n**d What blank from the search you did in the preceding example — presuming, of course, that you worked through that example right before you started this one. But the two things you *really* want to notice about the dialog box are the following:

✔ **The Where blank:** Make sure that you select "Any Part of Field." (The default is "Match Whole Field.") If the Where blank doesn't say "Any Part of Field," your search will not work properly.

✔ **The Search In radio buttons:** Directly under the Where blank are two Search In radio buttons: Current Field and All Fields. Unless you click on the radio button for All Fields, Access searches only the field where the cursor is positioned when you start the search.

If you see a group of dialog box options with radio buttons next to them, it means that only one of the options can be selected at any one time. For example, a thing can be both square and orange, but it *can't* be both square and triangular. Square and triangular could be radio-button choices. A black dot in the center of a radio button indicates that the option is on. An empty radio button indicates that the option is off.

Doing the search

To search all fields in the sample table for the letters *RR,* follow these steps:

1. **In the Find What blank, type RR.**

   (Don't type the period.) Because the *CA* is currently highlighted, it should automatically be erased when you start typing. If not, delete it so that only *RR* is in the blank.

2. **Click on the Search In All Fields radio button.**

   A black dot appears inside the radio button to indicate that the option is turned on.

3. **Click on the Find First button.**

   If you drag the Find dialog box out of the way, you can see that Access finds the record for Harriett Stowe, as shown in Figure 11-4.

4. **Search for other records with two *Rs.***

   Groggy as you are, you aren't sure if the record for Harriett Stowe is the one you want. Click on the Find Next button to see if any other customers have *RR* anywhere in their records. Access finds the record for Arnold Harris. You're pretty sure that this record is the one you want.

5. **Click on Find Next one more time just to make sure that there aren't any other matching records.**

   Access displays the end-of-table message box. Click on No.

6. **Close the Find box by clicking on Close.**

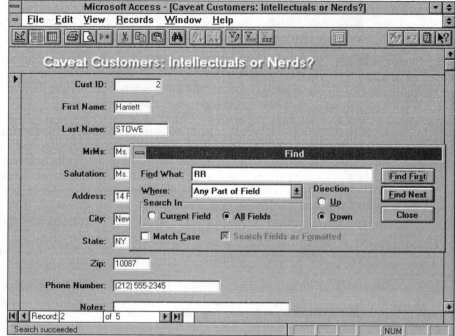

Figure 11-4:
Access
found a
record that
has a
double-r!

How the search worked

Trembling hands and all, you managed to find the right customer record. In the process, three remarkable things happened:

- ✔ First, Access searched all the fields in the table. You started out in the Cust ID field, but Access found an *RR* in the First Name field of one record and another *RR* in the Last Name field of another record.

- ✔ Second, Access ignored whether the letters were upper- or lowercase. You specified the letters to find as *RR,* but Access found one *rr* in the middle of *Harriett* and one *RR* in the middle of *HARRIS.*

- ✔ Finally, Access didn't just look at whole words. The two *RR*s it found were embedded in the middle of words.

Unless you say otherwise when you begin a search, Access doesn't pay any attention to whether letters are uppercase or lowercase. If you want an exact match with the case of what you type — for example, if you want Access to find *CA* but not *ca* — click in the Match Case checkbox in the lower left corner of the Find dialog box. (An X in the checkbox indicates that the option is turned on; an empty checkbox indicates that it's turned off.)

Match Whole Field for exact matches

If you want to find a field that *exactly matches* what you type, click on the list-box arrow next to the Where blank in the Find dialog box. Then select Match Whole Field. When you choose this option, Access finds only records in which the entire field matches what you type in the Find What blank.

If, for example, you type **Santa** and ask Access to search the sample database, it won't find any matching records. The closest match is *Santa Barbara* in the City field for Teri Lane. But because *Santa Barbara* doesn't exactly match your search specification — *Santa* — Access won't find the record.

Other Stuff to Know about Find

You may wonder if you should *always* click on the radio button for All Fields. The answer is no. Don't select that option unless you have to, because searching all the fields is slower than searching just one. In a small table (a few hundred records or less), it won't make a great deal of difference. But in a bigger table, it can take a lot of extra time.

Normally, Find searches *down* from wherever you are in the table. That is, if you're at record 15 in a table of 25 records, it starts searching at record 15 and goes to 25. If you want to search the whole table, it makes more sense to move to the first record before you begin the search. Also, if you want to search *up* in the table instead of down, just click on the Up radio button in the Find dialog box.

Remember that you can invoke the Find command in three ways. You can click on the Find (binoculars) button in the toolbar; you can open the Edit menu and select Find; or you can press Ctrl+F.

The 5th Wave
By Rich Tennant
Re·al Pro·gram·mers

Real Programmers don't sleep - their systems just temporarily go down.

Chapter 12

Queries Have "More Power!" to Find Stuff

*Y*ou have to put up with lots of weird words every day. For example, there's *microprocessor* (a boss who's always looking over your shoulder); *shortmeeting* (you should forget about getting anything done for the rest of the afternoon); *revenue enhancement* (which never seems to enhance *your* revenue); and even *epistemology* (the study of the nature of knowledge — always a favorite at parties). Well, get ready for another one: *query*.

Chapter 11 shows you how to use the Find command. Although it's quick and easy, it has some disadvantages. First, you can search for only *one thing* at a time. Second, you can't view just the fields that interest you. Third, you can only look for matches of one kind or another. In a sales table, for example, you can look for all records in which the price is *exactly* $10, but not for all records in which the sale price is *less than* or *more than* $10.

In this chapter, you learn how to find information in your database using queries. Queries require a little more effort than using the Find command, but they deliver a lot more power. You can handle it: You're *psycho-epistemologically well-integrated* (ready).

Query is just a fancy word for a question you ask Access about a table or database. *Running a query* just means asking the question. Without queries, you couldn't find your data as easily. And without words like *query*, database experts couldn't get $100 an hour.

Three Steps for Perfect Queries

Before you get into the specific steps of doing a query, it's important to understand the big picture, which is illustrated in Figure 12-1. When you set up a query, you specify three things:

1. **The fields you want to search.** For example, if you want the records for all customers named *Smith* who live in zip code 90210, you tell Access to search the Last Name and Zip fields.

2. **What you're looking for.** For the example just described, you'd tell Access to show you all the records in which *Smith* is in the Last Name field *and* 90210 is in the Zip field.

3. **What fields you want to see in the answer.** You may not want to see all the fields of the records found by the query. When you run a query, you must tell Access which fields you want to see when it displays the answer to your query.

You can also specify the order in which you want Access to display the records (A to Z or Z to A), but that's optional.

Because queries are often more complicated than simple searches you do with the Find command, it would be a pain in the neck if you had to redo them every time you needed to get the same information from your database. Therefore, you can also *save* queries and reuse them whenever you want.

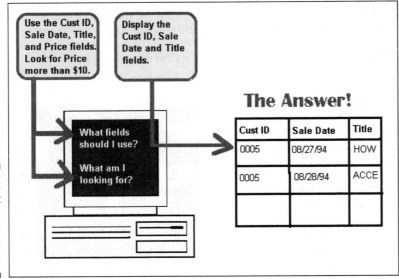

Figure 12-1:
What happens when you create and run a query.

Drudge Work Alert! Setting Up a Sales Table

To see the full power of queries, you first need to set up another sample table. This table will record all book sales at Caveat Emptor, the imaginary bookstore owned by the imaginary Honest Janis introduced in Chapter 2. If you've been playing hooky (hookey? hockey? hooey?) since you finished Chapter 11, start up Access again and load the Caveat database. Then create the Sales table with the fields listed in Table 12-1. Don't worry: You'll use the table *plenty* later in the book, too.

I show you how to set up a table in Chapter 3, so there's no point in repeating the information here. If you're a little hazy on the subject, follow the instructions in Chapter 3. But do *not* set the Cust ID field as the primary key. Note also that when you see N/A below, it means that something is *not applicable*. For example, for the Sale Date field, the Field Size column contains N/A because Access automatically sets the field size of a time/date field.

Table 12-1		Fields for the Sales Table			
Field Name	**Data Type**	**Field Size**	**Format**	**Indexed**	**Description**
Cust ID	Number (*not* Counter)	Integer	0000	Yes (Duplicates OK)	Buyer's account number
Sale Date	Date/Time	N/A	Short Date	No	Date of sale
Title	Text	50	>	No	Title of book sold
Author	Text	25	N/A	No	Author's name
Price	Currency	N/A	N/A	No	Price of book sold

Save the table under the name *Sales*. When Access asks whether you want to set a primary key, select No.

Now enter the following five records into the Sales table. (If you want to put in more records, Appendix A lists all 10 records for this table.) Because it contains numeric data, the Sales table is better for illustrating the power of queries than the Customer Records table.

Cust ID: 4
Sale Date: 8/21/94
Title: How to Write a Computer Book
Author: Obscurantis, Jargon
Price: 2.95

Cust ID: 1
Sale Date: 8/25/94
Title: In Praise of Idleness
Author: Russell, Bertrand
Price: 12.95

Cust ID: 2
Sale Date: 8/26/94
Title: Getting Your Husband Off His Lazy Butt
Author: Russell, Mrs. Bertrand
Price: 12.95

Cust ID: 5
Sale Date: 8/27/94
Title: How I Turned $25 Cash into a Successful Business
Author: Fleiss, Heidi
Price: 24.95

Cust ID: 5
Sale Date: 8/28/94
Title: Access 2 For Dummies
Author: Palmer, Scott
Price: 14799.95

Creating a Simple Query

Now that you've created the Sales table, it's time to do a simple query. This one will do just a little more than you can do using the Find command. In the next section, you learn how to do more powerful queries.

At this point, you should have the Caveat database loaded and the Database window on-screen. Click on the Query tab on the left side of the Database window, as shown in Figure 12-2.

No queries exist yet, so the Database window should be empty. To create your first query, click on the New button at the top of the Database window. The New Query dialog box appears, as shown in Figure 12-3.

Don't be disappointed, but you're not going to use the Query Wizards. It's so simple to create a query that Access provides wizards only to create the most difficult types of queries. So just click on the New Query button.

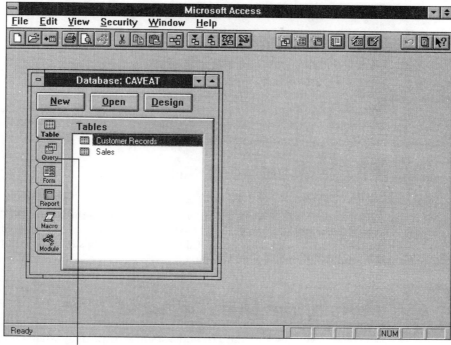

Figure 12-2:
Click on the
Query tab in
the
Database
window.

Click here and then click the
New button to create a query

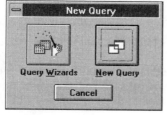

Figure 12-3:
The New
Query dialog
box.

With Query Wizards, you can create the following types of queries: *Crosstabs,* which shows the answer as a table with one field's values as row labels and another field's values as column labels; *Find Duplicates,* which searches your table for records that contain the same information; *Find Unmatched Query,* which searches your table for records that do *not* match a certain condition; and *Archive Query,* which takes the records in a table and copies them to a new table.

The next step is to tell Access what table you want to search, so Access displays the Add Table dialog box, shown in Figure 12-4. You're only going to use the Sales table, so double-click on it to add it to the query. Then click on the Close button.

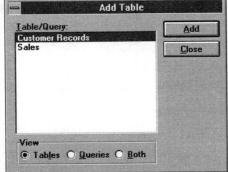

Figure 12-4:
The Add
Table dialog
box.

What you see now is the window where you'll create the query. Don't worry about the window's name: *Select Query: Query1*. It doesn't mean anything beyond what you already know. Click on the window's Maximize button so that the window fills the whole screen.

Parts of the Query window

The Query window isn't hard to understand — especially when you have a picture like Figure 12-5 that has circles and arrows and a paragraph telling what each thing is. The top part of the window shows the tables you selected to use in the query, along with a list of the fields in each table. When you create the query, you use the mouse to drag the fields you want from the list to the bottom half of the window.

The bottom half of the window contains four lines that you need to know about:

- ✔ **Field:** This is where you list the fields for the query. If you're actually going to *search* for something in a field, you must fill in the Criteria line. If you don't fill in the Criteria line, the field isn't used in the query but its value is displayed in the answer.

- ✔ **Sort:** This line just tells Access if you want the records in the query answer displayed in ascending order (A to Z), descending order (Z to A), or no particular order at all.

- ✔ **Show:** If you want the query's answer to include the field named in this column, this box should have an X in it. If the box is empty, the field won't show up in the answer, even if it's the one you use to find the records in the query.

- ✔ **Criteria:** This one is the biggie. It's where you put the stuff you're looking for in this column's field. If there's nothing on this line of a column, the field won't be searched in the query, though it can still be displayed in the answer.

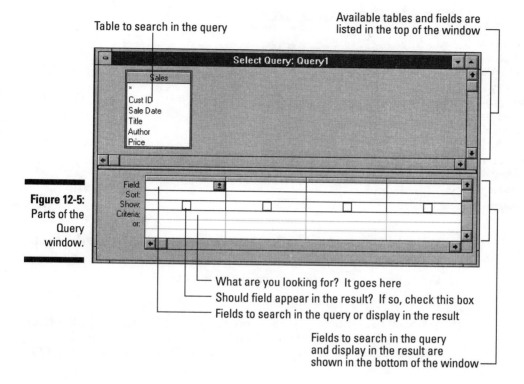

Table to search in the query

Available tables and fields are listed in the top of the window

Figure 12-5:
Parts of the Query window.

What are you looking for? It goes here

Should field appear in the result? If so, check this box

Fields to search in the query or display in the result

Fields to search in the query and display in the result are shown in the bottom of the window

Selecting the fields you want

Your next step is to select the fields to use in the sample query. To do so, follow these steps:

1. **Drag the Cust ID field from the Sales table field list to row one, column one of the query definition window, as shown in Figure 12-6.**

   Because you aren't doing anything else with the Cust ID field, that's all for this column.

To *drag* something, you position the mouse pointer over it. Then you hold down the left mouse button, move the mouse pointer to the position where you want to place the dragged object, and release the left mouse button.

2. **Click in the box in row one, column two to move the cursor to that position.**

3. **This time, double-click on the Sale Date field in the Sales field list.**

   It automatically appears at the cursor location.

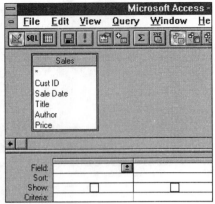

Figure 12-6:
Select the
first field for
the query by
dragging it
from the
Sales table
field list to
the query
definition
window.

4. **Move the Title field to row one, column three and move the Price field to row one, column four.**

Use either of the methods you used in Steps 1 and 2.

5. **Enter the query condition.**

You want to find all book sales where the price of the book is greater than $10. Therefore, click in row four (the Criteria row), column four (the Price column). Type > **10.** Your screen should look like the one shown in Figure 12-7.

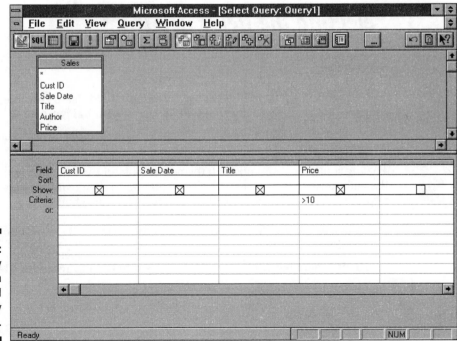

Figure 12-7:
The Query
window with
the finished
query
definition.

Relational Operators and Circus Cages

What you did in the preceding example was use a *relational operator* ("greater than") to prepare for a search that you can't do by using the Find command. Instead of telling Access to search for a specific text string or number, you asked it to look for records in which the price has a certain *relation* to $10 — in this case, a price that's greater than $10. You learn even more about relational operators in the next chapter — unless you run away and join the circus, in which case you'll be much too busy cleaning out the animal cages. Don't ask what you'll be cleaning out of them. You'd rather learn more about queries. Trust me.

Running the query

Running the query is the easiest part of all. Do you see the exclamation point button on the toolbar, shown in Figure 12-8? That's the Run Query button. Click on it, and Access finds all the Sales records that match what you specified in the query.

Click on this button to run the query

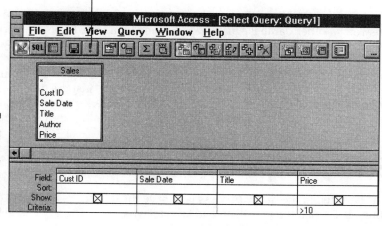

Figure 12-8:
Click on the Run Query button to do the deed.

Access displays the answer to the query in the form of a mini-datasheet, called a *dynaset.* In the dynaset, you see only the fields you requested and only the books that satisfied the query — that is, the ones costing more than $10. The dynaset is shown in Figure 12-9.

The answer to an Access query is called a *dynaset.* (Sure, it's jargon, but you need to know it: There's going to be a quiz next period.) If, for some reason, you ever use another database manager, you'll discover that other programs don't use the term *dynaset.* Paradox calls the answer to a query an *answer table,* for example, while dBASE and other database managers don't give it any special name at all.

Figure 12-9:
The answer
to your query
(sorry, not
the query
about which
horse to bet).

Cust ID	Sale Date	Title	Price
0001	8/25/94	IN PRAISE OF IDL	$12.95
0002	8/26/94	GETTING YOUR H	$12.95
0005	8/27/94	HOW I TURNED $	$24.95
0005	8/28/94	ACCESS 2 FOR DL	$14,799.95

Access calls the query answer a *dynaset* for a reason — another reason, that is, besides the need for one more confusing technical term. When you get a query answer in other database managers, such as Paradox or dBASE, the answer contains a *copy* of the data in your table. But in Access, a dynaset contains the actual "live" data in your table. If you change anything in the dynaset, it is changed in the table.

That means two things. First, dynasets give you more power than the query answers in other database managers. Second, you have to be a lot more careful about what you *do* to the data in a dynaset because it *isn't* just a copy.

A dynaset really *is* a mini-datasheet. You can resize the rows and columns just as you can in a normal datasheet. In the dynaset you just created, the Title column is too narrow and all the others are too wide. As an exercise, try resizing the dynaset's columns so that the answer data is easier to read.

Saving the query

The last step in the query process is to save the query. It's almost as easy as running it. Open the File menu and select Save Query. The Save As dialog box appears, as shown in Figure 12-10. If it looks familiar, that's because it's basically the same dialog box you used to name the form and the tables you created earlier in the book.

Figure 12-10:
The Save As
dialog box.

Save As

Query Name:
Query1

OK

Cancel

For the query name, type **Book Sales Over $10.** Then click on the OK button. Finally, close the Query window by double-clicking on the Window Control button in the top left corner.. (As usual, make sure that you don't accidentally click on the Window Control button for Access; the button you want is the one underneath the button in the top-left corner of the screen.) Access should return you to the Database window.

Rerunning a query

The sample query you just created was fairly simple. But when you get to be a real Access guru, you undoubtedly will want to create bigger databases and more complex queries — and to run the same query more than once. It would be wasteful and time-consuming to set up the same query each time you want to run it.

That's why Access makes it so *easy* to rerun a saved query. To rerun a query, just double-click on its name in the Database window. The dynaset should appear, just as before.

At the moment, the Book Sales Over $10 query is displayed in the Database window. If you were to rerun the query right now, Access would list the same book sales in the dynaset. But suppose that six months have passed since you ran the query the first time, and lots of new sales have taken place. No problem — you still have the query you created when you were getting started with Access. Simply rerun the query, and all those new books sales will be included in the dynaset.

Remember that the answer to a query is a dynaset: a kind of "mini-table." You can print the dynaset, just as you can print any table, by selecting "Print" from the File menu when the dynaset is displayed on your screen.

That's it for now! You worked hard in this chapter and you deserve a break. Hmm . . . "Melrose Place" looks pretty good tonight . . . maybe Billy will destroy another computer! Naaah . . .

Chapter 13

Using Logical Operators and Action Queries

The phrase *logical operators* sounds scary, like it might mean having your appendix taken out by a bunch of Vulcans. But logical operators are really just familiar words like *and, or,* and *not.* They were invented by George Boole, an English mathematician who lived from 1815 to 1864. That's why they're also called *Boolean operators.*

Before that time, nobody knew about logical operators, which made daily life rather difficult. If someone wanted to go to the store for a frozen pizza *and* a bottle of gin, he or she had to make two trips. People who needed to get a pound of liverwurst *or* a bag of potato chips *and* a six-pack of soda were often so befuddled by the problem that they gave up and entered a monastery or convent, where the food was lousy but at least they weren't required to make change.

Sometimes, history even shifted as a result. Marie Antoinette said, "Let them eat cake," after which she was beheaded by a mob of starving French peasants. What she *meant* to say was "Let them eat cake, *and* steak *and* french fries *and* have a nice bottle of wine." But because she didn't know about logical operators, she couldn't finish the sentence.

Creating Multiple-Condition Queries

In addition to making it easier to go to the store, logical operators are used to create queries that look for more than one thing at a time — also known as searching for *multiple conditions*. For example, you may want to look for every book sale that occurred before August 27th *and* was for more than $5. Access makes it simple.

Multiple-condition queries haven't always been so easy. In older versions of dBASE, which was the most popular database manager of the 1980s, you had to type things like

```
display fname, lname, city for zip = '90210' .and. lname =
          'spelling'
```

But these days, almost all database managers have adopted the simple *query by example* (QBE) approach used by Access.

Setting up the query

If you took a break after the preceding chapter, get back into Access and load the Caveat database. In this section, you create a sample query that searches for all records in the Sales table that have books sold before August 27th for more than $5. I'll take you through the process one step at a time so that you can see what's happening. If your doing a query with your own table, just follow along.

Start with these steps:

1. **Click on the Query tab in the Database window.**

2. **Click on the New button to create a new query.**

3. **In the New Query dialog box, click on the New Query button.**

   The Add Table dialog box appears.

4. **Double-click on the Sales table to add its field list to the Query window.**

   Then click on the Close button in the Add Table dialog box.

5. **Maximize the Query window.**

   Your screen should look like the one in Figure 13-1.

   Another way to maximize any window is to double-click on the title bar. That's the blue (or dark) area in the top border, where you see the window title. In Figure 13-1, it says *Select Query: Query1*.

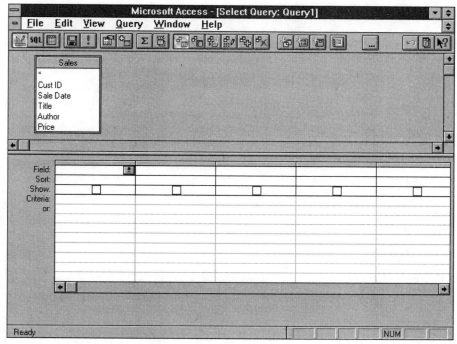

Figure 13-1:
The Query
window
with the
Sales table
fields
displayed.

6. Select all the fields.

In Step 7, you need to move all the fields from the field list into the *QBE grid* — that's the row-and-column table in the bottom half of the screen where you construct your query. You could drag the fields one at a time, but here's a shortcut: Double-click on the title bar of the field list, as shown in Figure 13-2. That action selects *all* the fields in the list. You then can drag them all at the same time.

7. Drag the fields to the QBE grid.

With the mouse, drag all the fields to the first cell of the QBE grid — that's the one on the Field row of the first column. When you release the mouse button, Access automatically places the fields in order in the columns of the grid — just as if you'd dragged them there one at a time.

Figure 13-2:
Click on the
title bar of
the field list
to select all
the fields.

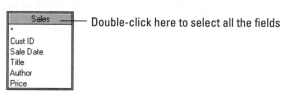 Double-click here to select all the fields

8. **Enter the first search condition.**

   In the Criteria row of the Sale Date column, type > **8-25-94** and press Enter. Notice that Access changes what you typed to > *#8/25/94#*, which is the format it uses for dates.

9. **Enter the second search condition.**

   In the Criteria row of the Price column, type >**5.** (It won't hurt if you type the period, but it isn't needed.)

10. **Click on either the Run Query (!) button or the Datasheet button in the toolbar.**

    The answer to the query appears, as shown in Figure 13-3.

Figure 13-3: Access displays the book sales for more than $5 that occurred after August 25th.

Cust ID	Sale Date	Title	Author	Price
0002	8/26/94	GETTING YOUR H	Russell, Mrs. Bertra	$12.95
0005	8/27/94	HOW I TURNED $	Fleiss, Heidi	$24.95
0005	8/28/94	ACCESS 2 FOR DU	Palmer, Scott	$14,799.95
0000				$0.00

 Click on the Design button in the toolbar to return to the Query window. Then open the File menu and save the query as *August Money-Makers*.

Did you notice something interesting? You didn't have to worry about the AND operator. Access took care of it for you. All you have to do in a query is tell Access what you want. It does all the work. Except for going to the store and serving dinner to the peasants.

 There's a lot more to using logical operators and multiple-condition queries than this book has room to talk about. If you want more information, take a look at the chapter on queries in your Access documentation or check out IDG's *PC World Microsoft Access 2 Bible, 2nd Edition.*

Twixt and between, or, "Looking for Mr. Range of Values"

You know how kids go through an awkward age — the time between their 13th birthday and when they get to be about 20 years older than *you* are now? Well, Access queries let you look for values that are between one thing and another. But it isn't awkward at all, as you discover in this section, when you create yet another sample query.

Suppose that after you created the query in the preceding section, the owner of the bookstore decides that he doesn't want to have one of the books, *Access 2 For Dummies,* included in the result. Because of the book's (entirely justified) list price of $14,799.95, he *knows* that the store will make money on it. In fact, sales of books for more than $200 are so exceptional that he doesn't want you to include any book that is priced higher than $200. So you need to alter the query you created in the preceding section to include all books sold after August 25th that cost at least $5 and at most $200. In computer lingo, you need to use a *Between X and Y* operator in your query.

The *Between X and Y* thing (called an operator) is *inclusive.* That means that if you put *Between 1 and 5* in a query, Access looks for all values between 1 and 5, *including* 1 and 5.

To set up the Between query, just click in the Criteria cell in the Price column, where it currently says *>5.* Delete the *>5* and type **Between 5 And 200.** Then click on either the Datasheet button or the Run button in the toolbar. The answer to the query appears, as shown in Figure 13-4. Notice that it's the same as the previous answer, *except* that the one book that had a price of more than $200 has been omitted.

Figure 13-4:
Books sold after August 25th for a price between $5 and $200.

Cust ID	Sale Date	Title	Author	Price
0002	8/26/94	GETTING YOUR H	Russell, Mrs. Bertra	$12.95
0005	8/27/94	HOW I TURNED $	Fleiss, Heidi	$24.95
0000				$0.00

You can use the *Between* operator with other values as well, including text values (such as zip codes) and date values. As an exercise, try setting up a query to find all books sold between August 26th and August 28th.

Saving a query under a different name

You want to keep the old version of the query instead of replacing it with your new version. The way to do this task is to save the query under a new name. Follow these steps:

1. **Switch back to the query window by clicking on the Design button on the left end of the toolbar.**

2. **Open the File menu and select Save As.**

3. **In the Save As dialog box, type August Money-Makers to $200.**

4. Click on OK.

Access saves the query under the new name.

Any time you need to save anything (a query, table, form, or even a whole database) under a different name, *always* select Save As from the File menu. If you make a mistake and select Save, Access saves the query (or whatever you're saving) under its current name and wipes out the old version of the query.

Using Multiple Tables in a Query

Remember all that fuss in Chapter 1 about Access being a relational database manager? You don't? Good. You shouldn't clutter up your mind with junk like that. But now, you're going to use a relational feature of Access to create a multi-table query.

A *what?!* A *multi-table query* is pretty much just what it sounds like. It's a query that gets information from more than one table.

Think about the answer to the query you created in the preceding section of this chapter. It includes the account number of the customer who bought each book. So in theory, you could open up the Customer Records table and look up the customer's name if you wanted to do so. But why should *you* do that extra work when Access is perfectly willing to do it *for* you?

All you need to do (well, pretty much) is bring the Customer Records table into the query so that you can get the name for each book sold.

Adding a table to the query

Adding a table to a query is easy. Just follow these steps:

1. Open the Query menu and select Add Table.

The Add Table dialog box appears.

2. In the dialog box, double-click on the table that you want to add.

Its field list should appear in the Query window.

3. Click on Close to close the dialog box.

Go ahead and add the Customer Records table to your sample query. First, make sure that you saved the August Money-Makers to $200 query and are at the query window. Then add the table following the steps just described.

Inserting a field in the QBE grid

After you add a table to the query, you have to select the fields you want to search and put them into the QBE grid in the bottom part of the screen. To add a field, drag it until your cursor is on the field that's just to the right of where you want the new field to go. When you release the mouse button, Access inserts the new field just to the left of where your cursor was positioned.

For the sample query, you want to insert the Last Name field from the Customer Records table into the QBE grid. Just drag the Last Name field from the field list until it's over the first row of the Sale Date column, as shown in Figure 13-5. When you release the mouse button, the Last Name field is automatically inserted to the left of the Sale Date field.

Running the query: Oops!

Now that you have the Last Name field in the query, click on the Datasheet button in the toolbar to run the query. The result is shown in Figure 13-6.

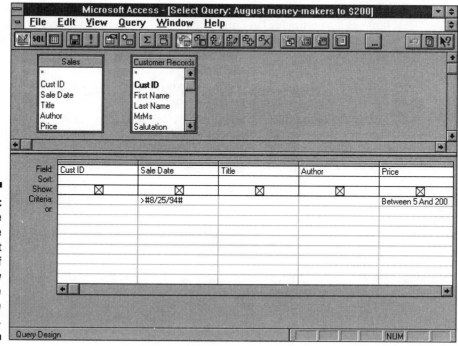

Figure 13-5:
Drag the Last Name field so that it's on top of the first row of the Sale Date column.

Figure 13-6:
The answer
to the multi-
table query.
What's
wrong with
this picture?

Cust ID	Last Name	Sale Date	Title	Author	Price
0002	WEST	8/26/94	GETTING YOUR H	Russell, Mrs. Bertra	$12.95
0002	STOWE	8/26/94	GETTING YOUR H	Russell, Mrs. Bertra	$12.95
0002	TWOMBLY	8/26/94	GETTING YOUR H	Russell, Mrs. Bertra	$12.95
0002	HARRIS	8/26/94	GETTING YOUR H	Russell, Mrs. Bertra	$12.95
0002	LANE	8/26/94	GETTING YOUR H	Russell, Mrs. Bertra	$12.95
0005	WEST	8/27/94	HOW I TURNED $	Fleiss, Heidi	$24.95
0005	STOWE	8/27/94	HOW I TURNED $	Fleiss, Heidi	$24.95
0005	TWOMBLY	8/27/94	HOW I TURNED $	Fleiss, Heidi	$24.95
0005	HARRIS	8/27/94	HOW I TURNED $	Fleiss, Heidi	$24.95
0005	LANE	8/27/94	HOW I TURNED $	Fleiss, Heidi	$24.95

As you can see, something is definitely screwy. Only two book sales satisfy the
query, but each one is listed five times — once for each customer in the
Customer Records table!

The problem is that right now, Access has no way to tell which sale goes with
which customer record. The obvious way is to use the Cust ID field, which is
the same in both tables. To make the query work right, you must tell Access to
use this field for matching the records from the two tables.

Your brain has more power than the most powerful computer on earth! It's easy
for *you* to see common-sense things, like the fact that the Cust ID field can be
used to match records in the Sales table with those in the Customer Records
table. But a computer isn't quite that smart. You must *tell* Access to use the
Cust ID field to match the records.

Linking tables for a multi-table query

Telling Access to match the records by using the Cust ID field is easy. Drag the
Cust ID field from the Customer Records field list until it's on top of the Cust ID
field in the Sales field list, as shown in Figure 13-7.

Figure 13-7:
Drag the Cust
ID field from
the Customer
Records field
list until it's on
top of the
Cust ID field
in the Sales
field list.

Sales
*
Cust ID
Sale Date
Title
Author
Price

Customer Records
*
Cust ID
First Name
Last Name
MrMs
Salutation

When you release the mouse button, Access creates a link between the Customer Records table Cust ID field and the Sales table Cust ID field. Access shows you that there's a link by adding a horizontal line connecting the two field lists.

Linking two tables in a query has no effect on the tables themselves. The link between the Cust ID field of the Customer Records table and the Cust ID field of the Sales table exists only in the query.

Deleting a field and running the query

After you tell Access how to match the records in the two tables, the sample multi-table query will actually work. But because the query answer (the *dynaset*) will include the customer's last name, there's no need to include the Cust ID field in the answer. To delete it from the QBE grid and run the query, follow these steps:

1. **Move the mouse pointer until it's directly over the gray area at the top of the Cust ID column.**

   The mouse pointer should turn into a little black downward-pointing arrow.

2. **Click the left mouse button to select the Cust ID column.**

   When it's selected, it should be highlighted in reverse video.

3. **Press the Delete key to delete the Cust ID column from the QBE grid.**

4. **Click on the Datasheet button in the toolbar to see the query answer.**

   It should look like the one shown in Figure 13-8.

Figure 13-8:
The answer to the sample multi-table query.

Last Name	Sale Date	Title	Author	Price
STOWE	8/26/94	GETTING YOUR H	Russell, Mrs. Bertra	$12.95
LANE	8/27/94	HOW I TURNED $	Fleiss, Heidi	$24.95
				$0.00

You may have been surprised that you could delete the Cust ID field from the bottom part of the query window because it's the field that you used to link the Customer Records and Sales tables. But remember that the fields you use to *construct the query* are not necessarily the same as the fields you *display in the answer.* In this case, the Cust ID field wasn't doing anything in the bottom part of the query window except telling Access to display account numbers. If you delete the Cust ID field from the bottom part of the query window (in the QBE grid), it has no effect on the link between the two tables.

Save the new query

Return to the Query window and save the multi-table query as *August Money-Makers w/Names.* Close the Query window and return to the Database window.

Creating Action Queries

As the final exercise in this chapter, you're going to create a different kind of query. All the queries you've done so far have been what are called *select queries.* That means that you tell Access what you want, and then it goes searching for the records that match. But you can also do *action queries,* which enable you to change or update the information in a table.

For this example, suppose that our imaginary bookstore owner, Honest Janis, just reminded you that all the book sales in the Sales table were made to regular customers, who get a 10 percent discount. Therefore, the prices currently in the Sales table are too high. Once again, you could do this on your own, calculating the correct sale prices and changing the records one at a time. But Access will do it *for* you, so why bother?

Doing a calculation in a query

Did you know that the word *calculate* is derived from the Latin word *calculus,* which is a word for a stone? Back in the old days — you know, like the 1950s — nobody had PCs or pocket calculators. And because most people had only 14 fingers, they counted stones on the ground to do simple arithmetic. Really. Honest.

Access doesn't require stones to do calculations, as you're about to learn.

Setting up a calculated field

Before doing the sample query to change the prices in the Sales table, try out the following basic calculation first. This will let you verify that everything is working right before you take the ultimate step of changing the prices in the sales table.

Different kinds of queries

In Access, you can create several other kinds of action queries in addition to the one covered in this chapter. You can perform *Crosstab queries,* which generate the answer in crosstab format;

Make Table queries, which create a new table to hold the answer; *Append queries,* which you can use to add records to a table; and *Delete queries,* which you can use to delete records from a table.

The first thing to do is start a new query. From the Database window and with the Query tab selected, click on the New button to create a new query. Then follow these steps:

1. **In the New Query dialog box, click on the New Query button.**
2. **In the Add Table dialog box, double-click on the Sales table.**

   The Sales table field list should appear. Click on the Close button.

3. **From the field list, drag (in order) the Cust ID, Sale Date, Title, and Price fields into the QBE grid in the bottom part of the screen.**
4. **In the Field row of the empty column to the right of the Price column, type** [Price] * .9 **and press the down-arrow key.**

   Be sure to type it exactly as shown in Figure 13-9. This little formula tells Access that for each record shown in the query answer, it should take whatever number is in the Price field, multiply it by 0.9, and display the result in the last column.

   Notice that as soon as you press the down-arrow key, Access changes the cell's contents to *Expr1: [Price] * 0.9.*

To see how the calculated field works, click on the Datasheet button. The query answer is shown in Figure 13-10.

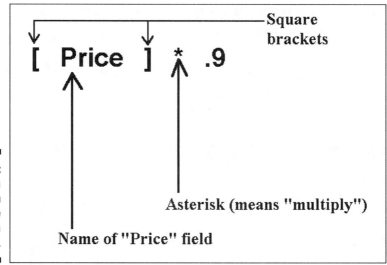

Figure 13-9:
Putting a
calculation
in one
column of a
query.

Figure 13-10:
The result of
a calculated
field in a
query.

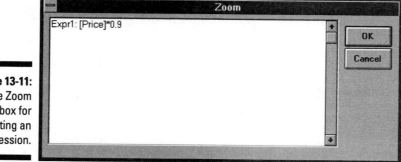

	Cust ID	Sale Date	Title	Price	Expr1
▶	0001	8/25/94	IN PRAISE OF IDL	$12.95	11.655
	0002	8/26/94	GETTING YOUR H	$12.95	11.655
	0004	8/21/94	HOW TO WRITE A	$2.95	2.655
	0005	8/27/94	HOW I TURNED $	$24.95	22.455
	0005	8/28/94	ACCESS 2 FOR DL	$14,799.95	13319.955
*	0000			$0.00	

The answer is all right, but it could be a lot better. First, the column heading *Expr1* is about as geeky and uninformative as computer jargon can get. Second, although the new column should contain dollar amounts, it contains numbers with three decimal places and no dollar signs. Now, you'll learn how to fix these problems.

Adding a new column in a query has no effect at all on the tables involved in the query. In this sample query, the calculated column exists only in the query itself, not in the Sales table.

Making it pretty

  Just a few changes will make the sample query answer much easier to read. Return to the Query window by clicking on the Design button on the left end of the toolbar. Then follow these steps:

1. **Click in the cell where you typed the expression for the calculated column.**

   That's the Field row of the column that is just to the right of the Price column.

2. **Press Shift+F2 (hold down the Shift key and press the F2 function key).**

   The Zoom box opens, as shown in Figure 13-11. In the Zoom box is the formula (sometimes called an expression) for calculating the amount.

Figure 13-11:
The Zoom
box for
editing an
expression.

```
Zoom
Expr1: [Price]*0.9                              OK
                                                Cancel
```

3. **Use the Delete key to erase *Expr1* at the beginning of the expression.**

   Don't erase the colon that comes after it.

4. **To the left of the colon — where *Expr1* used to be — type** Discounted Price.

5. **Press the right-arrow key twice so that the cursor is just to the left of the left square bracket.**

6. **Type** CCur(**and then press the End key.**

   That's the letters *CCur* followed by a left parenthesis. This tells Access to format the numbers as currency — meaning, as dollar amounts.

7. **Press the spacebar and type a right parenthesis.**

   When you're finished, the expression should look like the one in Figure 13-12.

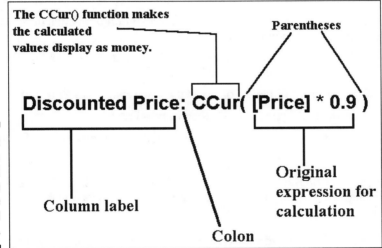

Figure 13-12: The modified expression for the calculated field.

Double-check your typing to make sure that the expression is like the one in Figure 13-12 (but without the arrows and all that other stuff). Then click on the OK button to close the Zoom box and click on the Datasheet button to run the query. The result should look perfect: The column label is *Discounted Price* and the numbers display as money.

Changing table data with an action query

So far, nothing you've done has changed the Sales table in any way. But the following steps take you through the process of creating a real action query that updates the prices in the Sales table:

1. **Return to the Query window by clicking on the Design button in the toolbar.**

2. **Move the mouse pointer to the gray area at the top of the Discounted Price column.**

    The pointer should turn into a black down-pointing arrow.

3. **Click the left mouse button to select the column.**

    Access displays the column in reverse video.

4. **Delete the Discounted Price column by pressing the Delete key.**

5. **Open the Query menu in the top-line menu bar. Click on Update to select that menu choice.**

    Notice that a new row appears in the QBE grid. The new row is right under the Field row and is labeled *Update To*.

6. **Click in the Update To row of the Price column, as shown in Figure 13-13.**

7. **In the cell, type** [Price] * .9 **and press Enter.**

    This time, you don't need to use the CCur() function because the Price field is already formatted as money.

If you click on the Run (!) button in the toolbar, Access displays a dialog box telling you that five records will be updated. Just click on OK, and Access changes the prices.

From the Query window, save this query as *Apply Discount* and then return to the Database window. In the Database window, the new query has an exclamation mark next to it. The exclamation mark indicates that it's an action query.

Finally, verify that the prices have been changed. Click on the Table tab in the Database window and open the Sales datasheet. It should look like the one in Figure 13-14.

That's it for this chapter! Take a break AND have a soda OR go to a movie.

[Price] * .9

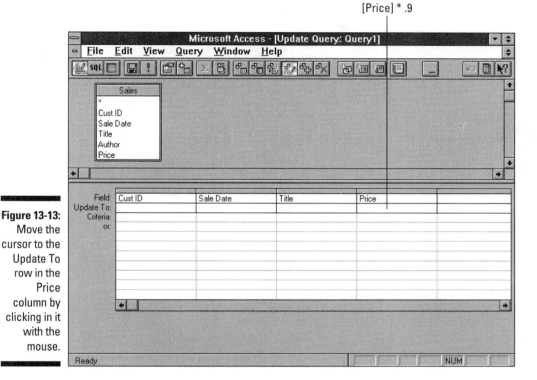

Figure 13-13:
Move the cursor to the Update To row in the Price column by clicking in it with the mouse.

Figure 13-14:
The Sales table with prices changed by the action query.

Cust ID	Sale Date	Title	Author	Price
0001	8/25/94	IN PRAISE OF IDL	Russell, Bertrand	$11.66
0002	8/26/94	GETTING YOUR H	Russell, Mrs. Bertra	$11.66
0004	8/21/94	HOW TO WRITE /	Obscurantis, Jargur	$2.66
0005	8/27/94	HOW I TURNED $	Fleiss, Heidi	$22.46
0005	8/28/94	ACCESS 2 FOR DL	Palmer, Scott	$13,319.96
0000				$0.00

Chapter 14

Hot Stuff! Customizing Your Forms

. . . .

In This Chapter

▶ Modifying a form design

▶ Moving and resizing fields

▶ Editing captions

▶ Changing colors

▶ Changing the look of captions

. . . .

*A*re you ready to be shocked and amazed? Sometimes, even database gurus (like you are becoming) don't do everything perfectly. The Access Form Wizard itself, which you find out how to use in Chapter 10, slips up here and there. If you did the exercises in that chapter, the form design it created for you isn't quite perfect yet.

In this chapter, you find out the basic ideas and skills for customizing and modifying forms. The good news is that Access makes it easy for you to change the features of a form. In this chapter, you discover how to move the fields and their captions around on the form. Then I show you how to change a field's caption. Finally, you find out how to change the color scheme and appearance of the form.

To understand the ideas in this chapter, you should know the concepts of a database (Chapter 2), a table (Chapter 3), and a form (Chapter 10). To do the exercises with the form in the book, you need to have created the Customer Records table (Chapter 3), put data in it (Chapter 5), and created a form (Chapter 10).

If you're customizing a form you've created for your own "real life" database, just read this chapter to get the basic ideas. Then use the ideas and techniques in the chapter to customize your own form.

Moving Fields and Captions

 The simplest thing you can do to customize a form is to move fields and captions around on it. The basic steps for moving fields and captions on a form are:

1. **In the Form Design window, open the form you want to modify.**

   If you're already designing a form, you're *already there.* If not, you just need to open the database you want in Access, click on the Form tab in the Database window, be sure that the highlight is on the form you want to modify, and then click on the Design button at the top right corner of the Database window.

2. **Select the item you want to move.**

   To select an item (a field, caption, etc.) in the Form Design window, just click on it with the mouse. When it's selected, it will be surrounded by a border with little black rectangles. If you're selecting a field and its caption, the black rectangles will be around only one of them, but a border will still be around the other.

3. **Position the mouse over the border until it turns into a little hand.**

   The little hand means that if you hold down the left mouse button, you can drag the item to a new location. When you release the mouse button, Access "drops" the item at the new location. If you're moving a field and its label, the little hand might have only one finger up, which means that it will move *only* the field or the label but not both, or all fingers up, with means that it will move the field and label together. Just move the mouse pointer around until you get the little hand you want.

Moving Stuff in the Customer Records Form

Now, it's time for a practical exercise. If you took a break after the last chapter, start up Access and load the Caveat database. Then:

1. **Click on the Form tab at the left side of the Database window.**

   Access displays all the forms that have been created for this database.

2. **Double-click on the Customer Records form in the Database window.**

   Access displays the form as it will appear when it's used to enter or view data.

3. **If needed, maximize the window so that it fills the whole screen.**

   Your screen should look like Figure 14-1.

 Moving fields and captions isn't difficult in principle: You just use the mouse to drag them from their old locations on the form to wherever you want them. But the details — well, let's tell the truth here — the details are a little messy.

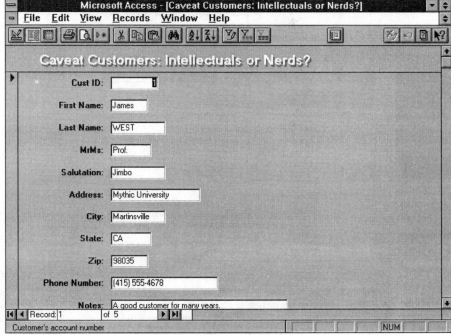

Figure 14-1:
The Caveat
Customers
form
created by
the Form
Wizard.

Selecting a field and caption

Before you can do anything with a field or its caption, you must select them. Now, the mere act of selecting a field and its caption is pretty simple. You just click on top of the field and its caption until you see both of them surrounded by a border with black rectangles in it, as shown in Figure 14-2.

In the figure, both the caption and field are selected. That's what the Last Name field and its caption look like if you click on the caption, which is on the left. If you click on the field instead, Access puts the six black rectangles around the field, and the caption has only one black dot in its upper left corner.

The double-arrow, the hand, and the finger

You can do three main things with a field or its caption:

- You can resize it vertically (to make it taller) or horizontally (to make it wider).
- You can move both the field and its caption at the same time by dragging them around the screen with the mouse.
- You can move just a field or its caption by dragging it with the mouse.

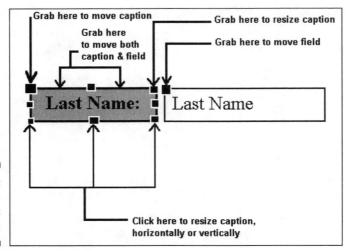

Figure 14-2:
Selecting a
field and its
caption.

Depending on where it's located over the field or its caption, the mouse pointer changes shape, as shown in Figure 14-3. When Access gives you the double arrow as a mouse pointer, it means that you can resize the field by holding down the left mouse button and dragging the field or caption border. When Access gives you the hand as a mouse pointer (also called a *grabber*), it means that you can move *both* the field and its caption simultaneously. And when Access gives you the finger, it means that you can move just the field or its caption, whichever is selected at the moment.

To become acquainted with this setup, play around a little bit to get the hang of moving and resizing fields and captions. Then move on to the next section, where you actually redesign the form layout.

Figure 14-3:
The shape
of the
mouse
pointer tells
you what
you can do
at the
moment.

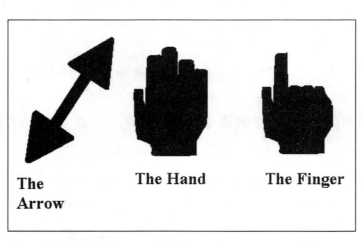

Control properties

Fields, captions, and all the other things you see in a form design screen are called *controls*. Each control has properties that you can set, such as its caption, its size, and any special jobs that it's supposed to do. Although the forms you're creat- ing here are simple, you can put push buttons, list boxes, and other advanced controls on the forms you design. Of course, that's all for when you become a real-life Access expert!

Dragging Fields Around

Suppose that you want to change the layout of the Caveat Customers form so that it looks like the one in Figure 14-4, with one exception — the caption for the Phone Number field. All you have to do is drag things around in the form design window to achieve your goal. To change the form, take the following steps, using Figure 14-4 as your guide.

1. Drag the right border of the form to the right.

Do this until the form is almost as wide as the screen. Don't let it get any closer than about a half inch from the right edge of the screen.

Figure 14-4: How the form should look when you're finished moving the fields and captions.

```
┌──────────────────────────────────────────────────────────────────────┐
│  =  Microsoft Access - Scott Palmer - [Caveat Customers: Intellectuals or Nerds?]  ▼ ÷ │
│  =  File   Edit   View   Records   Window   Help                          ÷ │
│  ────────────────────────────────────────────────────────────────────── │
│     Caveat Customers: Intellectuals or Nerds?                          ↕ │
│  ▶    Cust ID:  [        1]                                              │
│                                                                          │
│     First Name: [James]   Last Name: [WEST]      MrMs: [Prof.]          │
│                                                                          │
│     Salutation: [Jimbo]    Address: [Mythic University]                 │
│                                                                          │
│         City: [Martinsville]  State: [CA]       Zip: [98035]            │
│                                                                          │
│        Phone: [(415) 555-4678]                                          │
│                                                                          │
│        Notes: [A good customer for a long, long time.]                  │
│                                                                          │
│  ◄◄◄ Record: 1    of 5    ►►►                                           │
│     Customer's account number                             NUM            │
└──────────────────────────────────────────────────────────────────────┘
```

2. Drag the Cust ID field and caption to the left.

Drag the field and caption until the left end of the *field* is even with the first vertical grid line, shown in Figure 14-5.

Notice that Access makes things easy for you — anything you move on-screen automatically snaps into position along two of the window's grid lines.

3. Drag the First Name field and caption to the left until the left border of the *field* (not the caption) is even with the left end of the Cust ID field.

In the form design grid, fields are aligned horizontally by the left border of the field, *not* the left border of the caption.

4. Drag the Last Name and MrMs fields and captions so that they're on the same line as the First Name field.

5. Drag the Salutation field and caption up and to the left so that the left end of the field is even with the left end of the First Name field.

6. Drag the Address field up and to the right so that it's on the same line as the Salutation field.

Make sure that the left end of the field is even with the left end of the Last Name field above it.

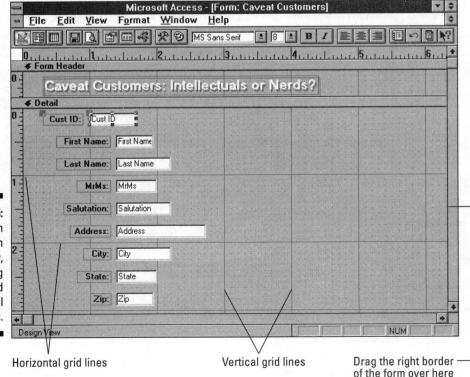

Figure 14-5:
The form design window, showing vertical and horizontal grid lines.

Horizontal grid lines   Vertical grid lines   Drag the right border of the form over here

7. **Do the same stuff to drag the City, State, and Zip fields and captions onto one line underneath the Salutation and Address fields.**

8. **Using the vertical scroll bar on the right side of the window, scroll down a little so that you can see the Phone Number and Notes fields.**

Changing a control's properties

Everything on a form design is called a *control*. The fields are controls, the form label is a control, and the field captions are controls. Moreover, all controls have *properties*.

Here, you'll change a control's Caption property. But you can use the same basic technique to change other properties. If you want more information about controls and their properties, you should consult IDG's *PC World Microsoft Access 2 Bible 2nd Edition* (Prague/Irwin, 1994).

The reason that this comes up at the moment is that the caption for the Phone Number field is too long. Because of that, you can't drag the Phone Number field far enough to the left to be even with the City field above it. But there's good news: all you need to do is change one of the caption's properties on the form. Follow these steps:

1. **Click on the caption for the Phone Number field so that it's surrounded by the six black (or gray) rectangles, as shown in Figure 14-2.**

2. **In the menu bar, click on <u>V</u>iew to open the <u>V</u>iew menu.**

3. **In the <u>V</u>iew menu, select <u>P</u>roperties.**

   The control properties window appears, as shown in Figure 14-6. The window contains a lot of stuff, but at the moment, you're only interested in the second line, Caption. Currently, it contains the words *Phone Number* followed by a colon.

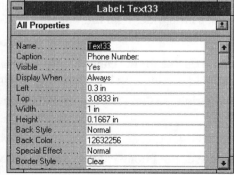

Figure 14-6: The control properties dialog box.

Label: Text33

All Properties

Name	Text33
Caption	Phone Number:
Visible	Yes
Display When	Always
Left	0.3 in
Top	3.0833 in
Width	1 in
Height	0.1667 in
Back Style	Normal
Back Color	12632256
Special Effect	Normal
Border Style	Clear

4. Click in the space just after the *e* in *Phone*.

5. Press the Delete key seven times.

The caption text should now be simply *Phone* followed by a colon.

6. Close the control properties window by double-clicking on its Window Control button in the top-left corner of the window.

The caption for the Phone Number field is now simply *Phone*.

Resizing a control

Now you need to make the Phone Number field caption a little narrower. First, click on the caption to select it. Then, using the mouse, grab the black rectangle at the caption's top right corner, as shown in Figure 14-7. The mouse pointer changes into a double arrow.

Figure 14-7:
Grab the caption by the rectangle at the top right corner.

Grab here

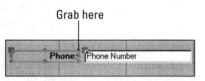

To grab something with the mouse position — whether it's a field or just one corner of a field — position the mouse pointer over it and hold down the left mouse button. To drag something with the mouse, grab it and then continue to hold down the left mouse button while you move the mouse.

Holding down the left mouse button, drag the mouse to the left. As you do so, the size of the box around the caption becomes narrower. Keep dragging the right edge of the box until it's just a little wider than the word *Phone*. To finish with the Phone Number field, follow these steps:

1. Position the mouse pointer over the Phone caption until Access gives you the finger, indicating that you can drag the caption by itself.

2. Drag the caption back to the right so that it's once again right next to the Phone Number field.

Then release the left mouse button.

3. Position the mouse pointer over the Phone caption until the mouse pointer becomes a hand.

The hand indicates that you can drag both the caption and the field at the same time.

4. **Drag the caption and the field up and to the left until the left border of the field is even with the left border of the City field above it.**

5. **Drag the Notes caption and field so that they're underneath the Phone Number field.**

   The left border of the Notes field should be even with the left border of the Phone Number field.

6. **Click on the Datasheet button in the toolbar to see how your form looks.**

   It should look like the one in Figure 14-4, shown earlier in this chapter.

7. **If the form looks all right, click on the Design button on the left end of the toolbar to switch back to the form design window.**

8. **Save the form by opening the File menu and selecting Save.**

Changing a Form's Colors

Changing colors on a form is easy. With the form displayed in the Form Design window, the basic steps are:

1. **Select the part of the form whose colors you want to change.**

   This can be a field, caption, floating text, or the whole form itself.

2. **From the View menu, select Palette.**

   The Palette dialog box appears.

3. **In the Palette dialog box, select the color for foreground (text), background, and border.**

4. **Close the Palette dialog box by clicking on the little control button at the dialog box's top left corner.**

Changing Colors in the Customer Records Form

Now, try a practical exercise. With the Customer Records form displayed in the Form Design window, open the View menu and select Palette, or click on the Palette button in the toolbar. The Palette dialog box appears, as shown in Figure 14-8.

As usual, anything you do in the color palette applies only to the thing that's currently selected in the form. You can change the foreground color, which is usually the text in a label or field; the background color, which is the color of the screen behind the text; and the way a caption looks on-screen.

These buttons control the "look" of
captions — boxed, raised, or sunken

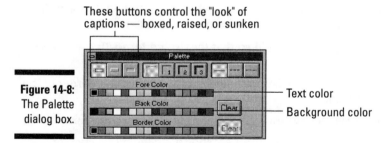

Figure 14-8:
The Palette
dialog box.

Text color
Background color

To see how these features work, use Figure 14-9 as a guide and follow these steps:

1. **Click at location 1 (see Figure 14-9) to select the *Caveat Customers:* *Intellectuals or Nerds?* label.**

2. **In the color palette, click on yellow in the ForeColor bar.**

   The text color changes to yellow.

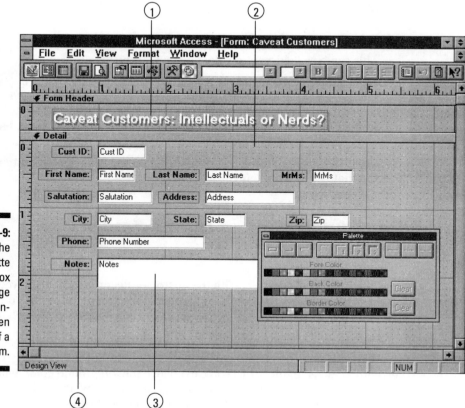

Figure 14-9:
Use the
Palette
dialog box
to change
the on-
screen
colors of a
form.

3. **Click at location 2 to select the form background.**

   Experiment by clicking on different colors in the Palette's BackColor bar. If you find one that you like better than basic gray, keep it. Otherwise, click on gray to change back to the form's original background color.

4. **Click at location 3 to select the Notes field.**

   Experiment with different foreground and background colors in the Palette. Then switch the field back to its original colors of black text on a white background.

If you wanted to stop at this point, you'd close the Palette dialog box by clicking on the control button at the top left corner of the dialog box. However, if you want to go on with the exercise, don't close the dialog box quite yet.

Changing the Look of a Caption

The final thing to do in this chapter is to learn how to change the look of a caption on a form. Three buttons in the top left corner of the Palette dialog box (see Figure 14-8) enable you to do this. From left to right, your choices are

- ✔ **Normal appearance,** which means that the caption is surrounded by a little box.
- ✔ **Raised appearance,** which means that the caption looks like it's raised above the form background.
- ✔ **Sunken appearance,** which means that the caption looks like it's sunk below the form background.

Like a lot of things, you really have to see these options in use to understand them. So, using Figure 14-9 as a guide, click at location 4 to select the caption for the Notes field. Then try experimenting with the three Appearance buttons in the top left corner of the Palette.

Finally, close the Palette dialog box by clicking on the control button at the top left corner of the dialog box.

Save your new form design by selecting Save from the File menu or clicking on the Save button in the toolbar. Then relax for a bit. In the next chapter, you learn how to sort and filter your data. (What the heck is that? Don't worry — it's going to be tons of fun!)

Part III
Organizing and Printing Your Data

The 5th Wave   **By Rich Tennant**

Bob, the laser printer repairman, finds an idle moment that costs him his sideburns.

©RICHTENNANT

TECHNICALLY, YOU SHOULD BE ABLE TO LIGHT YOUR CIGARETTE ON THIS THING PRETTY EASY.

In this part ...

Putting data into a database is one thing. Parts I and II cover all the ways to do that. Organizing data and getting it *out* of a database are something else. This part shows you how to sort the data in your database in any way you like.

This part also shows you how to print out your data: either the quick and dirty way, by printing directly from a datasheet or form, or the easy but pretty way, by creating simple reports.

Chapter 15

Sorting Stuff and Using Filters (Not Including Coffee Filters)

Consider the Customer Records table you created in earlier chapters. At the moment, the records are in order by account number. But suppose that you want to view customer records in order by last name or zip code? Likewise, records in the sample Sales table are in order by the date that the record was entered into the table. What if you want to see the sales records organized according to the amount of the sale or alphabetically by the name of the book?

In this chapter, you find out how to sort your database records so that they appear in whatever order suits your purpose.

You also use *filters*. You can use filters to tell Access to hide some of your records so that it's easier to see the ones you want. Filters are a lot like queries, except that they're quicker and you can't save them for later use — unless, of course, they're coffee filters, which you can use over and over for up to three months, if it's just the office coffeemaker, anyway.

To understand the ideas in this chapter, you should know the concepts of a database (Chapter 2) and a table (Chapter 3). To do the exercises with the example database in the book, you need to have created the Sales table (Chapter 12).

If you're sorting records in your own "real life" database, just read this chapter to get the basic ideas. Then use the ideas and techniques in the chapter to customize your own form.

Doing a Simple Sort

When you see the term *simple sort,* you may think of Jethro Clampett or Gomer Pyle. But though these fictional characters are indeed simple sorts, it's a different kind of simple sort from those you do in Access. In Access, a simple sort puts records in order by one field, such as Sale Date or Last Name. You can also sort your records on more than one field, but that comes later.

The following example illustrates the process of doing a simple sort.

Drudgework alert! Add more sales records

If you took a break after you finished the last chapter, start Access again and load the Caveat database. Then open the Sales database and add five more records to make the sort more interesting:

Cust ID: 5
Sale Date: 8/26/94
Title: Fershlugginers I Have Known
Author: Smith, Joe
Price: 11.66

Cust ID: 1
Sale Date: 8/27/94
Title: Atlas Shrugged
Author: Rand, Ayn
Price: 11.66

Cust ID: 2
Sale Date: 8/28/94
Title: Love in the Time of Cholera
Author: Garcia Marquez, Gabriel
Price: 10.80

Cust ID: 4
Sale Date: 8/30/94
Title: Deep Thoughts
Author: Clinton & Quayle
Price: 1.75

Cust ID: 3
Sale Date: 8/31/94
Title: "Supertrain" Forever!
Author: Silverman, Fred
Price: 1.75

Sort the sales records

After you enter the new records, display the datasheet for the Sales table, as shown in Figure 15-1. (The column widths have been changed to make the datasheet easier to read. You learned how to do that in Chapter 7.) Notice that the records, as you enter them, were in order by date. Apart from that, they aren't in any real order at all.

Figure 15-1:
Sales records are no longer in order by date.

Cust ID	Sale Date	Title	Author	Price
0001	8/25/94	IN PRAISE OF IDLENESS	Russell, Bertrand	$11.66
0001	8/27/94	ATLAS SHRUGGED	Rand, Ayn	$11.66
0002	8/26/94	GETTING YOUR HUSBAND OFF HIS LAZY BUTT	Russell, Mrs. Bertrand	$11.66
0002	8/28/94	LOVE IN THE TIME OF CHOLERA	Garcia Marquez, Gabriel	$10.80
0003	8/31/94	"SUPERTRAIN" FOREVER!	Silverman, Fred	$1.75
0004	8/21/94	HOW TO WRITE A COMPUTER BOOK	Obscurantis, Jargun	$2.66
0004	8/30/94	DEEP THOUGHTS	Clinton & Quayle	$1.75
0005	8/27/94	HOW I TURNED $25 CASH INTO A SUCCESSFUL BUSINESS	Fleiss, Heidi	$22.46
0005	8/28/94	ACCESS 2 FOR DUMMIES	Palmer, Scott	$13,319.96
0005	8/26/94	FERSHLUGGINERS I HAVE KNOWN	Smith, Joe	$11.66
0000				$0.00

Ascending and descending sorts

The easiest way to sort your records is to use one of the two Sort buttons in the toolbar, shown in Figure 15-2. Access gives you two buttons because you can sort things in either *ascending order* (A to Z) or *descending order* (Z to A).

Figure 15-2:
The Sort Up (ascending sort) and Sort Down (descending sort) buttons on the toolbar.

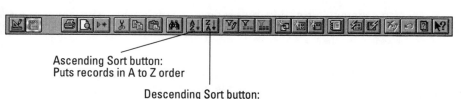

Ascending Sort button:
Puts records in A to Z order

Descending Sort button:
Puts records in Z to A order

The general method for sorting records involves two steps. First, click in the field you want to use for the sort. For example, if you want to put the sales records in order by book title, you would click in the Title field. After you select a field, click on one of the Sort buttons. Try it now to put the Sales records in order by date:

1. Click in the Sale Date column to select it.

2. Click on the Sort Up button in the toolbar.

As you can see, the records almost instantly jump into a date-sorted order, from August 21 (the first sale in the table) to August 31 (the last sale in the table).

Now try a descending sort. Click in the Sale Date field again to select it and then click on the Sort Down button. Once again, the effect is almost immediate: The records jump into order, with the last date first and the first date last.

Finally, select the Sale Date field and click once again on the Sort Up button to put the records in ascending order by date.

Sorting on more than one field

If you haven't done much of this sorting stuff, you probably have two questions at this point:

1. What the heck is "sorting on more than one field?"

2. Why the heck would any sane person do something like that, what with all the traffic jams and pollution and bad Top 40s music that's already in the world?

The answer is simple. Yes, the records in the Sales table are in order by date. Does that mean that all's well with the world? No. For one thing, Pauly Shore makes a *lot* more money than you do. And if that isn't enough to convince you that something is *seriously* wrong in the universe, take a look at Figure 15-3. Even though the records are in order by date, they're out of order *within* particular dates.

Using the Sort buttons is quick and easy. But the more common — and powerful — way to sort records is by creating a query.

Figure 15-3:
The records
are out of
order within
particular
dates.

	Cust ID	Sale Date	Title	Author	Price
▶	0004	8/21/94	HOW TO WRITE A COMPUTER BOOK	Obscurantis, Jargun	$2.66
	0001	8/25/94	IN PRAISE OF IDLENESS	Russell, Bertrand	$11.66
	0005	8/26/94	FERSHLUGGINERS I HAVE KNOWN	Smith, Joe	$11.66
	0002	8/26/94	GETTING YOUR HUSBAND OFF HIS LAZY BUTT	Russell, Mrs. Bertrand	$11.66
	0001	8/27/94	ATLAS SHRUGGED	Rand, Ayn	$11.66
	0005	8/27/94	HOW I TURNED $25 CASH INTO A SUCCESSFUL BUSINESS	Fleiss, Heidi	$22.46
	0002	8/28/94	LOVE IN THE TIME OF CHOLERA	Garcia Marquez, Gabriel	$10.80
	0005	8/28/94	ACCESS 2 FOR DUMMIES	Palmer, Scott	$13,319.96
	0004	8/30/94	DEEP THOUGHTS	Clinton & Quayle	$1.75
	0003	8/31/94	"SUPERTRAIN" FOREVER!	Silverman, Fred	$1.75
*	0000				$0.00

The Sale Date column looks fine. But look at the Author column. The authors' names are completely out of order. More than that, they're out of order in two ways:

- ✔ If you look at *all* the author names, the whole group is out of order. You get books by Obscurantis, Russell, Smith, Russell, Rand, and so on.

- ✔ Within some of the dates, the author names for that date are out of order. For sales dated August 27, for example, the book by Ayn Rand appears in the datasheet before the book by Heidi Fleiss.

There's really nothing you can (or should) worry about doing with the overall order of the author names. If you sort on one field, then in general, the other fields will be out of order. It would be an incredible coincidence if on Monday, the bookstore sold only books whose author names began with *A,* sold *B* authors on Tuesday, *C* authors on Wednesday, and so on. That just doesn't happen, except in California, where the weather is nice but the people are weird — at least, so you hear if you ask people in other parts of the country.

But you *can* do something about the order of records within each date. That's why you want to sort on more than one field. Unfortunately, you can't do it with the Sort Up and Sort Down buttons. But wait: There's good news. You can do it with the Filter/Sort buttons.

Setting Up the Multi Field Sort

Don't worry too much at the moment about what filters are: In essence, a filter is just a "quick and dirty" query. The Filter/Sort buttons you're going to use in the example in this section are shown in Figure 15-4.

Apply a filter/sort to data

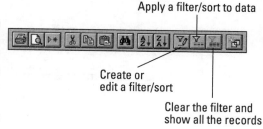

Figure 15-4:
The Filter/
Sort buttons
in the
toolbar.

Create or
edit a filter/sort

Clear the filter and
show all the records

Access sorts fields from left to right in the QBE grid. The general steps for doing a multi-field sort are as follows:

1. Drag the most important sorting field into the QBE grid. For instance, if you wanted to sort records by Last Name and First Name, the Last Name field would be the most important. Overall, the records would be in order by last name.

2. Drag the second most important field into the grid so that it's in the column to the right of the first field. In the Last Name/First Name example, this would be the First Name field. Within each group of records with the same last name, the records would be in order by first name.

3. Drag any additional sorting fields into the QBE grid, in their order of importance.

4. Run the query to sort the records.

Access sorts fields from left to right in the QBE grid.

To sort the Sales table on both the Sale Date and Author fields, click on the Create/Edit button. The Filter window appears on your screen, looking an awful lot like the Query window, as shown in Figure 15-5. Because you're filtering the Sales table, its field list is automatically displayed in the window. And because the Sale Date field was the last one you sorted on, Access automatically puts it in the first column of the filter grid in the bottom part of the screen.

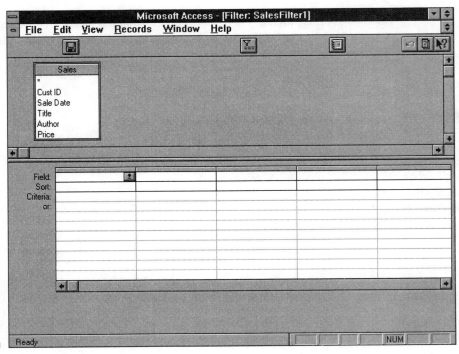

Figure 15-5:
The Filter
window.

To set up the filter, follow these steps:

1. **Drag the Cust ID field from the field list to the cell where Sale Date is currently shown.**

   (That's the top cell in the leftmost column.) When you release the mouse button, Access puts the Cust ID field in that column and bumps the Sale Date field over one column to the right.

2. **Click on the Title field in the field list.**

3. **Hold down the Shift key on your keyboard and press the down-arrow key twice.**

   This selects the Author and Price fields, so that all three fields are highlighted.

4. **Drag the fields to the Field row of the column to the right of Sale Date.**

   Access automatically inserts the three new fields in the grid.

5. **Click in the Sort row of the Author column.**

6. **Click on the arrow at the right end of the cell. In the list, select Ascending.**

7. **And that's it! Click on the Apply Filter button in the toolbar to see the result.**

   The records are in order by Sale Date, and within each date, they are in order by author name, as shown in Figure 15-6.

Figure 15-6:
Result of the
simple Filter/
Sort. The
records are
now in order
by sale date,
and within
each date,
they are in
order by
author name.

Cust ID	Sale Date	Title	Author	Price
0004	8/21/94	HOW TO WRITE A COMPUTER BOOK	Obscurantis, Jargun	$2.66
0001	8/25/94	IN PRAISE OF IDLENESS	Russell, Bertrand	$11.66
0002	8/26/94	GETTING YOUR HUSBAND OFF HIS LAZY BUTT	Russell, Mrs. Bertrand	$11.66
0005	8/26/94	FERSHLUGGINERS I HAVE KNOWN	Smith, Joe	$11.66
0005	8/27/94	HOW I TURNED $25 CASH INTO A SUCCESSFUL BUSINESS	Fleiss, Heidi	$22.46
0001	8/27/94	ATLAS SHRUGGED	Rand, Ayn	$11.66
0002	8/28/94	LOVE IN THE TIME OF CHOLERA	Garcia Marquez, Gabriel	$10.80
0005	8/28/94	ACCESS 2 FOR DUMMIES	Palmer, Scott	$13,319.96
0004	8/30/94	DEEP THOUGHTS	Clinton & Quayle	$1.75
0003	8/31/94	"SUPERTRAIN" FOREVER!	Silverman, Fred	$1.75
0000				$0.00

Understanding Indexes — and When to Use Them

The subject of sorting wouldn't be complete without at least a look at indexes. In real life, an index usually helps you find information, as shown in Figure 15-7. The index of a book, for example, lists topics and has a page number for each topic — a kind of "pointer" to the place where you can read about the topic.

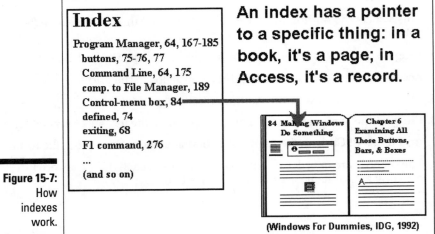

Index

Program Manager, 64, 167-185
  buttons, 75-76, 77
  Command Line, 64, 175
  comp. to File Manager, 189
  Control-menu box, 84
  defined, 74
  exiting, 68
  F1 command, 276
  ...
  (and so on)

An index has a pointer to a specific thing: in a book, it's a page; in Access, it's a record.

84 Making Windows Do Something

Chapter 6 Examining All Those Buttons, Bars, & Boxes

(Windows For Dummies, IDG, 1992)

Figure 15-7: How indexes work.

TIP

When you index a field, Access can find stuff in that field faster than it can in a non-indexed field. *However* — and it's a big however — in smaller databases, indexing makes very little difference. If you have only a few hundred records in a table, indexing *slightly* speeds up Find operations and queries, but not enough so that you'll be able to notice it.

An index in Access works almost exactly like a computerized book index. When Access needs to search for a particular in an index field, it simply looks in the index to find the location of the records that have that value. When you first create a table, you can set up each field so that Access does or doesn't create an index for it. Whether or not a field is indexed is one of the field properties you set in the bottom of the table design screen, shown in Figure 15-8.

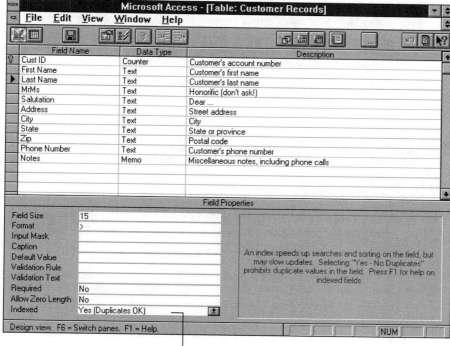

Figure 15-8:
When you create or modify a table design, you can tell Access to index a field.

Here's where you tell Access whether you want a field to be indexed

When you're deciding if a field should be indexed, you have three choices:

✔ **Not indexed.** If you choose this option, Access doesn't create an index for the field. Everything will work fine, but searching for stuff in this field will be a little slower than it would be if the field were indexed. It's sort of like trying to find things in a book that has no index. Sure, you can still find everything — it just takes longer.

✔ **Indexed, Duplicates OK:** This option tells Access to create an index but also to let more than one record have the same value in the field. It's the option you would use if you wanted to index a Last Name field, because many people can have the same last name.

✔ **Indexed, No Duplicates:** This option tells Access to create an index but *never* to let more than one record have the same value in this field. It's the option you would use for customer account numbers because you never want two customers to have the same account number.

If indexing helps Access find stuff more quickly, why not just index every field? The reason is that every index you create makes Access do more work to manage your records — and that takes extra time.

If a table has one indexed field, Access must create a new entry in the index every time you enter a new record. If the table has 10 indexed fields, Access has to create *10* new entries in *10* different indexes (indices? *naaah*) for each new record. Even with a fast program like Access and a fast PC, the slowdown can become significant. So you shouldn't automatically index every field. If you know that you'll be searching a particular field often or that you need to use it to link up with other tables, indexing is a good move. Otherwise, don't do it.

Filtering Stuff (Not Coffee!) With the Filter Buttons

As you learned earlier in this chapter, one of the things you can do with the filter buttons is to sort tables on more than one field. But there's another important use for filters: to display only certain records in a table.

Suppose that you want to know which recent book sales in your sample Sales table had a price over $15. Because the table is small, that's not a problem. There are only 10 records, so you can just look at the datasheet.

But imagine for a moment that your bookstore sold 5,000 books in the last week. Sure, you could still go through the table record by record or skim down through the datasheet a screen at a time. But it would be a *lot* of work and take a lot of time.

You really have two options. First, you could run a query. As you saw in Chapter 12, running a query isn't terribly hard. But there's an even easier way: Use a filter. With a filter, you can make the datasheet (or a form) show only those records for book sales over $15. When you're finished looking at the over-$15 books, you can just click another button in the toolbar, and presto! All the records are displayed again.

Setting up a filter

You actually set up a filter before, when you sorted the Sales table on both the Sale Date and Author fields. The only difference between what you did then and what you're about to do is that before, you didn't fill in any criteria for matching records. As a result, Access simply sorted the records and displayed all of them — with no criteria, they were *all* matching records.

This time, however, you're less interested in sorting the records than in displaying only those where the Price is more than $15. Follow these steps:

1. **In the Datasheet window with the Sales table displayed, click on the Create/Edit Filter button in the toolbar.**

   The Filter window appears, as before.

2. **Click in the Criteria row of the Price column, which is the rightmost column of the grid.**

3. **In the Price/Criteria cell, type** >15.

4. **Click on the Apply Filter button in the toolbar. The datasheet reappears.**

   This time, only two records are displayed: the Heidi Fleiss book and this book, both of which cost more than $15.

You can create many other kinds of filters. You could, for example, display only those records in which the author's name started with *B*. Or you could create a filter that displayed a record only if the customer's account number was 0005, the sale date was after August 25, and the price of the book was under $10. The possibilities are limited only by your imagination and your needs for information.

Removing the filter

After you set up a filter, Access no longer displays all your records. To redisplay all the records in your table, simply click on the Show All Records button in the toolbar.

Save the filter — not!

One thing you *can't* do with a filter is save it to use again in the future. That's where the similarity between filters and queries breaks down. But if you don't need a full-blown query, filters can save you time by providing a quick and easy alternative.

Speaking of time, it's about time for a break. If you want, put down the book, rest your eyes, dust off that exercise bicycle you've had in the closet for the last six months, or just kick back for a while.

Chapter 16

Quick and Easy Ways to Print Database Stuff

In This Chapter

▶ What are reports?

▶ Using Print Preview to see how something will look on paper

▶ Printing stuff from a datasheet

▶ Printing stuff from a form

*D*id you ever notice that the word *report* always seems to mean something bad? There's the report *card,* which usually means no TV for a month; the *credit* report, which recounts in loving detail the $11.75 dry cleaning bill you forgot to pay six years ago; the *gunshot* report, which you usually hear a split-second after you accidentally propel a bullet through your foot; and, of course, the ever-popular *tax* report, by which you render unto Caesar everything you've earned since his last April 15th payday.

The good news is that in Access, *report* means something *good.* A report is just a printout of your database data. It can be plain or it can be fancy. It can have all your data or just some of it. It can be grouped and organized, include totals and summaries, use boldface type and other printing effects — or not. Everything is up to you. And the *great* news is that Access makes it easy to create all these types of reports.

Here are some examples of reports you can produce from the Caveat Emptor bookstore database you created in earlier chapters:

- ✔ A simple printout from a datasheet or form
- ✔ A name, address, and phone number list for all bookstore customers
- ✔ A list of all sales for a given month, with sales broken down by state

✔ A customer list that includes the items each customer purchased and the total amount spent by each customer. This report would involve information from both the Customer Records and Sales tables.

✔ A summary of sales for the entire year, with revenues broken down by quarter (three-month periods) and graphed in a bar chart

To understand this chapter, and to create reports with the sample database, you should read Chapters 3, 5, and 10 before you read this chapter.

Different Kinds of Reports

All the different variations of reports really boil down into three categories. First, you can produce an *informal report,* which basically is just a printout of a datasheet or form in your database. The big advantage of an informal report is that it takes about 10 seconds to create. The big *dis*advantage is that it presents your data just as it appears in the datasheet or form. Informal reports aren't very flexible.

Second, if you have something appropriate to wear, you can produce a *formal report.* A formal report is what you normally think of as a snazzy business report. It can present your database information in rows and columns, include page numbers, footers, and totals, and so on. The report doesn't have to use a row and column format: if you prefer, you can select a different layout, such as for a single-column or summary report. You can even include graphs and bar charts.

Third, you can create a *special-purpose report.* This type of report lets you create mailing labels and form letters.

In this chapter, you learn how to create informal reports. Formal reports are covered in the next chapter, with mailing labels and form letters coming along a bit later.

For most of the exercises in this chapter, you need to use your printer. Make sure that your printer is turned on, has plenty of paper, and is ready to print. If you see the word *online* somewhere on the front of the printer, the little light next to it should be turned on — it means that the printer is ready to go.

If you're in a big hurry, you can create an informal report just by opening the datasheet or form you want to print, opening the File menu, and clicking on Print. But if you have at least two minutes, you can use a few tricks to make even your informal reports look great. The following exercises show you how to print a quick report.

Printing from a Datasheet

If you haven't done so already, start Access and open the Caveat database. Make sure that the Database window is displayed and the Table tab is selected. Double-click on the Customer Records table to open its datasheet and then follow these steps:

1. **Make sure that your printer is on and ready to print.**

2. **Open the File menu and select Print.**

   The Print dialog box appears, as shown in Figure 16-1.

3. **Click on OK.**

   Your printer prints the datasheet.

Figure 16-1:
The Print
dialog box.
It may look
a little
different on
your screen,
depending
on what
kind of
printer you
have.

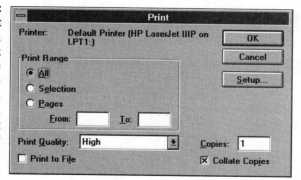

Did it occur to you that when you run a query or a filter, the result is a *dynaset* — and a dynaset is just another kind of datasheet? When you run a query or filter, you can print the result just as you can any other datasheet.

But it doesn't all fit on one page!

The datasheet printout you just produced includes all the data in your table. But unless you have a very unusual printer, the printout looks pretty weird. What's weird is that on the first page of the report, Access printed only the first few columns of the datasheet. All the columns farther to the right are printed on the second page.

No, you didn't do anything wrong. That's just the way it works when you print a datasheet. Any columns that don't fit on the first page are kicked over to the second page. If you want to blame someone, blame the people who invented computerized spreadsheets in the first place: That's how *they've* always printed data, and it's not for nothing that the Access datasheet is often described as being "in spreadsheet format."

You can do one of three things to resolve the problem:

✔ You can narrow some of the columns in the datasheet. In some tables — not the sample one you're working with, unfortunately — narrowing the columns is enough to fix the problem. See Chapter 7.

✔ If you don't actually *need* to print all the columns in the datasheet, you can hide some of them so that Access prints only the ones you want. If those columns fit in the width of a single page, the problem is solved.

✔ When you print the datasheet, you can switch from *Portrait* to *Landscape* mode. Landscape mode prints the datasheet sideways on the page, as shown in Figure 16-2. Because normal printer paper is longer than it is wide, this option can often solve the problem. (It works for 8½ × 11-inch paper used in the U.S. and the A4-size paper used in other countries.)

Because Chapter 7 covers how to change column widths, try using the other two methods with the sample printout: hiding columns and printing in Landscape mode. The following sections take you through each process.

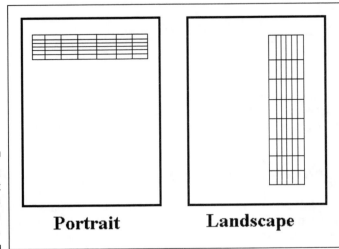

Figure 16-2:
Portrait
versus
Landscape
printing.

Portrait   **Landscape**

Hiding columns in the datasheet

Hiding columns is very simple. Here's an example. Suppose that you decide that you don't need the MrMs, Salutation, Address, Phone Number, and Notes fields in the quick datasheet printout. To hide them, follow these steps:

1. **Click in the gray field selector area of the MrMs column, as shown in Figure 16-3.**

   Access highlights the column to show that it is selected.

2. **Hold down the Shift key and press the right-arrow key twice.**

   Access expands the highlight to include the Salutation and Address columns.

3. **Open the F̲ormat menu and select H̲ide Columns.**

   The columns you selected disappear. They're still in the datasheet; you just can't see them anymore.

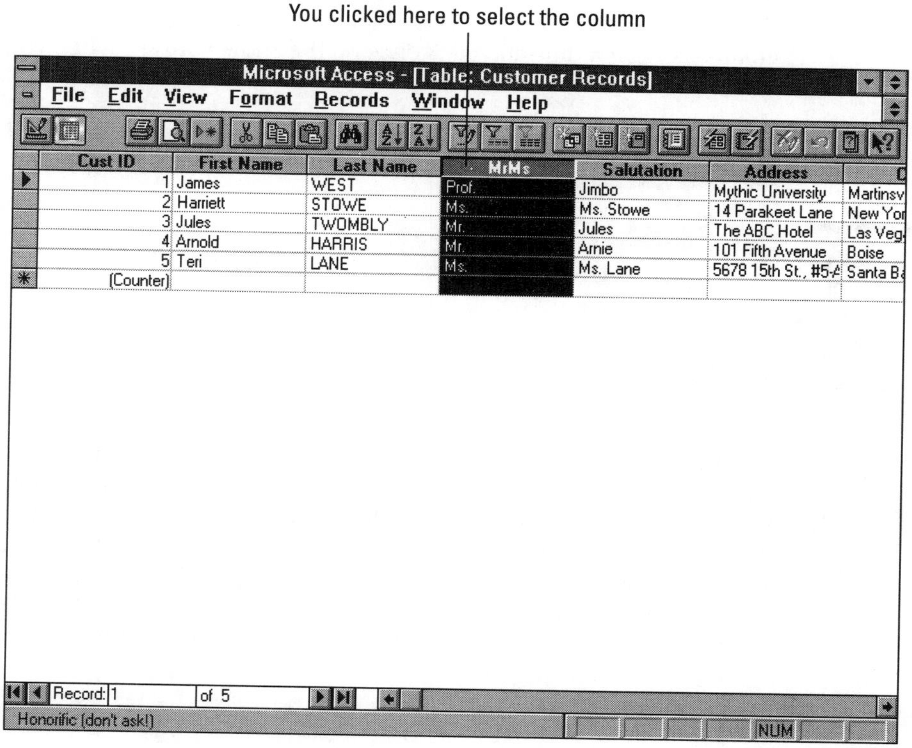

You clicked here to select the column

Figure 16-3:
Click in the gray field selector area to select the column.

4. **Move to the right in the datasheet by clicking on the right-arrow button in the bottom-right corner of the window.**

   Do this until the Phone Number and Notes columns are visible.

5. **Hide the Phone Number and Notes columns in the same way you hid the other columns.**

6. **Print the datasheet.**

   Open the File menu, select Print, and click on OK in the dialog box. This time, the printout looks fine.

Making hidden columns visible again

To make the hidden columns visible again, open the Format menu and select Show Columns. The Show Columns dialog box appears, as shown in Figure 16-4. Only the columns with check marks next to them are currently visible in the datasheet.

By double-clicking on the names of the hidden columns, you can check them so that they reappear. Do that now. (If you don't like to double-click, highlight the columns one at a time and click once on the Show button.) When you're finished, click on the Close button.

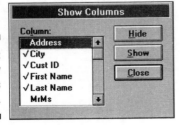

Figure 16-4:
The Show
Columns
dialog box.

Hiding columns is just one way to print part of a datasheet. Another thing you can do is use the mouse to *select* only the columns you want to print. Then, in the Print dialog box, click on the Selection radio button (see Figure 16-1). This method can be quicker and easier than hiding columns. However, the columns you print must be next to each other in the datasheet. And Print Preview won't be an accurate reflection of how your printed page will look. Instead of displaying only the selected columns, Print Preview displays *all* the columns.

Printing a datasheet in Landscape mode

If you want to print a datasheet in Landscape mode, you need to do only one thing differently from what you do when you print in Portrait mode. As you do when you print in Portrait mode, open the File menu and select Print. This time, when the Print dialog box appears, click on the Setup button on the right. Then follow these steps:

1. **When you see the Print Setup dialog box, click on the Landscape radio button, as shown in Figure 16-5.**

   Your click tells Access to print the datasheet in Landscape mode.

2. **Click on the OK button to return to the Print dialog box.**

3. **Click on OK to print the datasheet in Landscape mode.**

4. **When you finish printing, open the File menu and select Print Setup.**

5. **In the Print Setup dialog box, click on the Portrait radio button to switch back to normal printing.**

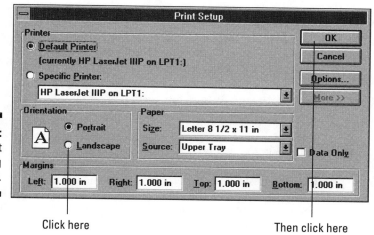

Figure 16-5:
The Print Setup dialog box.

Click here   Then click here

Using Print Preview

Another tool you can use with every Access printout — whether it's a datasheet, a form, or a formal report — is Print Preview. Print Preview shows you on-screen what your current datasheet, form, or report will look like when it's printed.

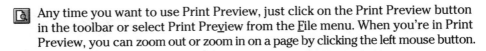 Any time you want to use Print Preview, just click on the Print Preview button in the toolbar or select Print Preview from the File menu. When you're in Print Preview, you can zoom out or zoom in on a page by clicking the left mouse button.

To close the Print Preview window and return to the datasheet, form, or report screen, either click on the Close Window button in the toolbar or press the Esc key on your keyboard.

Printing from a Form

Printing your table from a form is almost exactly like printing it from a datasheet. The main difference is that you don't have to worry about columns disappearing off the right side of the page. To print the customer records using a form, follow these steps:

1. **Close the Datasheet window.**

2. **When Access asks whether you want to save the layout changes in the datasheet, click on No.**

3. **In the Database window, click on the Form tab at the left.**

4. **Double-click on the Caveat Customers form to display it on-screen.**

 5. **To print the table using the form, click on the Print button in the toolbar.**

6. **When the Print dialog box appears, just click on OK.**

   The result should look something like Figure 16-6, which is the Print Preview screen for the form. (Your screen may differ depending on what printer you're using.)

If you're printing a big table, you don't have to print the whole thing. To tell Access how many pages to print, the simplest approach is to use the Print dialog box. In the left side of the box, click on the Pages radio button. Then click in the From blank and type in the starting page number. Click in the To blank and fill in the ending page.

When you print data using a form, Access prints however much will fit on each page, which may not be an even number of records per page. Thus, you may end up with half of a record at the bottom of a page and the other half at the top of the next page.

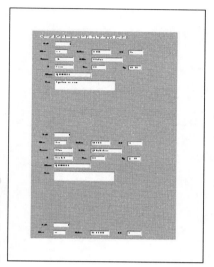

Figure 16-6:
How a form
looks when
printed.

That's it for this chapter. In the next chapter, you learn how to create formal reports with Access Report Wizards!

Chapter 17

Creating Simple Reports with Report Wizards

*P*rinting datasheets and forms, as demonstrated in Chapter 16, is fine when you need a quick and dirty list of the stuff in your database. But if you're printing the data for somebody else — for example, to present at a meeting — the report needs to be a little nicer. It should not only *look* nicer, but it should *do* more, such as group your records or calculate totals. And for that, you need to create a *formal report.*

Now, don't worry too much about the word *formal.* It does *not* mean difficult. All it means is that your report is going to look good and do more than a simple printout from a table. Of course, if you love to play around on your PC, you can create a report that's as complicated as you want. But producing a formal report that includes the basic stuff — columns, totals, and so on — is simple, especially with the help of Access's Report Wizards.

To do the exercises in this chapter, you need the bookstore database (created in Chapter 2) and the Customer Records table (Chapter 3). You also need at least five records in the Customer Records table; the data for the table is in Appendix A. If you're creating a report for your own real-life database, just follow along, doing the same steps with your own database.

Creating a Simple Report

In this section, you'll use a Report Wizard to create a simple row and column report. Because the Wizard doesn't do everything quite the way you want it, you'll then learn how to modify the report design on your own.

Start up Access and load the Caveat database. In the left side of the Database window, click on the Report tab. Then click on the New button in the top of the Database window. The New Report dialog box appears, as shown in Figure 17-1.

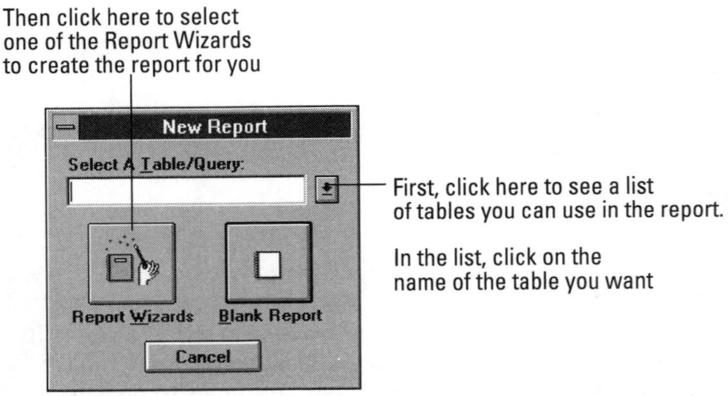

Figure 17-1: The New Report dialog box. This dialog box is where you select a table for the report and decide whether you want to use Report Wizards.

Then click here to select one of the Report Wizards to create the report for you

New Report

Select A Table/Query:

First, click here to see a list of tables you can use in the report.

In the list, click on the name of the table you want

Report Wizards   Blank Report

Cancel

To create the report, follow these steps:

1. **Click on the arrow on the right end of the Select A Table/Query blank.**

   Access presents a list of the tables for which you can create a report.

2. **In the list of tables, click on the table you want.**

   For this example, click on Customer Records.

3. **Click on the Report Wizards button.**

   When Access asks *Which Wizard do you want,* click on Tabular to highlight it. Then click on the OK button. The field selection dialog box appears, as shown in Figure 17-2.

   Tabular reports are the simplest reports, so they're also the easiest to use when you're learning basic techniques.

   You can select a Wizard in two ways. You can double-click on its name in the list or, if you don't like to double-click, you can click on its name once and then click on the OK button.

Click on a field
name to highlight it

Then click here to
select it for a report

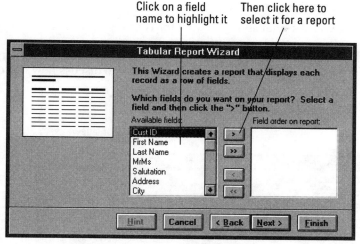

Figure 17-2:
The field
selection
dialog box.
This dialog
box is
where you
pick the
fields (data
items) that
you want to
include in
your report.

4. **In the Available fields list (see Figure 17-2), click on the Cust ID field to highlight it.**

   Then click on the button with the single right-pointing arrow to move the field into the list of fields selected for the report. (If you prefer, you can just double-click on the field name, which automatically moves it into the selected fields list.)

5. **In the same way, select the First Name, Last Name, Address, City, State, and Zip fields to be included in the report.**

6. **Click on the Next button.**

   A new dialog box appears, asking which fields you want to sort by. If you pick the Zip field, for example, the report lists your records in zip code order. For this example, assume that you want the records listed in order by the customer's last name. So, in the Available fields list, click on the Last Name field to highlight it. Then click on the single right-arrow button to select it.

   If you want to select *all* the table's fields for the report, you can click on the button with the double right-pointing arrow. The buttons underneath, with the single and double left-pointing arrows, "unselect" one or all of the fields you've selected.

7. **Here's a trick question: What will Access do if two customers have the same last name?**

   The answer is: nothing much. *You* know that if two or more people have the same last name, their records should be placed in order by their first names. But Access doesn't know that unless you say so. Therefore, say so by selecting the First Name field in the same way that you just selected the Last Name field.

8. Click on the <u>N</u>ext button.

Access asks what style you want for your report, as shown in Figure 17-3.

You'll finish this report in an upcoming section. Now that you've arrived at the report style dialog box, it's a good time to discuss how this dialog box is used.

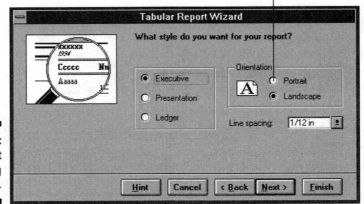

Click here to select "normal" printing instead of sideways

Figure 17-3:
The report style dialog box.

Report styles and — what? Sideways printing?

The different report styles (Executive, Presentation, and Ledger) don't alter the content of your report. They simply affect its look — what kind of type face is used, where lines are drawn, and so forth. The best way to learn about these styles is to try each one and decide which you like. In a nutshell, however, here's what the different styles are:

- **Executive-style** reports are basic, not fancy looking. They're fine, but they're obviously something you'd use internally in the office — not something you'd give to the big boss or anyone you needed to impress.

- **Presentation-style** reports look really nice. They use a better-looking type face and don't have some of the messy-looking lines that you get in an executive-style report.

- **Ledger-style** reports print the data in a boxed grid that looks like an Access datasheet.

The really big thing to notice in the report style dialog box isn't the report style, however — it's the *orientation*. Unless you say otherwise, Access prints your report sideways on the page, in what's called *Landscape* orientation. Usually, however, you'll want normal, or *Portrait* orientation. To change to Portrait orientation, click on the Portrait radio button, as shown in Figure 17-3.

After you select the orientation and style you like, just click on the Next button.

Finishing the report layout

Next, Access asks you to name your report. In the blank under *What title do you want,* type **Customer Names and Addresses.** Then click on the Finish button. The Wizard designs your report and opens a Print Preview window to show you how it looks. Maximize the preview window and inspect the result. The preview window is shown in Figure 17-4.

When the mouse pointer is over the Print Preview part of the screen, it changes into a little picture of a magnifying glass. By clicking the left mouse button, you can flip back and forth between seeing the report up close and seeing a full page preview that shows you the report's overall layout.

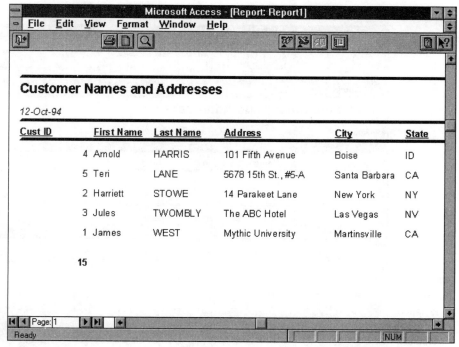

Figure 17-4: Print preview of the tabular name and address report.

Customer Names and Addresses

12-Oct-94

Cust ID	First Name	Last Name	Address	City	State
4	Arnold	HARRIS	101 Fifth Avenue	Boise	ID
5	Teri	LANE	5678 15th St., #5-A	Santa Barbara	CA
2	Harriett	STOWE	14 Parakeet Lane	New York	NY
3	Jules	TWOMBLY	The ABC Hotel	Las Vegas	NV
1	James	WEST	Mythic University	Martinsville	CA

15

Understanding Parts of a Report Layout

The way the Report Wizard laid out the sample report is all right, but the layout needs a little fine-tuning. The Wizard's biggest goof was assuming that because Cust ID is a number field, the report should add up the customer ID numbers. (Microsoft may fix this problem at some point, so if your copy of Access doesn't add up the numbers, don't panic. Everything is fine.) Also, the report would look better if the numbers in the Cust ID column were aligned with the left side of the column, like the label above them, instead of the right side.

Before you can make any of these changes, however, you need to become familiar with the different parts of a report layout. Click on the Close Window button on the left side of the screen, third line from the top. Access displays the Report Layout window, as shown in Figure 17-5.

There's no denying it: The Report Layout window looks *pretty scary*. But it's really much simpler than it looks, so don't let it worry you too much.

A report is divided into horizontal sections called *bands*. The name of each one appears in a horizontal gray line just above and to the left of the band. The band is the white part underneath each gray line. Here's what the bands are used for:

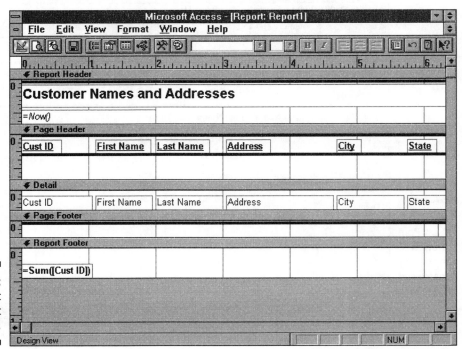

Figure 17-5:
The Report
Layout
window.

✔ **Report Header:** The Report Header contains stuff that you want to print at the very beginning of the report but nowhere else — such as the report's title, the date it was printed, and so on.

✔ **Page Header:** The Page Header contains stuff that you want to print at the top of each page, such as the title of each column in the report.

✔ **Detail:** The Detail section contains the actual data from your table, such as each customer's first name, last name, and street address.

✔ **Page Footer:** The Page Footer contains stuff that you want to print at the bottom of each page, such as page numbers.

✔ **Report Footer:** The Report Footer contains stuff that you want to print at the end of the report. If you were printing a sales report, for example, the Report Footer might contain a total of the sales in the report.

Changing the Wizard's Report Layout

It would be nice to change four things about the report layout that the Wizard created. First, as I mentioned earlier, it makes no sense at all for the report to add up the customer ID numbers. Second, the report would look nicer if the customer ID numbers were aligned with the left side of the column, just like normal text. Third, the Page Header band is just too tall. The report would look better if the column titles were closer to the data. Finally, the report title would look better if it were in a different type font.

If the Report Design Toolbox is in your way on the Design window, you can use the mouse to drag it to another position on the screen.

Selecting and deleting a report item

The first step is to get rid of that idiotic total in the Cust ID column. In the report layout, it's actually way down in the bottom left corner of the screen, in the Report Footer band. If you need to, scroll down a bit until you can see a little box that says *=Sum([Cust ID])*. Then click on the box to select it. When the box is selected, it should be surrounded by little black squares. After you select the total, press the Delete key to get rid of it.

You need to delete just two more things. Directly above where the total used to be, there are two horizontal lines. The Report Wizard added these lines either to make the report look nicer (which they don't), or to make your life miserable. But don't worry about the reason. Just select and delete them, the same way as you did with the total.

When Access sees a number field in a report, it automatically assumes that the report should show the total of the numbers. Here, that's a nuisance. But when you're creating a report with numbers that you *do* want to add, this Access feature comes in handy. It's a lot easier to delete a total that *shouldn't* be in a report than it is to set up a total in the first place.

Changing how a column (or anything else) is formatted

The next step is to change how the Cust ID data is formatted. You want the customer ID numbers to align with the left edge of the column, just as if they were text.

To make this change — or to make *any* change in how a column is formatted — you just follow these two steps:

1. **In the Detail band, select the data item you want to format.**

2. **Using the Format menu or the toolbar, apply whatever format you want — text alignment, boldface, a bigger type size, and so on.**

You're not restricted to formatting stuff that's in the Detail band, either. You can use these same two steps to change the formatting of pretty much anything in the report — for example, the title or the page numbers.

For this example, click on the Cust ID box in the Detail band to select it. Then, in the toolbar, click on the Left Alignment button, as shown in Figure 17-6. When you print the report, the customer ID numbers will be left-aligned.

If you use a Windows word processor, the formatting buttons in Access are almost exactly the same as the ones you already know.

Changing the height of report sections

Another problem with the layout created by the Report Wizard is that the Page Header band is too tall, making the column labels too far above the data in the columns. If you've ever used the mouse to drag things on-screen, you'll find that changing the height of a report band is easy.

Depending on the font you chose for the column labels, Access will insist that the Page Header band be a certain minimum height. If the Page Header band is already at its minimum height, you can't make it any smaller. In that case, the following steps don't work. If you want to see how they work, first make the Page Header band bigger by dragging its bottom border down on the screen. Then make it smaller by dragging the border back up the screen.

Figure 17-6:
The toolbar
for the
Report
Layout
window.

Click here to align the data
at the left side of the column

To try out the process, position the mouse pointer over the bottom border of
the Page Header band. That's the thin black line at the top of the gray area with
the word Detail at the left. When the mouse is in the right place, the mouse
pointer changes to a black up-and-down arrow. Hold down the left mouse
button and drag the border up until it's just a little bit underneath the items in
the Page Header band (Cust ID, First Name, etc.). Then release the left mouse
button. It's done!

You can use the same method to make any section of the report taller or shorter.

Changing text in a report layout

The final step in fine-tuning the sample report is to change the type font used in
the report title (Customer Names and Addresses) to make it look a little
snazzier. Basically, you change the type font in the same way that you make
other changes to a report: You select the item you want to change and then use
the menus or the toolbar to pick the new format.

To change the font, click on *Customer Names and Addresses* in the Report
Header band. Then, in the toolbar, click on the down arrow next to the font list,
as shown in Figure 17-7. In the list, click on the font you want — Arial is always a
good choice. Access automatically changes the type font for you.

To the right of the type font list in the toolbar is a list of available type *sizes*. If
you like, you can use this to make the type bigger or smaller. Use it the same
way as any other list box. To select a different type size, open the list box by
clicking on the downward arrow button at the right end of the size blank. Then,
in the list, click on the size you want.

You can use these same methods to change the type font and size of any text
that appears in the report.

Click here to select a new type font

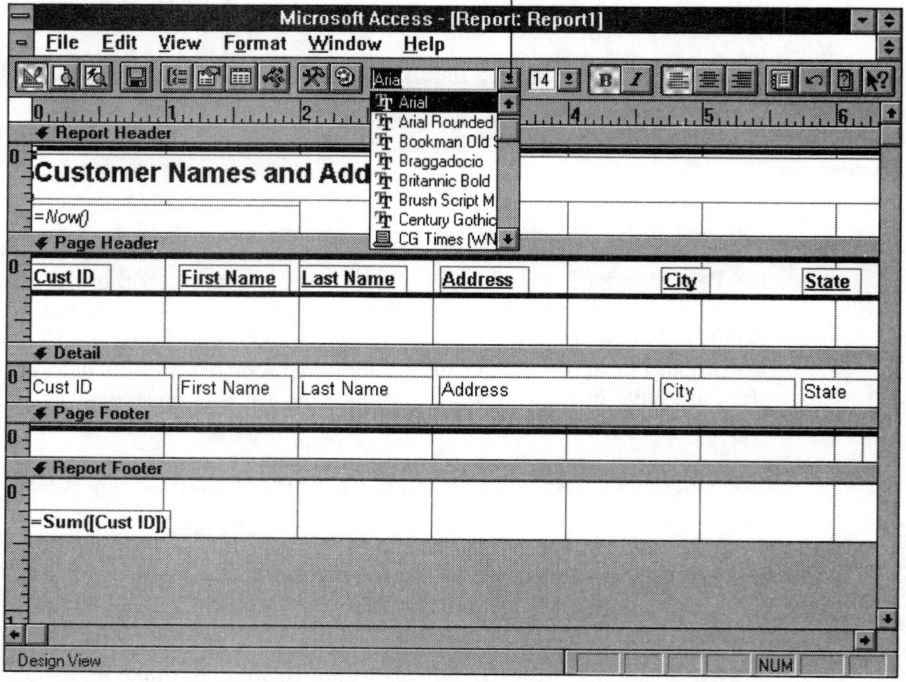

Figure 17-7:
Click on the
down arrow
next to the
font list in
the toolbar.

Viewing the Finished Report

Now that you've done all the work, it's time for the fun part. First, save your report layout by opening the File menu and selecting Save. In the dialog box, type **Customer Names and Addresses** as the report title. Then click on OK.

Finally, click on the Print Preview button on the left side of the toolbar to see what your report will look like.

You can use these same methods to change the layout of any type of formal report — whether it's a tabular report, a single-column report, or an auto report. Some other types of Access reports are discussed in Chapter 19.

Chapter 18

Divvy Up Your Database and Then Put It Back Together

*T*ables are the building blocks of a database. Most people, when they design a database for the first time, try to cram everything into a single table: customer records, sales records, Bob Dylan records, and even world bungee-jumping records.

But that's not the right way to do it. One of the great strengths of Access is that it lets you divide your data into different tables. That way, you have one table for customer records, another for sales records, and so on. Each table contains data about a different kind of thing.

Dividing up your data would be pretty useless, however, unless you could put it back together when necessary. And that's just what you do when you link two or more tables together: You tell Access to treat them temporarily as a single table.

To understand the ideas in this chapter, you should know about tables, records, and fields. To do the exercises with the book's example database, you should have created the Customer Records table (Chapter 3) and the Sales table (Chapter 12). Data for these tables is in Appendix A. If you're working with your own "real life" database, you can just follow along, learning the basic concepts and techinques. Then apply them to your own database.

The Basic Idea: Divide and Conquer

You *could* put all your data in one table. But remember that all the records in a table must be the same size. If you put all your data in a single table, some records would contain a lot of information and others would contain very little. *Every* record, however, takes up the same amount of disk space, so records with little information would take as much disk space as ones that are packed to the gills.

This concept is pretty abstract, so consider the Customer Records and Sales tables as an example. Each customer record must have the customer's name, address, account number, and a few other pieces of information. Each sales record must have the buyer's account number, the date, a description of the item, and the amount of money received for the item.

Suppose that you put all the data from these two tables into a single table. Some customers might make 25 purchases a month, while others might make only one or two. That means that the records for customers who buy 25 times a month would need 75 extra fields to hold their monthly sales data (25 purchases x 3 fields per purchase). But because all records in a table have to be the same size, the records for customers who buy once or twice a month would *also* need 75 extra fields — and most of those fields would be empty all the time. That's incredibly inefficient.

This approach presents another problem, too. What if a customer makes 26 purchases in a month? In that case, you're simply out of luck. There are no more fields to record the data for the 26th sale. You could add more fields, but that would require you to restructure the table (Chapter 8), which is a waste of time if you can avoid it.

Dividing your data into different tables

Access enables you to divide up your data into different tables. Instead of creating one big Customer/Sales table, you created a Customer Records table and a Sales table. Each customer record includes the same information (account number, name, and so on), and each sales record includes the same information (account number, sale date, item, and price). No disk space is wasted, and customers can make as many purchases as their probably-over-the-limit credit cards allow.

But suppose that you want to print a report showing each customer's name and purchases for the month. The customer information is in one table, and the sales information is in another. You need a way to bring the two together. And that's what links between tables are all about.

Linking tables, temporarily and permanently

You can bring tables together in two ways: temporarily and permanently (at least, as permanently as anything in this world of fast food, fast cars, and fast changes in everything). In Chapter 13, you see how to join two tables together temporarily in a query.

A query, if you recall, is just a question that you ask about your data. In Chapter 13, you ask the question, "What are the top money-making books for the month and the names of the people who bought them?" In order to get the answer, you join the Customer Records and Sales tables by the account number field that they both contain. Because each customer has a unique account number and each sales record includes the account number of the customer who made the purchase, it is easy for Access to match up the sales records with the customer records — and give you the answer you need.

But when you join two tables in a query, the link is strictly temporary. It exists only for that query. When you *relate* two tables, on the other hand, the link is permanent. You can remove the link, but if you don't remove it, it stays in effect. That means that you can now treat the *two* tables as if they were a *single* table — but still enjoy all the efficiency of keeping their data separate.

When two tables are related, the link is already established whenever you want to create a form, report, or query that uses data from both tables.

Different types of relations between tables

In Access, you can set up two types of relations between tables: *one-to-one* and *one-to-many*.

An example of a one-to-one relation would be that of husband and wife. In Western countries (at least in theory), each husband has only one wife, and each wife has only one husband. An example of a one-to-many relation would be that of a customer record to sales records: Each customer might make many sales, but each sale can only be made by one customer. This type of relation is illustrated in Figure 18-1.

One-to-one relations between tables aren't used that often. Most of the time, you'll find yourself setting up one-to-many relations, as in the example of the customer table — each customer record can have many sales records associated with it.

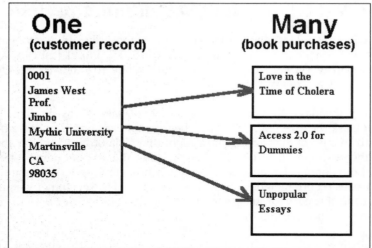

One
(customer record)

Many
(book purchases)

0001
James West
Prof.
Jimbo
Mythic University
Martinsville
CA
98035

Love in the
Time of Cholera

Access 2.0 for
Dummies

Unpopular
Essays

Figure 18-1:
An example
of a one-to-
many
relation.

You should realize that for a one-to-many relation, each "one" record need not in fact have many records related to it. If you set up a one-to-many relation between a customer records table and a sales table, some customers may have only one sale, while others may have many or none at all!

To be related, tables must share a field

For two tables to be joined or related, they must have a common field, such as an account number field. You need to know four main things about this shared field:

- ✔ The field does not need to have the same name in both tables, but it must contain the same data. In other words, it doesn't matter if the account number field is called *Cust ID* in the Customer Records table and *Madonna* in the Sales table, as long as both fields contain account numbers.

- ✔ Access works faster if the common field is indexed in both tables. In a one-to-many relation, the common field will usually be the Primary Key field in the "one" table (also called the *master table*). If it's indexed in the "many" table, the common field *cannot* be the Primary Key field and should be indexed so that it allows duplicates. Otherwise, the table could not have more than one sale record for the same account number. If a customer made two purchases, you'd be out of luck.

- ✔ The shared field must be the same data type in both tables. The only exception is if the field is a Counter data type in the master table. If it were also a Counter data type in the related table, a one-to-many relation would be impossible. Therefore, if the shared field is a Counter data type in the master table, it can be a Number data type in the related table, and its Field Size must be set to Long Integer.

- ✔ Usually, the common field is the *first* field in the table.

The Practical Part: Here's How You Do It

In the following exercise, you actually set up a relation between the Customer Records table and the Sales table. To begin, make sure that the Caveat database is loaded and that the Database window is on-screen.

This chapter assumes that you're using Access 2.0. If you're using Access 1.0 or 1.1, the process is somewhat more complicated. Just follow along to get the basic techniques. I provide a brief explanation of Access 1.0/1.1 techniques at the end of the chapter.

Changing the Sales table

Setting up the relationship requires one minor change in the Sales table. Because its Cust ID field is going to be the link field in the relationship, you need to change its Field Size from Integer to Long Integer. To do this, highlight the Sales table in the Database window and click on the Design button. The Table Design window will appear. Then follow these steps:

1. **Click in the Data Type column of the Cust ID row, which is the *first* row in the table design.**

2. **In the Field Properties part of the window, click in the Field Size blank, which currently says *Integer*.**

3. **Click on the down-arrow button on the right side of the blank to display the list of field sizes. In the list, click on Long Integer.**

4. **Open the File menu and select Save. Then close the Design window and return to the Database window.**

Setting up the relationship

Open the Edit menu and select Relationships. The Relationships window appears, as shown in Figure 18-2. Maximize the window.

Now, if Access were a 1980s-style database manager, you'd have to type something awful, like **set relation from "customer" into "sales" on "custID"** or a variation on that theme. But in Access, establishing the relationship is as easy as rolling the mouse:

1. **In the field list for the Customer Records table (that's the list on the left), click on the Cust ID field to select it.**

2. **With the mouse pointer still on the Cust ID field, hold down the left mouse button.**

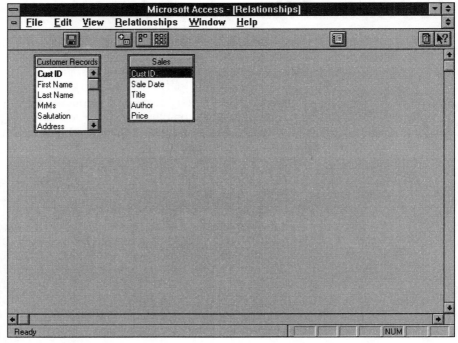

Figure 18-2:
The
Relationships
window.
This window
is where
you link
tables in
Access.

3. Drag the Cust ID field until it's directly on top of the Cust ID field in the Sales table.

4. Release the left mouse button.

The Relationships dialog box appears, as shown in Figure 18-3. Everything looks all right, so click on the Create button in the top right corner of the dialog box.

5. Close the Relationships window. When Access asks whether you want to save layout changes, click on Yes.

You're done! Access shows the relationship with a horizontal black line connecting the two fields. You can now easily consolidate the information from the two tables in reports, queries, and forms.

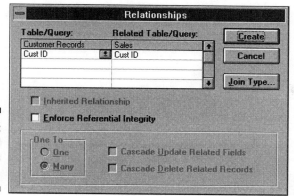

Figure 18-3:
The second
Relationships
dialog box.

If you're using Access 1.0 or 1.1, the procedure for setting up a relation is slightly different. When you select Relationships from the Edit menu, the Relationships dialog box appears. In the Related Table blank, click on the down-arrow button and select Sales. Access automatically fills in the Select Matching Fields blank with the field that it thinks should be the link field. Click on the Close button to establish the relationship.

Deleting a relationship

Deleting a relationship is even easier than creating it. Simply open the Relationships window, click on the black line for the relation you want to delete, and press the Delete key on your keyboard. You're going to use the relation between the Customer Records and Sales tables in later chapters, so don't delete that one. But if you ever do need to delete a relation, you know how to do it.

Part IV
Really Advanced Stuff to Impress Your Friends

The 5th Wave

Re·al Pro·gram·mers

By Rich Tennant

ELEVATOR CAPACITY 2100 LBS.

1000110111
0101100110
101KLUGEO
10011101

0011010
11000101
01MACRO11
01000101
0101001

Real Programmers love to talk "computer-eze" while ordinary citizens are listening.

In this part ...

Often, the simple kinds of reports like those covered in Part III aren't enough. This part shows you how to create really sophisticated reports that group your data and do calculations. You also learn how to use Access to create form letters and mailing labels in case you want to do one of those annoying mass mailings.

Finally, this part shows how to create beautiful 2-D and 3-D graphs and bar charts in Access. You can embed these graphs and bar charts in reports and forms, and they provide a way to make your data come alive.

Chapter 19

Hot Stuff! Creating Sophisticated Reports

● ●

In This Chapter

▶ Different types of Report Wizards

▶ How to create a grouped report

▶ Parts of a grouped report design

▶ Basing a report on a query instead of a table

▶ How to create a multi-table report

● ●

*W*hen most people hear the term *sophisticated reports,* they naturally assume that it has something to do with tea and crumpets, watching "Masterpiece Theatre" on public television, or putting on a tie and jacket before they sit down at the computer.

Not true! It certainly *helps* if you wear a tie and jacket while using Access — at least, it helps the people who sell ties and jackets — but sophisticated reports are just another way for Access to print out your database information. Chapter 16 covers simple datasheet and form printouts, and Chapter 17 covers simple reports. This chapter shows you how to create and print fancier reports that organize your database information in a variety of different ways.

So make yourself a nice cup of tea (Earl Grey, hot), eat a crumpet (whatever the heck *that* is), and get ready to create some kick-it reports! Formal dress is optional.

To understand the ideas in this chapter, you should understand the concepts of a database (Chapter 2), a table (Chapter 3), a query (Chapter 12), and a link between two tables (Chapter 18). To do the exercises, you need to have created the sample Customer Records table (Chapter 3) and the Sales table (Chapter 12). The data for these tables is in Appendix A. To do the multi-table report, you also need to have created the multi-table query (Chapter 13).

If you're creating reports for your own "real life" database, just read this chapter to get the basic ideas and techniques. Then follow the steps in the exercises using your own database and tables instead of the ones in the book.

The Basic Ideas

The basic ideas behind creating a report are the same no matter what kind of report you're talking about. A report is just a printout of the information in your database. You can print all the information or just some; put the information in alphabetical order or not; and include groups and totals or not.

Before you can print a report, you first have to create the *report layout.* The report layout shows where the parts of the report will appear on the printed page. When you create the layout, you also can *format* the parts of the report to control the type style, left or right text alignment, and so on.

Access provides Wizards that make it easy to create several different types of report layouts:

- ✔ **Single-Column:** This layout puts each field in the report (account number, first name, last name, etc.) on a separate line of the printed page.

- ✔ **Groups/Totals:** This layout enables you to group your database records and add up any numbers in them. For example, you can use this layout to create a report that groups sales transactions by state and includes a subtotal of the money from each state and a grand total of all sales revenue at the end of the report.

- ✔ **Mailing Label:** This layout enables you to design and print name and address labels to put on envelopes.

- ✔ **Summary:** This layout creates a report that's similar to a Groups/Totals report. The difference is that it *only* prints the totals of the records, not each individual record.

- ✔ **Tabular:** This layout creates a standard row-and-column report that doesn't include grouping or totals. You can add those elements on your own, but the Wizard doesn't do it for you.

- ✔ **AutoReport:** This layout creates a report that's essentially the same as a Single-Column report.

- ✔ **MS Word Mail Merge:** This layout prepares your records so that you can use them with Word for Windows to print form letters. Because this option involves really advanced features, it requires Version 6.0 (or later) of Word for Windows.

After you use a Wizard to create the report layout, you can use Print Preview to see how it will look on paper. Then you can switch to the Design window and change the layout. You go back and forth from Print Preview to the Design window, adjusting the layout until it's exactly the way you want it. Then you save the report layout to disk. Any time you want to view or print the report, you just click on the Report tab in the Database window and double-click on the report you want.

The Basic Steps

You'll work through a specific example in the next section. However, the basic steps in creating any report are the same whether it's a simple Tabular report, a Groups/Totals report, or another other kind of report. Just follow these steps:

1. **Start Access and load the database for which you want to do a report.**

2. **Click on the Report tab in the Database window. Then click on the <u>N</u>ew button at the top of the window.**

3. **Pick the table or query that will provide the data for your report. Then click on the Report <u>W</u>izards button.**

4. **Select the Report Wizard you want to use.**

5. **In the dialog boxes that follow, select the fields that should be printed in the report, how records should be sorted and/or grouped, the report style, and the printing direction (Portrait or Landscape).**

6. **Use Print Preview to see how the report will look on paper.**

   Switch from close-up view to full-page view by clicking the mouse button. (You can do this whenever the mouse pointer looks like a magnifying glass.)

7. **If needed, switch back to the report design window and modify the report layout created by the Wizard.**

   Switch back and forth between Design Mode and Print Preview until the report looks exactly the way you want it.

8. **From the report design window, save the report layout to disk by selecting <u>S</u>ave from the <u>F</u>ile menu.**

Whenever you want to use the report layout, click on the Report tab in the Database window. Then double-click on the name of the report you want. To print the report, either click on the Print button in the toolbar or open the <u>F</u>ile menu and select <u>P</u>rint.

Creating a Grouped Report

A Groups/Totals report is similar to the Tabular report you created in Chapter 17 but lets you divide up the records. If, for example, you want a report that lists customers by state and also includes totals of how many customers are in each state, you use a Groups/Totals report.

The following steps walk you through the process of creating just such a report. First, get to the Caveat database window. Then click on the Report tab and follow these steps:

1. **Click on the <u>N</u>ew button.**

2. **When the Report Wizard dialog box opens, open the Select a <u>T</u>able/ Query list box.**

3. **Click on Customer Records in the list and then click on the Report <u>W</u>izards button, as shown in Figure 19-1.**

4. **When Access asks which Wizard you want, click on Groups/Totals.**

   The Field Selection dialog box appears. In this dialog box, you pick the fields that you want to appear in the report.

5. **In the Available Fields list, double-click on each of the following fields: First Name, Last Name, City, State, Zip.**

   After you click on a field, it should appear in the Field Order on Report list at the right.

6. **Click on the <u>N</u>ext button in the lower-right part of the dialog box.**

   A new dialog box appears, asking which field you want to use for grouping the report.

7. **In the Available Fields list, double-click on the State field. Then click on the <u>N</u>ext button.**

You don't have to select *any* fields to group your report. If you don't select any grouping fields, the report will be the same as a simple Tabular report, like the one in Chapter 17. If you want to create a Tabular report in an older version of Access (1.0 or 1.1), this is how you *have* to do it, because those versions have no Report Wizard for creating Tabular reports.

Figure 19-1:
Start a report by selecting the table and clicking on the Report <u>W</u>izards button.

Then click here to tell Access that you want to use Report Wizards

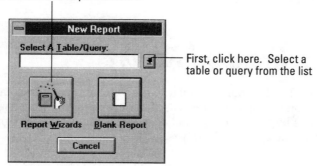

First, click here. Select a table or query from the list

8. **In the next dialog box, you don't need to do anything. Just click on the <u>N</u>ext button.**

   The report style dialog box appears, as shown in Figure 19-2.

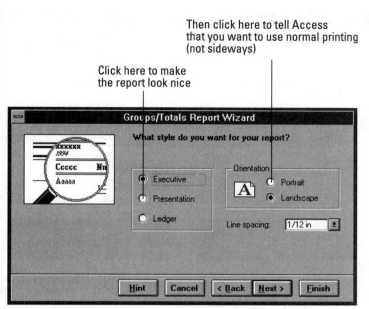

Figure 19-2:
The report
style dialog
box is where
you specify
the style (type
font and
general
appearance)
of the report,
as well as
whether you
want Access
to print the
report
normally
(Portrait) or
sideways
(Landscape)
on the page.

Then click here to tell Access
that you want to use normal printing
(not sideways)

Click here to make
the report look nice

9. **Click on the Portrait radio button so that the report will print normally on the page.**

10. **Click on the Presentation radio button to tell Access to make the report look nice. (Refer to Figure 19-2 if you need help.) Then click on the Next button.**

    A dialog box appears and Access asks for the title of your report.

11. **Enter the report title.**

    For this example, type **Customers by State** in the blank.

12. **Underneath the title blank, there's an X in the Calculate percentages of the total check box. Click in the box to remove the X.**

    If there's an X in this box, Acess will calculate what percentage of the records are in each group — for example, 45.3 percent of customers are in California, 22.1 percent are in New York, and so forth. In case such information is totally useless, tell Access to skip it.

13. **Click on the Finish button.**

    Access works for a few seconds and then displays a window with a Print Preview of your report. Maximize the window to get a good look at the report, shown in Figure 19-3.

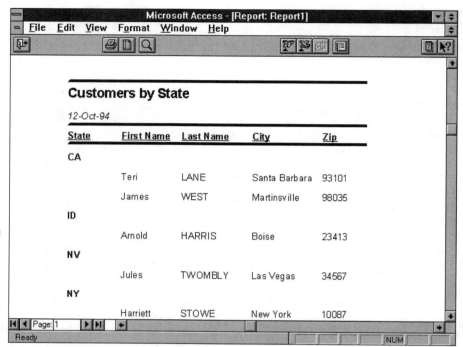

Remember that whenever you're in Print Preview and the mouse pointer looks like a magnifying glass, you can switch between close-up and full-page view by clicking the mouse button.

 Now, return to the report design window by clicking on the Design button on the left end of the toolbar. Then save the report design by opening the File menu and selecting Save. When the dialog box asks what name to save the design under, type **Customers by State.** Then click on OK.

 The name you just gave the report design is used differently from the one you gave it earlier, when you were first creating the report. The earlier name was used as the report title and is printed at the top of the report's first page. The one you typed when you saved the report is the name used by Access to keep track of the report design. It's what appears in the Database window when the Report tab is selected. Using the same name both times makes things easier to remember.

Modifying the Wizard's Report Layout

The report you created in the preceding section looks pretty good. You can see that the records are grouped by state: The report shows that you have two customers in California, one in Idaho, and so forth. The grouping field is in the first (leftmost) column of the report.

When you created this report, you didn't include the Cust ID field, which eliminates a little bit of hassle. In Chapter 17, you see that the Report Wizard assumes that any number field should be added up. By omitting the Cust ID field from this report, you avoided having to delete the "total" of the Cust ID numbers. Deleting the total wouldn't have been a big problem — but it would have been one more thing you had to do before you printed the report.

Even though you don't have that particular problem to worry about, you can improve the report in two other ways. First, it would be nice if, at the end of each state group, Access told you how many customers are in that state. And second, the groups aren't separated very clearly. It would help if there were a horizontal line after each state to set it apart from the next one. Of course, in a report with five records, neither of these issues is terribly important. But if the report had 500 or 5,000 records, both the state totals and the line separators would be great additions.

Parts of the grouped report design

Take a look at the report design window, shown in Figure 19-4. This report design, just like the simpler one in Chapter 17, consists of horizontal bands. Each band contains a different kind of information to print on the page. The bands are:

- ✔ **Report Header band:** This band contains stuff that prints at the beginning of the report, such as the report title and the date the report was printed.

- ✔ **Page Header band:** This band contains stuff that prints at the top of each page, such as the titles of the columns in the report (State, First Name, and so on).

- ✔ **State Header band:** This band contains stuff that prints at the top of each group in the report. Here, the report is grouped by State, so the band label is *State Header*. Access will print the name of the state for each group of records.

- ✔ **Detail band:** The Detail band contains the actual data from the Customer Records table: names, cities, and so on.

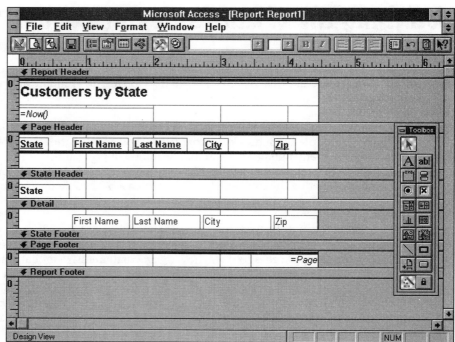

Figure 19-4:
The report design window, showing the bands of the grouped report. On the right side of the figure, you see the Toolbox, which contains stuff that helps you modify a design. The Toolbox may be in a different place on your screen, or you may not see it at all.

- ✔ **State Footer band:** The State Footer band contains stuff that prints at the bottom of each group. This is where you tell Access to count the number of customer records for each state.

- ✔ **Page Footer band:** This band contains stuff that prints at the bottom of each page, such as the page number.

- ✔ **Report Footer band:** This band contains stuff that prints at the end of the report.

- ✔ **New Trier High School Marching Band:** This band contains immensely talented but sometimes out-of-step high school students. If it appears on your screen, you are in serious trouble and should call 911 immediately.

Counting the records in each group

In this exercise, you add some stuff to the State Footer band so that the report shows the total number of customer records in each state. At the moment, the State Footer band is empty. You need to open up the band so that you have someplace to put the total.

First, position the mouse pointer on the horizontal line between the words *State Footer* and *Page Footer* in the bottom left section of the window, as shown in Figure 19-5. The mouse pointer should change to an up-and-down arrow.

After the mouse pointer turns into an up-and-down arrow, hold down the left mouse button and drag the pointer downward until the State Footer band is about the same height as the Detail band above it. You may need to fool around with the band a little until you get it right.

Figure 19-5:
Position the mouse pointer, hold down the left mouse button, and drag the State Footer's border down to open up the band.

Position the mouse pointer right there.
It should change to an up-and-down arrow

State Footer
Page Footer

Using the Toolbox

Now you need to use the Toolbox, shown back in Figure 19-4. If the Toolbox isn't visible on-screen, open the View menu and select Toolbox to make it appear.

Figure 19-6 shows a close-up view of the Toolbox. For the purposes of this book, you really need to know about only four of the buttons in the Toolbox:

✔ **Mouse Pointer button:** You use this button when you've changed the mouse pointer into a tool and want to change it back to a plain mouse pointer.

✔ **Label button:** You use this button to insert labels into the report layout.

✔ **Text Box button:** You use this button to insert *text boxes,* which can contain formulas like the one you'll use to count records in each state.

✔ **Line Drawing button:** The Line Drawing button is used for . . . naah, you have to figure out that one for yourself. (Hint: It has to do with drawing lines.)

Figure 19-6:
The report
design
Toolbox,
showing the
tool buttons for
the mouse
pointer,
creating a
label, inserting
a text box, and
drawing a line.

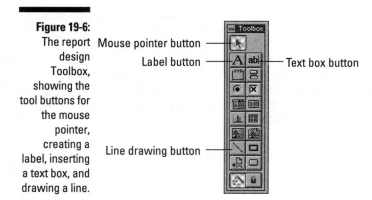

Mouse pointer button

Label button ——— Text box button

Line drawing button

To make a record count appear under each state's group of records in the sample report, follow these steps:

1. **Click on the Label button in the Toolbox.**

   Notice that when you move the mouse pointer over the report layout, the pointer changes into an *A* with a plus sign (+) just to its left. The plus sign indicates where Access will put the label on the report layout if you click the mouse.

2. **Move the mouse pointer so that the plus sign is right under the *S* in *State Footer* and the pointer's *A* is vertically centered in the State Footer band.**

3. **Click the mouse button.**

   Access anchors the label at the spot where the plus sign was located. (You can move the label later if you want. You just select it and drag it with the mouse.)

4. **Create the label text.**

   Type **Number in this state:** and press Enter. The label is done. Next, you're going to position the text box to count the records.

5. **Click on the Text Box button in the Toolbox.**

   When you move the mouse pointer over the layout, it changes into a plus sign and a little *ab* in a box. (Nice hint, huh?)

6. **Position the plus sign so that it's just a little to the right of the box around the *Number in this state:* label.**

7. **Click the left mouse button.**

   The text box is now anchored.

8. **Click inside the text box.**

   The vertical-line text cursor should appear, indicating that you can start typing. (If clicking inside the text box doesn't seem to work, you can press the F2 function key instead.)

9. **Enter the formula in the text box.**

   In the text box, *carefully* type **=Count([City])** and press Enter. What you type should exactly match Figure 19-7.

10. **With the text box still selected (you can tell because it's surrounded by those little black rectangles), click on the left-alignment button in the toolbar.**

    That's the one over on the right, next to the slanted *I* that stands for *Italic*.

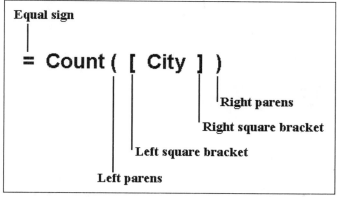

Figure 19-7: The formula you type to tell Access to count records in each state group.

Take a look at the result of your work. Click on the Print Preview button in the toolbar. Your report should look like the one in Figure 19-8.

If the report looks okay, switch back to the report design window. Open the File menu and select Save to save the design to disk.

What field should I be in?

If you have an inquiring mind, you're probably wondering what the City field has to do with counting the records in each state group. The answer is: *nothing.* When you use the Count function to count records in a report, it doesn't matter what field you tell Access to count — you can use any field you want. In this example, you used the City field, but you would get the same total if you used any of the other fields.

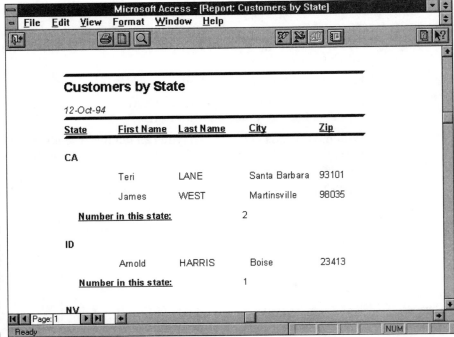

Figure 19-8:
The report
showing
totals for
each state
group.

Adding a line

Whew! Getting Access to include the totals by state took a few steps, didn't it? Don't worry. Do it one or two more times, and you'll be able to whip these things out like lightning. For now, do something simple and easy. (No, not going to sleep. That's *too* easy.) Draw a line at the bottom of the State Footer band:

1. **Click on the Line Drawing button in the Toolbox.**

2. **Position the mouse pointer's plus sign directly underneath the *N* in** *Number in this state.*

3. **Hold down the left mouse button.**

4. **Hold down the Shift key on your keyboard.**

5. **Drag the mouse to the right until the line reaches all the way across the report layout.**

6. **Release the left mouse button.**

   Presto! The line appears. Check it out in Print Preview and then save the report design.

You're done with this report, so close the report design window and return to the Caveat database window.

Basing a Report on a Query

So far, all the reports you've created have used information from a table. But you can also base a report on a query. If you think about it, that shouldn't be too surprising, because the result of a query is a dynaset, which is sort of like a table.

By using a query instead of a table, you can restrict the information that appears in a report. Suppose that you want a report that just includes information about customers who live in California. The easiest way to produce such a report is to create a query that asks, "Which customers live in California?" The answer to the query contains the records you want for the report. When you base the report on the query, Access automatically prints information about California customers only.

In the exercise in the next section, you use the query-report combination for another very special purpose: to create a report that draws information from more than one table.

Creating a Multi-Table Report

The multi-table report you're about to create isn't fancy. But you can use the same process you learn in this example to create more interesting reports.

To create the sample multi-table report, you'll use the August Money-Makers w/ Names query that you created in Chapter 13. The reason I want you to use this query is that it *already* draws information from both the Customer Records and Sales tables. By basing the report on this query, all the data that the query draws from both tables can be printed in the report.

If you haven't created the August Money-Makers w/Names query, you have two options. You can go back to Chapter 13 and create the query. Or, if you like, you can just follow along, perhaps using your own real life database and query, to learn the steps.

To create a multi-table report, follow these steps:

1. **Make sure that the Report tab is selected in the Database window. Then click on the <u>N</u>ew button.**

2. **In the dialog box, select August Money-Makers w/Names and click on the Report <u>W</u>izards button.**

3. **When Access asks which Wizard you want, select Tabular. Then click on OK.**

4. **In the Field Selection dialog box, double-click on the Last Name, Title, and Price fields in the Available Fields list.**

They should appear in the Field Order list at the right.

5. **Click on the Next button.**

6. **When Access asks which field(s) you want to sort by, double-click on the Last Name field. Then click on the Next button.**

7. **In the Report Style dialog box, select Presentation as the style and Portrait as the orientation.**

8. **Click on the Finish button.**

Access displays a Print Preview of the report, as shown in Figure 19-9.

You're not limited to having only two tables in a report or query. You can include as many as you need.

It's easy to see how you could fine-tune the report layout using the same tricks you learned earlier in this chapter. You can also create other queries to get different information from the two tables and print that information in a report.

Figure 19-9:
Print
Preview
shows the
multi-table
report. The
report
contains
information
from both
the
Customer
Records
table and
the Sales
table.

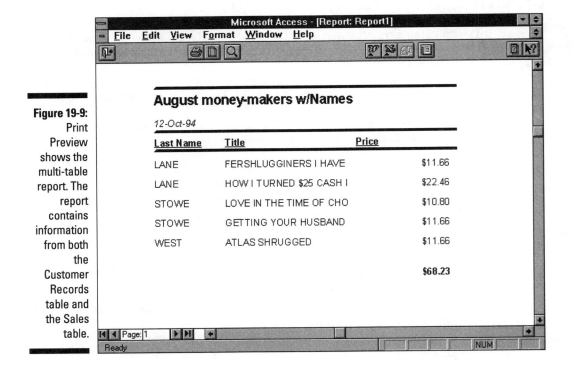

Microsoft Access - [Report: Report1]

File   Edit   View   Format   Window   Help

August money-makers w/Names

12-Oct-94

Last Name	Title	Price
LANE	FERSHLUGGINERS I HAVE	$11.66
LANE	HOW I TURNED $25 CASH I	$22.46
STOWE	LOVE IN THE TIME OF CHO	$10.80
STOWE	GETTING YOUR HUSBAND	$11.66
WEST	ATLAS SHRUGGED	$11.66
		$68.23

Page: 1

Ready   NUM

Save the multi-table report as **Last Name/Sales.** Then close the report design window.

That's it for this chapter! The next chapter shows you how to use Access to create those annoying form letters that are always jamming your mailbox. But this time, you'll be able to send them to *other* people! (Plan on sending at least a thousand to Ed McMahon.)

Chapter 20

Create and Print Form Letters with Access

Dear [MrMs] [First Name] [Last Name]:

You may ***already have won*** a valuable ballpoint pen in the *Access 2.0 For Dummies* Miracle Sweepstakes! Yes, [First Name], I personally selected you from *millions of suckers* to get this valuable prize! All you need to do to get your prize is to pay a one-time shipping fee of $29.95, and your pen (in an attractive gift box made of sturdy recycled cardboard) will be *rushed* directly to your home in beautiful [City] via fourth-class mail!

Sincerely, Joe Jones

*Y*ou get them all the time: personalized form letters. Your mailbox is stuffed with them. Even your dog gets them. And although some of them are just junk mail, others are really important.

Because you may need to send out the *important* kind of form letters — whether to customers, to patrons of charitable groups, or even to family members (if you have a very large family!) — Access enables you to create them from your table data.

Notice what I did *not* say: "Access makes it *really easy* to create form letters." I've said that a lot in this book, but in this case, it just isn't true. Not that creating form letters in Access is really *hard* — but you do need to know a few things before you can do the job. By the end of this chapter, you won't need a "Form Letter Wizard" — you'll *be* one.

To understand the ideas in this chapter, you should understand the concepts of a database (Chapter 2), a table (Chapter 3), and a report (Chapter 19). To do the exercises, you need the Customer Records table (created in Chapter 3). The data for this table is in Appendix A. You should also be familiar with the basic techniques of creating a report (Chapter 19), using Print Preview, and working in the report design window.

If you're creating form letters with your own "real life" database, just read this chapter to get the basic ideas. Then follow the steps using your own table instead of the one in the book.

The Basic Ideas

The first thing you need to understand about creating a form letter is what the term *form letter* really means. A form letter is a document that combines standard, boilerplate text with information from a database or a mail merge file. If you've ever created a form letter in your word processor, you should understand the concept. It's illustrated in Figure 20-1.

In Access, you can use either a table or a query answer as the basis for a form letter. For example, if you wanted to send the form letter to *all* customers listed in your customer table, you'd use the Customer Records table as the data source for the form letter. But if you wanted to send the letter only to customers in California or those with an overdue account balance (requiring you to combine data from both the Customer Records table and the Sales table), you'd use a query.

Figure 20-1:
Take a data source such as an Access table. Add a document with slots for the data. Put the two together, stirring gently. Bake 20 minutes in a preheated oven. Cover with chocolate syrup and eat. Serves thousands.

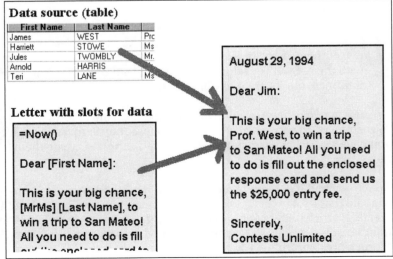

In Access, a form letter is a report

The idea of taking data from a table or query and printing it on a page may sound a little familiar. If you guessed that a form letter in Access is a kind of report, you guessed right. You design a form letter exactly the same way you designed reports in earlier chapters. The only difference is that a form letter is just a *teensy* bit more complicated than the reports you've created so far.

Actually, you can use two *other* methods to create form letters in Access. This book doesn't cover them in detail because they require you to use Access in conjunction with other software packages — which you may not have. But here are the nutshell versions of the two other methods:

- **Use the Mail Merge Report Wizard.** This Report Wizard is designed to work with Microsoft Word for Windows Version 6.0. When you start the Wizard, it tells Word that you want to create a form letter. Word and the Wizard (sounds like a new TV show!) then cooperate to lead you through all the steps. But you must have Word Version 6.0 or later; earlier versions won't work.

- **Export a table and then use it with your word processor.** Access can *export* a table — in other words, convert the table so that you can use it with your word processor to create form letters. To see your options here, open the File menu and select Export. Access displays a dialog box showing the ways that it can convert a table.

Everything in a report design has "properties"

One issue that you haven't needed to worry about very much — until now — is that everything in a report design has *properties*. Properties are just attributes — or characteristics — of a thing. A baseball, for instance, has the properties of roundness, whiteness, and hardness, as well as a certain weight. A basketball has roundness, brownness, and hardness, as well as being a tool that provides a somewhat more profitable way to earn a living than throwing a baseball.

Just like a baseball or a basketball, the parts of a report design have properties, too. To create form letters, you need to fool around with some of these properties. And to do that, you use what Access calls the Properties window. You learn how the Properties window is used when you create the sample form letter in this chapter.

A formula is just like you learned in school

There's just one more idea to understand before you can get down to business. Form letters usually contain *formulas*. Formulas (which are also sometimes called "expressions") are just special instructions — *not* in English, unfortunately — that tell Access how to handle certain things in the letter.

For instance, at the top of the letter, you might put the formula =*Now()*. This formula tells Access that when it prints the letters, it should print the current date at the top of each one. Another formula would be something like = *"Dear |[First Name]|"*, which tells Access to print the word *Dear* and then the first name from the current customer record.

Formulas are *not* hard to use — you just need to make sure that you don't let them intimidate you. The form letter you create in this chapter requires only a few simple formulas, so it'll be a walk in the park. (Hopefully, *not* a walk in New York's Central Park at night.)

A detailed explanation of formulas and how to use them is beyond the scope of this book. If you want to learn more about formulas, consult your Access manuals or IDG's *PC World Microsoft Access 2 Bible 2nd Edition* (Prague/Irwin, 1994).

The Basic Steps

In the next sections, you learn the details about creating form letters. But here are the basic steps you follow:

1. **Select or create the data source for the form letters. The source can be a table or a query.**

2. **Create the form letter as a report in the same database as the data source.**

   You can't use a Wizard because Access doesn't have one that works for creating form letters.

3. **Change the "Force New Page" property of the Detail band, and change the "Auto Label" property of the Text Box tool.**

   For a fancier form letter, you can change properties of other things, too. But here, you're just doing the basic stuff. Changing the Force New Page and Auto Label properties makes Access print the form letters right — not quite as exactly as it would print a normal report.

4. **In the Page Header band, put anything that should appear at the top of each letter, such as a return address or the current date.**

5. **In the Detail band, put the body of the form letter, including slots for the name, address, city, state, and zip code of each person who should receive it.**

Access will fill these slots with data from the data source.

6. **Use Print Preview to make sure that the form letter looks the way that you want it to look.**

7. **Save the form letter as a report.**

The name of the report should indicate that it's a form letter.

8. **Print the form letter.**

Here's How To Do It

The sample form letter uses the Customer Records table as your data source. Remember the report design Toolbox? To create the form letter, you need to use two of the tools — the Label and Text Box tools — to put text and data slots onto the page layout. The tools are shown in Figure 20-2.

Figure 20-2: The Label and Text Box tools in the report design Toolbox.

The Label tool: Use for paragraphs that don't need to contain data.

The Text Box tool: Use for paragraphs that contain data. Also use it to put formulas in the form letter design.

Getting started

In the Caveat Database window, click on the Report tab on the left. Then click on the New button. When the New Report dialog box appears, select the Customer Records table and click on the Blank Report button, as shown in Figure 20-3.

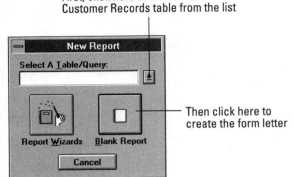

First, click here and select the
Customer Records table from the list

Figure 20-3:
Select the
Customer
Records
table as the
data source
and then
click on the
Blank
Report
button.

Then click here to
create the form letter

Changing some properties

The first step in creating the sample form letter — or *any* form letter — is to
change one property of the Detail band and one property of the Text Box tool.
Here's some advice: *Don't worry* about what the properties are, what they mean,
or stuff like that. You don't need to understand that to use them in creating
form letters.

If the Properties window, the Toolbox, or anything else on-screen is getting in
your way, you can just use the mouse to drag it to another location. Likewise,
you can easily change the size of any part of the report — whether it's one of
the bands, a label, or a text box. If it's too big, too small, in the wrong place, or
whatever, just use the mouse to drag or resize it.

Follow these steps:

1. **Select the Detail band of the report by clicking in the white area underneath the word *Detail*, as shown in Figure 20-4.**

2. **Click on the Properties button in the toolbar, as shown in Figure 20-4.**

   The Properties window opens. The properties displayed in the window
   apply to the Detail band because it was selected when you clicked the
   button.

3. **In the Properties window, the second line should say *Force New Page*. Click in the blank next to those words.**

   A down-pointing arrow button appears on the right end of the blank,
   indicating that the blank has a list box.

4. **Click on the arrow button to open the list box. Then select the Before Section option.**

Click here to open
the Properties window.

Click here to select
the Detail band.

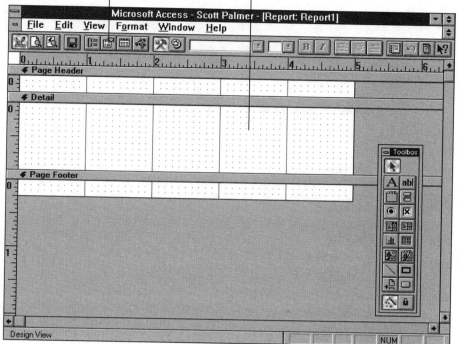

Figure 20-4:
Select the
Detail band
and then
click on the
Properties
button.

This selection tells Access to make each letter print on a separate page.
Now, if you need to, drag the Properties window out of the way so that you
can see the Toolbox on-screen.

5. Click on the Text Box tool.

Check Figure 20-2 if you need a refresher on which button is the Text Box tool.

6. Look for the Auto Label line in the Properties window.

Use the scroll bar on the right side of the window to move down in the
properties list until you see the Auto Label line. (If you're hazy on scroll
bars, see IDG Books' *Windows 3.11 For Dummies,* 3rd Edition.)

7. Click in the Auto Label blank.

As usual, a button indicating a list box appears on the right end of the blank.

8. Click on the button. In the list, select No.

**9. Close the Properties window by clicking on the Window Control button
in the top left corner of the window.**

If you look at the Properties window when the Text Box or Label tools are selected, you can see that one of the lines in the window says *Font Name.* If you click in this blank, you can see a list box of available type fonts. By selecting a different font, you can make your form letter look even fancier. One word of advice: Use the *same* font for both the Label and Text Box tools. If you use the Label tool to create one paragraph and the Text Box tool to create another paragraph, it will look *really* weird if the fonts are different.

Enlarging the page area

Next, you need to make the page a little wider so that it can accommodate the text that you're going to put in the letter. In addition, you need to make the Page Header band taller so that it's big enough for the return address and make the Detail band tall enough to hold the body of the letter. None of this will affect the page margins; it just affects how much text will print inside of the margins.

To make these changes, follow these steps:

1. **Enlarge the Detail band.**

   Position the mouse pointer over the right edge of the white area in the Detail band. Holding down the left mouse button, drag the edge to the right until it's even with the six-inch mark in the ruler at the top of your screen. Then release the mouse button, and the white area should be wider.

2. **Make the Page Header band taller.**

   Position the mouse pointer on the thin horizontal line at the top of the gray bar marked *Detail.* (This is also the bottom edge of the Page Header band.) Drag the border downward until it's at the half-inch mark in the ruler on the left side of your screen. Then release the mouse button. The Page Header band should now be taller.

3. **Make the Detail band taller.**

   Using the same method described in Step 2, drag the bottom border of the Detail band downward until it's almost to the bottom of the screen. Then release the mouse button. The Detail band should be taller.

Putting in a return address

The next step is to put a return address in the Page Header band. This tells Access to print the return address at the top of each letter. Follow these steps:

1. **Click on the Label tool in the Toolbox.**

2. **Position the mouse pointer so that it's near the top of the Page Header band.**

The mouse pointer's plus sign should be even with the two-inch mark in the ruler at the top of your screen.

3. Click the left mouse button to anchor the label.

4. Type the first line of the return address.

Type **Caveat Emptor Bookstore.** After you enter this line, you need to create a new line and type the second line of the return address. But if you just press the Enter key, Access thinks that you're finished typing the label. So instead, hold down the Shift key and press Enter. That's how you start a new line in a label.

5. Enter the second and third lines of the return address.

On the new line you created in Step 4, type **123 Lane Street.** Create another new line and type **San Mateo, CA 94402.**

6. Press Enter to tell Access that you're finished typing.

While the label is still selected, you can use the buttons in the toolbar to center the text, boldface the type, or change the type size. If you make the type size bigger, you need to use the mouse to make the label bigger. You can do this by positioning the mouse pointer until it turns into a double arrow and then dragging the label border in the direction you want.

To start a new line in a label or a text box, you hold down the Shift key and press the Enter key. But technically, you don't really need to do this when you're working in a text box because text automatically wraps down to the next line.

Putting in slots for fields

To simplify matters, the sample form letter will contain only one slot for a field from the Customer Records table. However, you can use the same techniques you learn here to put in slots for all the fields you'd normally include.

Follow these steps:

1. Click on the Text Box tool in the Toolbox.

2. Near the top left corner of the Detail band (under the word *Detail*), click the mouse button to anchor the text box.

3. Press the F2 function key on your keyboard to tell Access that you want to type in the text box.

4. In the text box, type ="Dear |[First Name]|:" **and press Enter.**

What you type should match Figure 20-5. On your keyboard, the vertical slash is usually on the same key as the backslash and is often next to the Backspace key. This formula tells Access to insert the word *Dear,* and then a space, and then the contents of the First Name field in the current record of the table.

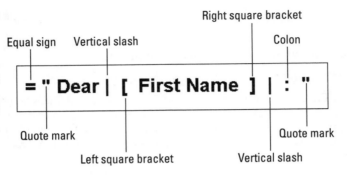

Figure 20-5:
What you should type in the text box.

5. **If needed, resize the text box so that all of what you typed is visible.**

6. **Click on the Label tool in the Toolbox.**

7. **To anchor the label, click directly under the text box you just typed.**

8. **Type the following text to begin the body of the letter:** It's been a pleasure serving you with fine books all these years. If you come into the store,

9. **Hold down the Shift key and press Enter to start a new line.**

10. **Type the following:** I'll give you some passes to the movies.

11. **Holding down the Shift key, press Enter twice. Then type the text:** Your friend,

12. **Press Shift+Enter three more times. Then type the word:** Janis.

13. **Press Enter to tell Access you're finished typing.**

14. **If you need to, resize the text box so that everything you typed is visible on the screen.**

Finally, click on the Print Preview button in the toolbar. Your form letter should look like the one in Figure 20-6.

Return to the report design screen and save the form letter under the name *Customer Form Letter.*

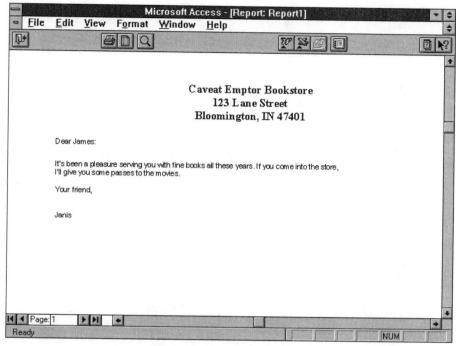

File   Edit   View   Format   Window   Help

Caveat Emptor Bookstore
123 Lane Street
Bloomington, IN 47401

Dear James:

It's been a pleasure serving you with fine books all these years. If you come into the store, I'll give you some passes to the movies.

Your friend,

Janis

Page: 1

Ready   NUM

Figure 20-6:
The finished
form letter.
The name is
from the first
record in the
Customer
Records
table.

Printing the form letter

If you wish, you can now print the letter just like any other report. To do so, make sure that your printer is turned on and ready to print. Then simply open the File menu and select Print. Access does the rest.

If you want to print only some of the records in a table, you should first create a query that displays only the records you want to print. Then base the form letter (which is, after all, a report) on the query instead of on the table.

"I'M ALWAYS AMAZED AT THE TECHNOLOGICAL ADVANCES MADE AT PR FIRMS."

Chapter 21
Design and Print Mailing Labels

· ·

· ·

*M*ailing labels are another kind of report you can create with Access. And because Access provides a Mailing Label Wizard, you hardly have to do any of the work unless you want something *really* weird. You can create any normal mailing label in a minute or two.

To understand the ideas in this chapter, you should understand the concepts of a database (Chapter 2), a table (Chapter 3), and a report (Chapter 19). To create the example labels, you need to have created the Customer Records table (Chapter 3); the data for this table is in Appendix A. You should also know how to use Print Preview.

If you're creating labels with your own "real life" database, just read this chapter to get the basic ideas and techniques. Then follow the steps using your own table instead of the one in the book.

The Basic Ideas

The basic concept of a mailing label is probably familiar to you: It's about 2 inches by 3 inches, has someone's name and address on the front, and has glue on the back so you can stick it to an envelope.

You may not have considered, however, that when you design and print "mailing labels" in Access, you're really just creating a very simple kind of report. Normally, you'd print mailing labels on special mailing label paper, but there's no law (except in Indiana) that you *must* do so. You can print out a mailing label report on plain paper to create a simple, quick-and-dirty customer list, for example. (Believe it or not, with some older database managers, that was the only way to produce simple reports!)

In addition, you don't have to put names and addresses on your labels. Instead, you can create videotape labels, inventory labels, and so on. Just as you can use a "mailing label" report for just about anything, you can use the labels themselves for just about anything, depending on the data source of your mailing label report.

The Basic Steps

The basic steps in creating and printing mailing labels are very similar to those for producing any other kind of report. Here's a brief look at the process:

1. **Select the data source for the mailing label report.**

   If you want to print labels for all the records in a table, simply use the table itself as the data source. If you want to print only some of the records, first create a query that selects only the records you want. Then, use the query instead of the table itself as your data source.

2. **Tell Access that you want to use the Mailing Label Report Wizard.**

3. **Lay out the mailing label by positioning the fields from the data source on a screen picture of the label.**

4. **Tell Access how to sort the labels.**

   Normally, if you're doing a mass mailing, you want the labels sorted by zip code.

5. **Select the type of label you want to use.**

   Access lets you pick from a list of over 40 pre-defined label sizes. You can print labels either one at a time or up to four across on a large sheet of labels.

6. **Save the mailing label report and print the labels.**

Here's How To Do It

The following exercise, in which you create labels for a mass mailing to customers of the Caveat Emptor bookstore, shows you the specific steps involved in producing labels.

If you need to, start up Access and load the Caveat database. The Database window should be on your screen. Click on the Report tab on the left side of the window. Then click on the New button to create a mailing label report. The New Report dialog box appears, as shown in Figure 21-1.

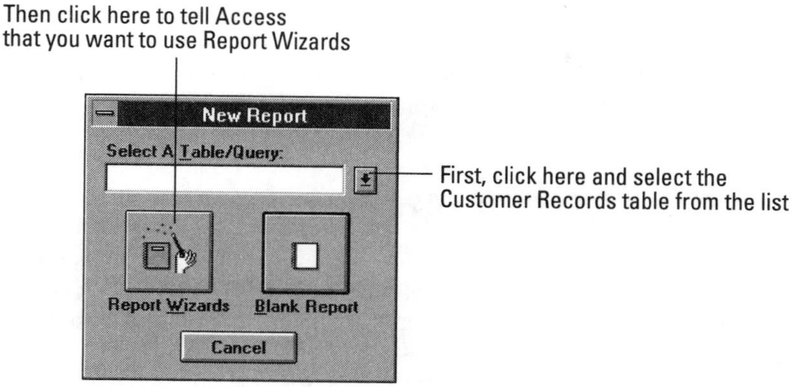

Then click here to tell Access
that you want to use Report Wizards

Figure 21-1:
The New
Report
dialog box.

First, click here and select the
Customer Records table from the list

From the list box, select the Customer Records table. Then click on the Report
Wizards button. When Access asks which Wizard you want to use, double-click
on Mailing Labels. The label design window appears, as shown in Figure 21-2.

The main parts of the label design window are pretty self-explanatory. On the
left is a list of available fields, just as you'd have in any other report. Underneath the field list is a blank in which you can type any special text you want on
your label. Just to the right of the blank is a button marked _Text ->_, and if you're
a _particularly_ astute guesser, you probably figured out that this moves the
special text into the label.

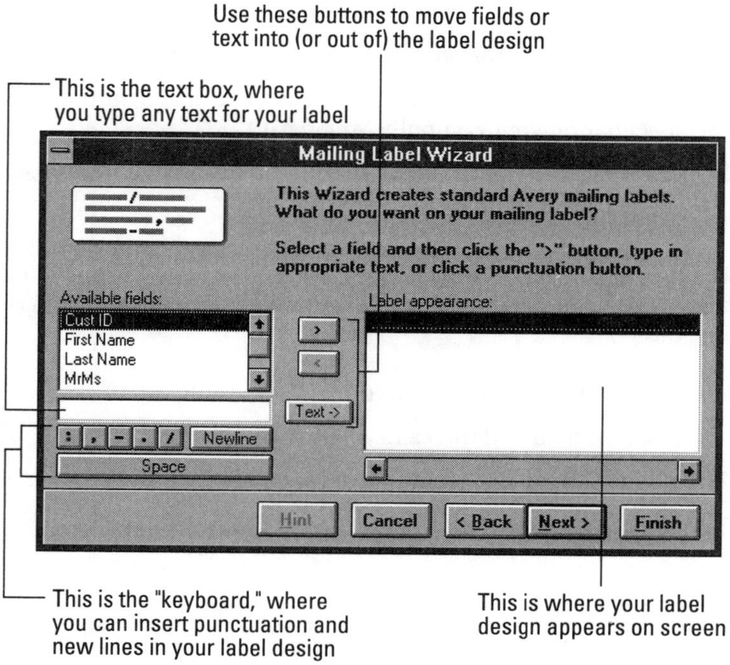

Use these buttons to move fields or
text into (or out of) the label design

This is the text box, where
you type any text for your label

Figure 21-2:
The label
design
window.

This is the "keyboard," where
you can insert punctuation and
new lines in your label design

This is where your label
design appears on screen

In the middle of the dialog box, above the Text button, is a right-pointing arrow button. This button moves a field into the label design. Just underneath it is a left-pointing arrow button that *removes* a field from the label design. And, of course, the label design itself appears over on the right.

Putting special text on a label

As the first step in the exercise, put some special text on the label design. Click in the text box blank and type **IMPORTANT MAIL FOR**. Then click on the Text button. What you typed is now on the first line of the label design.

Though the text you just entered was on the first line of the label, you can put it anywhere you like. When you click the right-pointing arrow button or the Text button, Access places the currently selected text at the current "cursor position" in the label. With a blank label design, of course, that's always the first line.

Putting data fields on a label

Now follow these steps to finish the label. They're all little and very simple:

1. **Click on the New Line button in the on-screen keyboard.**

2. **Double-click on the MrMs field in the Available fields list.**

   (If you prefer, click on the field once to highlight it and then click on the right-pointing arrow button.) Access puts the field into the label design.

3. **Click on the Space button in the on-screen keyboard.**

   Access puts a space after the MrMs field. (The Space button works just like the spacebar on your computer keyboard.)

4. **Double-click on the First Name field in the Available fields list.**

   Access places the First Name field on the label.

Simple enough? Then try it on your own for the rest of the label. Using the same techniques described in Steps 1 to 4, add the following elements (in order) to the label design:

A space, the Last Name field, and then a new line

The Address field and then a new line

The City field, a comma, and then a space

The State field, a space, and then the Zip field

When you're finished, the label design window should look exactly like the one in Figure 21-3, except that it should be bigger. When you're sure that your label design window matches the figure, click on the Next button.

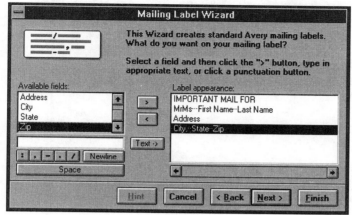

Figure 21-3: The completed label design.

Sorting the labels

The Wizard next asks how you want to sort the labels when you print them. Normally, with mailing labels, you'd sort by zip code, so scroll down in the Available fields list until you can see the Zip field. Then double-click on the Zip field to move it into the Sort Order list. Finally, click on the Next button.

Selecting a label size

Access now displays a window in which you can select the size of your label, as well as how many labels are on each horizontal row of the label sheets. Figure 21-4 shows this window.

Somewhere on your mailing label box or packaging, you should find an *Avery number*. In the dialog box, select the label size that has the same Avery number as your mailing labels. Notice that there's a scroll bar on the right side of the Avery number list: This means that you can scroll down to see more of the list. Access supports over 40 different label types.

Underneath the Avery number list are two Label Type radio buttons — that is, two circles next to two lines of text. If you're using a laser printer or any other type of printer that uses separate sheets of paper (labels usually come on such sheets), the normal setting of Sheet feed is fine.

Click in one of these circles
to select separate label sheets
or continuous-feed labels

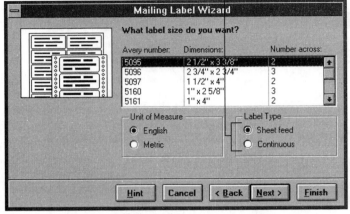

Figure 21-4:
The label
size
window.

On the other hand, if you're using continuous-feed labels, such as those
typically used with a dot-matrix printer, click on the Continuous radio button.
The black dot should disappear from the Sheet feed radio button (circle) and
appear next to Continuous. Do this *only* if you're using continuous-feed labels.
Otherwise, use the normal setting of Sheet feed.

Selecting a font and type style

After you select a label size, click on the Next button. The font selection dialog
box appears, as shown in Figure 21-5.

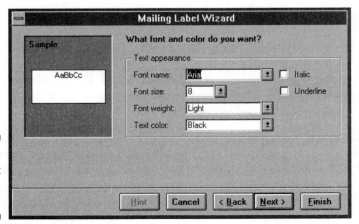

Figure 21-5:
The font
selection
dialog box.

This dialog box is pretty self-explanatory, but just in case, here's the explanation:

- ✔ On the left side of the dialog box, Access displays a preview of what the text will look like if you use the currently selected font and style.

- ✔ Use the Font name list box to select the font you want to use with your labels. You can select any font available on your PC. The specific fonts are installed with Windows and vary from one person's PC to another's. (Times New Roman is very nice.)

- ✔ Underneath the Font name list box is the Font size list box. Type size is measured in points; 72 points equals one inch. Thus, 72-point type is an inch tall. Normal-sized type is 12 points. The specific point sizes available depend on the font selected in the Font name list.

- ✔ Use the Font weight list box to specify how bold you want the letters on your labels to appear.

- ✔ If you have a color printer, select the label text color using the Text color list box. If you don't have a color printer, don't worry about this option at all.

- ✔ Just to the right of the Font name and Font size list boxes are boxes you can check if you want the label text to be italicized or underlined.

After you select the options you want in this dialog box, click on the Next button.

Previewing the labels

In the dialog box that appears next, simply click on the Finish button. Access displays a Print Preview of how the labels will look, as shown in Figure 21-6. Depending on the label size, font, and printing effects you selected, your screen may look slightly different from the one in Figure 21-6.

Click on the Close Window button on the far left end of the toolbar. Access returns you to the report design window. Open the File menu and save the label design as *Customer Mail Labels*.

Using these same techniques, you can design any kind of labels you need, using any data source you want.

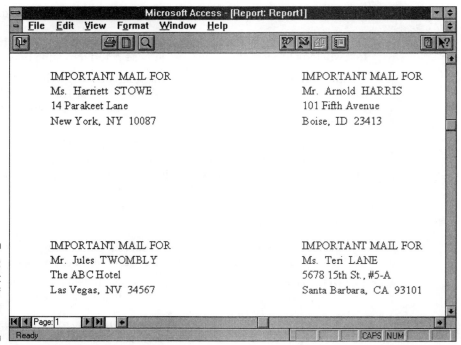

Figure 21-6:
A Print
Preview of
the mailing
labels.

Chapter 22

Create Dazzling Graphs
From Your Data

• •

In This Chapter

▶ Why use graphs and bar charts?

▶ Different kinds of graphs in Access

▶ Putting graphs in forms and reports

▶ Using Access Graph Wizards

• •

Seeing is believing — but some things are a lot easier to see than others. If you set up a database, it's easy for *you* to understand a printout of your own data. But suppose that you show the printout to a corporate big shot or a particularly rich customer who inherited his parents' cotton-candy farm? Would *they* understand it? (Are you sure they can read, anyway?)

The fact is that lots of times, graphs and bar charts make it a lot easier to understand stuff that's in your database. Even when you know what's in your data, a picture can make everything clearer. If you don't believe it, take a look at Figure 22-1. The numbers on the left contain exactly the same information as the bar chart on the right — but do they tell you as much?

Figure 22-1:
A graph
makes it
clear what
the numbers
mean.

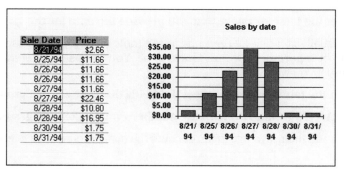

Sale Date	Price
8/21/94	$2.66
8/25/94	$11.66
8/26/94	$11.66
8/26/94	$11.66
8/27/94	$11.66
8/27/94	$22.46
8/28/94	$10.80
8/28/94	$16.95
8/30/94	$1.75
8/31/94	$1.75

If you want to know which day had the highest sales, it's not easy to find the answer by looking at the report on the left, even though there is a column showing dollar amounts. But when you look at the bar chart, the answer is crystal clear at a glance. That's the big advantage of using Access graphs: When your data includes numbers, it's often easier to understand when presented in a graph or bar chart.

To understand the ideas in this chapter, you should understand the concepts of a database (Chapter 2), a table (Chapter 3), a query (Chapter 12), and a report (Chapter 17). To create the graphs, you need to have created the Sales table (Chapter 22); the data for this table is in Appendix A. You should also know the basic techniques for designing a report (Chapter 17).

Be sure to change the price of the Access 2 For Dummies book in your example database (if you've been following along) to $19.95; otherwise, your graphs will look a little strange.

If you're creating graphs with your own "real life" database, just read this chapter to get the basic ideas. Then follow the steps using your own database instead of the one in the book.

The Basic Steps

You can place an Access graph on any form or report. When you create a graph in Access, you need to perform several basic steps. Don't do anything just yet; this is an overview.

1. **Decide which form or report design you want to put the graph on.**

   You can either create a completely new design or add the graph to a design you've already created.

2. **In the design window, use the Graph tool to position the graph on your form or report.**

3. **Select the table or query that will provide the data for the graph.**

   It's usually going to be the same as the table or query that's used with the form or report, but it doesn't have to be. You can use a different table or query if you want.

4. **From the table or query, select the fields that you want to graph.**

5. **Tell Access what to do with the numbers you're going to graph.**

   It can add them, average them, or count the number of records in each group.

6. **Select the type of graph you want.**

    Access can create both 2-D and 3-D bar charts, pie charts, line graphs, area graphs, and a bunch of other weird types of graphs that you've never even heard of (donut, radar, etc.).

7. **After Access creates the graph, look it over in Print Preview and then fine-tune the graph design until it looks just right.**

Adding a Graph to a Report

In the following example, you create a bar chart like the one in Figure 22-1. Your sample chart will show how much money the Caveat Emptor bookstore made on each day between August 21 and August 31, 1994. Days on which the bookstore made *no* money aren't shown in the graph because there are no sales records for those days.

Access lets you create all kinds of fancy 2-D and 3-D graphs. But when you choose a graph type, remember that *fancy* is not always best unless you're simply trying to impress the boss. A simple 2-D graph often can show information better than a fancy 3-D graph. So when you look at your graph, don't just ask how pretty it is; ask how well it shows the information you need to convey.

If you quit Access after the last chapter, start it up again and load the Caveat database. In the example, you add the graph to a report. However, you can use precisely the same techniques you learn in the example to add a graph to a form.

Setting up a simple report for the graph

Start out by clicking on the Report tab on the left side of the Database window. The report part of this exercise is unimportant — you just need someplace to put the graph you're going to create. Do the following:

1. **Click on the New button to create a new report.**

2. **In the New Report dialog box, select the Sales table as the basis for the report. Then click on the Report Wizards button.**

3. **In the Report Wizards dialog box, double-click on AutoReport.**

    Access designs the report and shows you a Print Preview of what the report would look like if you printed it.

 4. **Maximize the Report window. After looking over the Print Preview, click on the Close Window button on the left end of the toolbar.**

    Access returns you to the report design screen.

TIP

If the Toolbox is in the way, just use the mouse to grab it by the top border and drag it somewhere else on your screen.

5. Fine-tune the report.

You're going to put the graph in the Report Header band at the top of the design. At the moment, however, you don't have enough space to put a graph there. Open up some space by dragging the bottom border of the Report Header band about halfway down the screen. Then drag the report layout's right edge so that it's about even with the 6-inch mark on the ruler at the top of the window, as shown in Figure 22-2.

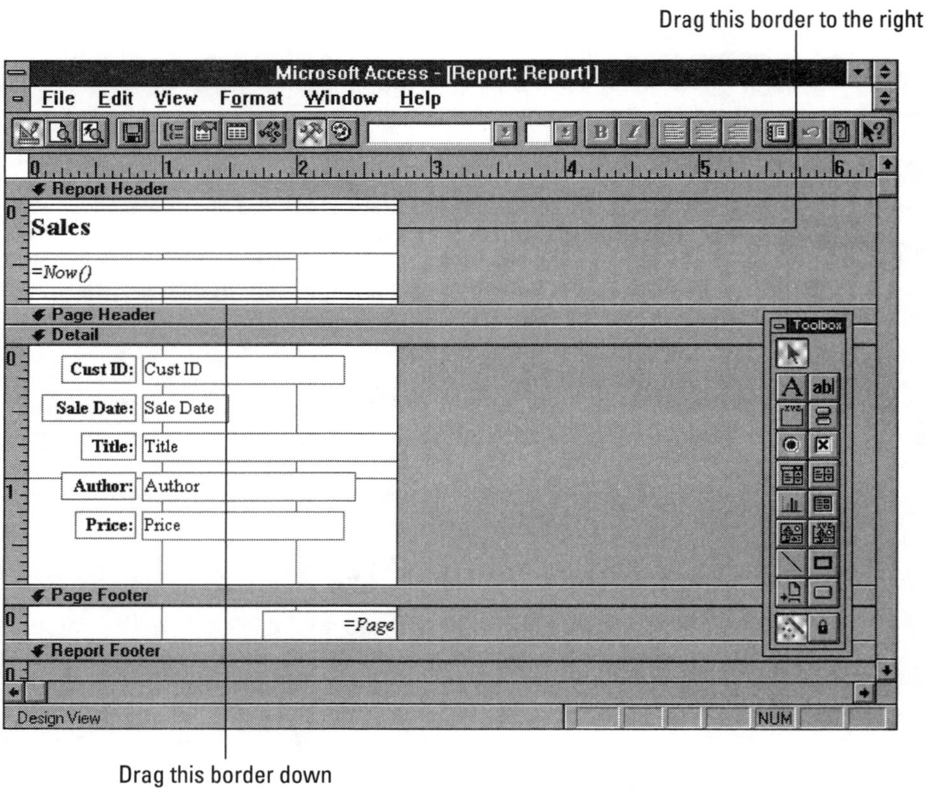

Drag this border to the right

Figure 22-2:
Expanding
the Report
Header
band to
make space
for a graph.

Drag this border down

Using the Graph tool

You use the Graph tool in the same way as all the other tools in the Toolbox. First, click on it. Access changes the mouse pointer into a picture of a graph. Move the mouse pointer to the place on the design where you want to put the graph. Click the left mouse button, and presto! Access starts up the Graph Wizard and puts a graph at that location on the report (or form).

That's the general idea. To create the example graph for this report, follow these steps:

1. **Click on the Graph tool in the Toolbox and then click again in the report design window to position the graph as shown in Figure 22-3.**

   As soon as you position the graph, the Graph Wizard dialog box appears, and Access asks what data you want to graph. The bottom right portion of the dialog box has three radio buttons: Tables, Queries, and Both. These buttons indicate that you can use either tables or queries as the data

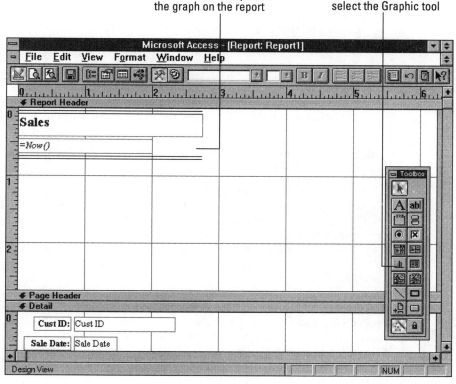

Then click here to position the graph on the report

Click here first to select the Graphic tool

Figure 22-3: Click on the Graph tool and then click in the Report Header band to position the graph.

source for your graph. If you want to use a table as your data source, click in the button next to Tables. If you want to use a query, click next to Queries. If you want to use both, click next to Both.

2. **Click on the Sales table and then click on the Next button.**

   You've just selected the Sales table as the source for your graph. The next dialog box should be familiar by now. It lets you tell Access which fields in the Sales table have the data you want to graph.

 If the wrong fields appear in the field list, it means that you selected the wrong table or query in the previous dialog box. Don't worry! Just click on the Back button, and Access takes you back to the previous dialog box to fix your mistake.

3. **In the Available fields list, double-click on the Sale Date field and the Price field.**

   These two fields should appear in the Fields for graph list on the right. Click on the Next button.

4. **When the next dialog box appears, just click on the Next button.**

   For this graph, you don't need to do anything in that dialog box. In the next dialog box that appears, Access asks how you want to group the data in the date field.

5. **Tell Access how to group the data.**

   In the top right section of the dialog box is a list box (remember them?) that lets you select how you want to group the dates. Click on the down-arrow button on the right end of the blank and select Day from the list. Then click on the Next button.

6. **In the next dialog box, tell Access how to handle the numbers in the Sale Price field.**

   For each date, you could add the numbers, average them, or just count how many sales were made. For this example, you want to add them, so just click on the Next button. Access displays a dialog box asking if you want to link the graph to the report. Answer No. Access then shows you a dialog box asking what kind of graph you want, as shown in Figure 22-4. (You choose the graph and finish the sample graph in the next section of this chapter.)

 The graph you're creating uses the same data source (the Sales table) as the report itself. But you can graph data from a different source if you want. In a report about customers, for example, you could put a graph with data from the Sales table or from a query.

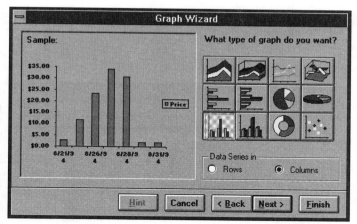

Figure 22-4:
Selecting a
graph type
with the
Graph
Wizard.

Another important thing to remember is that even though this report has text on it, you can create a report that contains *nothing* but a graph. After you click on the New button to create a new report, just click on the Blank Report button in the New Report dialog box. Then position your graph on the blank report without adding anything else to the layout.

Finishing the graph

In the dialog box that shows you all the different chart types available, each of the pictures acts as a button. To select a graph type, you just click on the picture. For the example, you want a graph that is simple and clear, so click on the Column button in the top row. Then finish the graph by following these steps:

1. **Click on the Next button.**

   When Access asks what format you want for your chart, you can select any of the formats shown by clicking on its picture. In this case, format 6 is already chosen, and that's the one you want. So just click on the Next button.

2. **Preview the graph.**

   Access shows you a sample of what your graph will look like. It looks good, so just click again on the Next button.

3. **Yet *another* dialog box appears, this one asking if you want to add a title to your graph. You don't, so just click on the Finish button.**

Presto! Your graph is done. To see what it will look like in the printed report, click on the Print Preview button in the toolbar. Your report should look like the one shown in Figure 22-5.

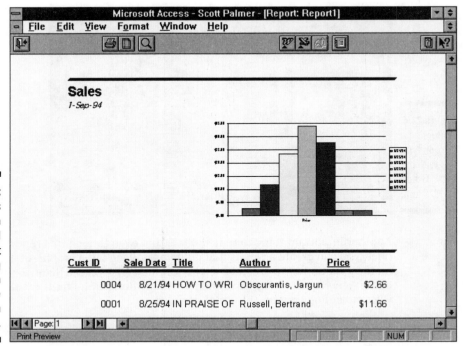

Figure 22-5:
The Sales
report with
the finished
bar chart
showing
how much
money came
in on each
day.

Click on the Close Window button on the left end of the toolbar, and Access returns you to the report design window. Save the report under the filename *Sales Report with Graph*.

Creating pie charts and other graph types

Creating other types of graphs is just as easy as creating a bar chart. You simply select the data you want to graph, select the graph type you want, and let the Access Graph Wizards do the rest!

To create a pie chart, follow the same steps as you did before. However, in the graph type dialog box shown in Figure 22-4, select a pie chart instead of a column chart. Just for fun, select a 3-D format in the chart format dialog box. A few more steps, and you'll get a graph like the one shown in Figure 22-6.

Figure 22-6:
An "exploded" pie chart of the same data used for the bar chart in Figure 22-5.

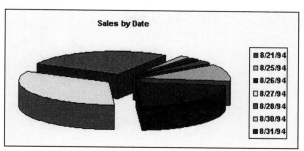

There's a lot more to learn about creating graphs with Access, but most of it will be easy now that you know the basic ideas and techniques. The best way to learn is to experiment and have fun.

Shut down Access if you want to take a break. And if you're *really* in trouble (your spouse has just announced that "We have to talk," or your house is surrounded by ATF agents), turn to the next chapter. It has some tips that will help you get out of trouble with your PC intact.

Part V
The Part of Tens

The 5th Wave   By Rich Tennant

PORTRAIT OF A
CYBERHOLIC

CYBERHOLICS SPEND HOURS BALANCING
THEIR CHECKBOOKS ON A COMPUTER,
WHEN THEY COULD DO IT IN MINUTES
WITH A PEN AND CALCULATOR.

In this part ...

This part talks about things you'd probably rather not think about. What if you get in trouble on your PC while using Access? What are the secrets of Access that those M.I.T. computer wizards are hiding from you? And what will you do if a computer wizard corners you at a party and starts to spout a lot of database jargon?

In this part, you find out how to handle *all* those situations. Except how to get invited to a party in the first place. You already know that. (Don't you?)

Chapter 23

Ten Things To Do When You're *Really* In Trouble

*I*n California, people are blasé about what they call "The Big One." They know that a catastrophic earthquake is coming. It's not a matter of *if*, only *when* it hits.

Database disaster is the same kind of thing. It's out there waiting for you, just around a corner, down a dark street, at three in the morning when a big report is due to the boss at eight. That's when it falls on you like a truckload of bricks — or at least a minivan full of football equipment. The main difference between your imminent database disaster and "The Big One" is that your house won't slide into the middle of the street. Thank goodness for small blessings.

 To understand the ideas in this chapter, you should know the concepts of a database (Chapter 2), a table (Chapter 3), data entry (Chapter 5), and printing data (Chapters 16, 17, and 19). You also need to have experienced *suffering* — the hopeless feeling you get when the PC has just gone "Kapow!" while you're writing an important letter to your parole officer.

If you're in the middle of a real-life database disaster, thumb through the chapter until you spot the section you need. Then follow the steps with your own database. And don't *worry*. It will be all right. Unless it isn't.

Before Disaster Hits: Back Up, Back Up, Back Up!

The most important thing you can do to prepare for a database disaster is to back up your database.

Backing up means copying your database to one floppy disk or more — or, if you have the equipment, to a tape cassette. After you've done a backup, you should store the backup disks or tapes in a different place from your PC. That way, even if your building burns down, you'll still have your data. And your data is more valuable than your computer. Replacing a PC may cost a few thousand dollars. If you run a business, losing your customer records could cost you the business.

You should back up all your databases every day. And backing up isn't the only way to protect your data. It's a good idea to *save your work* every few minutes.

The most common way to back up your database (and anything else on your PC's hard disk) is to use the MS-DOS or Windows backup command. Here, it's assumed that you installed "Windows Tools" when you set up Windows and that you're using MS-DOS Version 6.0 or later.

If you prefer to back up from MS-DOS, exit Windows and type **help msbackup** at the C: prompt. If you want to back up from Windows, open the Microsoft Tools window and double-click on the Backup icon, shown in Figure 23-1. The Windows Backup program appears (see Figure 23-2).

If your database fits on a single floppy disk, you can just copy it to the disk by using the Windows File Manager or the MS-DOS copy command. If you need more help with MS-DOS, check out IDG Books' *DOS For Dummies,* 2nd Edition; for help with Windows or Windows Backup, try IDG Books' *Windows 3.11 For Dummies,* 3rd Edition.

Figure 23-1:
The Backup
icon in the
Microsoft
Tools
window.

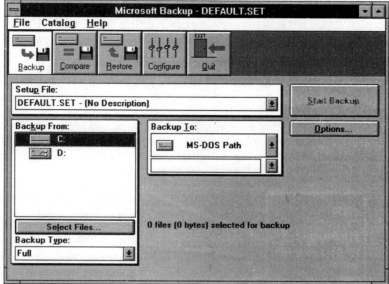

Figure 23-2:
The
Windows
Backup
program.

When Access Locks Up

Sometimes, Access locks up — no matter what you do, the program just sits there and refuses to work. This lockup can happen for several reasons: some of them minor, some of them a real pain to fix. But if you follow my advice from the preceding section — back up, back up, back up — you have very little to worry about. Except maybe that tooth that's been hurting since you crunched it on a macadamia nut.

It's worth mentioning that lockups do not mean that Access is a bad program. Access is a *great* program. But so many things can go on at once in Windows that any program can lock up once in a while.

The simplest solution: Reboot

Unless your keyboard locks up, too, the simplest solution is to *reboot*. In other words, you tell Windows that you need to shut it down because the program you're in has stopped working. To reboot, press Ctrl+Alt+Delete. After you tell Windows you want to reboot, your next step depends on whether Windows can detect that Access has locked up.

If Windows sees that there's a problem, you're in luck: Windows lets you shut down Access but leave everything else running. To do that simply press Enter. If you're running other programs in Windows, you then can switch back to them and save your work. After you do so, it's a good idea to shut down and restart Windows. You don't have to, but restarting is an extra safety measure. Sometimes a lockup can "destabilize" Windows and cause problems with other programs. If you shut down and restart Windows, however, you avoid this risk.

If Windows thinks that everything is OK, though, you have to press Ctrl+Alt+Delete again. When you do so, you shut down Windows and reboot the entire PC. If you're running any other programs, you lose any unsaved work in them, as well as your unsaved work in Access.

If your keyboard locks up, you can't reboot in the normal way. Instead, press the little button marked Reset on your PC. If your computer doesn't have a reset button, you have to turn your PC off. Once you turn it off, wait at least 30 seconds before turning it on again so that the hard disk has a chance to stop spinning. After you turn your PC back on, you should check your hard disk for errors by running the MS-DOS CHKDSK command. See *DOS For Dummies* if you need help.

Common reasons for lockups

The most common causes of Access locking up are

- **No printer driver is installed.** A printer driver is a little piece of software that tells Windows how to format text for a particular type of printer. Although setting up a default printer driver is a normal part of installing Windows, you may have skipped this step if your PC isn't hooked up to a printer. Access needs a printer driver, *any* printer driver, however, so that it can figure out how to display a Print Preview on-screen. If you haven't installed a default printer driver, Access locks up when you try to use Print Preview.

  The solution is to install a default printer driver in Windows. See *Windows For Dummies* if you need help.

- **Access doesn't get along with your Windows video driver.** Just as a printer driver tells Windows how to work with a printer, a video driver tells Windows how to work with your PC's screen. If you have an out-of-date or slightly weird video driver installed in Windows, Access can lock up.

  The solution is to get an up-to-date video driver or install a *generic* video driver that corresponds to your monitor type. Again, see *Windows For Dummies* if you need help.

✓ **While running a really complicated query, Access hits a snag.** None of the queries in this book are very complicated, but after you become a real expert (and you will!), you'll probably run some fancier queries. If you make even a minor mistake, Access sometimes locks up.

The easiest and safest solution is to press Ctrl+Break to stop the query (don't reboot). After you do so, it's still a good idea to save your work and then shut down and restart Access.

✓ **Access just decides to lock up for no particular reason.** Anyone who tells you that computers are perfectly logical has never worked with one. Computers and programs are just like people: each has a personality, and sometimes they just feel ornery and want to give you a scare.

If this happens, just reboot and don't worry about it too much. Access may never lock up again. If it does, _then_ you can try to find the problem. Remember to back up once a day and save your work every few minutes.

When Access Is Really Slow

To work properly, Access requires that your PC have a lot of electronic memory — called _RAM_ (random-access memory).

You don't need to know all the technical stuff, but Access needs an absolute minimum of 4MB of RAM to work at all.

If Access is running short of memory, it slows down. If you have other programs running in Windows, the easiest solution is to switch to those programs and close them. That way, the memory they were using becomes available to Access.

Another thing that eats up memory is Windows wallpaper, which you can turn off through the Windows Control Panel. Finally, if you're running a disk cache program, such as Microsoft's SmartDrive, you can reduce the amount of memory it uses. See _Windows For Dummies_ if you need help with the Control Panel and _DOS For Dummies_ for help with SmartDrive.

Unfortunately, the best solution costs money. The best solution is to take your PC back to the store and get more RAM. Eight megabytes is good, 16 is even better.

When You Make a Terrible Mistake in Data Entry

As usual, the best defense against data entry mistakes is to back up your database at least once a day.

But Access also provides a couple of ways for you to save yourself after you enter incorrect information, delete a record, or make some other horrific change in your database. If you've left the record — and you haven't changed another record since — you can choose Undo Saved Record from the Edit menu. If you make a data entry error and you're still in the record where you made the error, you can just go back and retype whatever you entered incorrectly.

When You Make a Terrible Mistake in Design

If you make a mistake when designing tables, forms, and reports, you can often undo a change simply by opening the Edit menu and choosing Undo. If you've already saved the changes, however, you can do two things:

- ✔ Go back into the Design window and change things back
- ✔ Restore your database from the backup copy, which, of course, you made yesterday

When You Accidentally Delete a Table

If you accidentally delete a table, you have only one way to get it back: retrieve it from your backup copy.

When Access Can't Load a Database

There are two reasons why Access may not be able to load a database that you've created:

- ✔ Access can't *find* the file.
- ✔ Access can't *read* the file.

Searching for the database file on your disk

Remember that your hard disk is divided into lots of little folders, called *directories*. If Access looks in the wrong directory, it won't find and therefore can't load the database. No big deal: the file is probably just in a different directory.

The name of the database should be the name you chose when you created it (such as *Caveat*, the example database in this book), plus a period and three letters, MDB. So when you're looking for the Caveat database, you look for the following file:

```
CAVEAT.MDB
```

If you look through all your Access directories and still can't find the database, have Windows scan your entire hard disk for it. The easiest way to do so is to go into the Windows File Manager (in the "main" program goup), open the File menu, and choose Search. When the Search dialog box appears, type ***.MDB** in the blank (see Figure 23-3). Make sure that the little box next to "Search all Subdirectories" has an x in it.

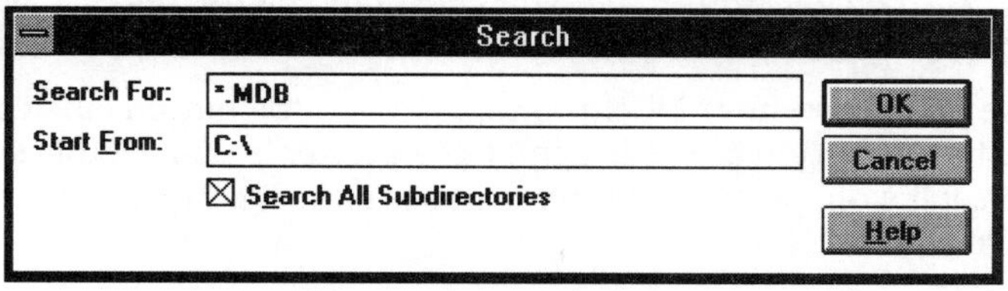

Figure 23-3:
The Search
dialog box
from the
Windows File
Manager.

Search
Search For: `*.MDB`
Start From: `C:\`
☒ S**e**arch All Subdirectories

OK · Cancel · Help

By typing ***.MDB**, you ask Windows File Manager to list all the Access database files on your disk, no matter what they're called. (You want Access to do so because you may have saved the database with a different name than you thought.) If you see a database whose name you don't remember or one that's in the wrong directory, that file's probably the one you want.

Repairing a corrupted database file

Sometimes when you try to load a file, Access tells you that the database has become *corrupted* — in other words, the file looks strange. Access expects all database files to look a certain way. If a database file looks funny, Access suspects that there's something wrong with it.

Remember, if Access or Windows locks up, and you have to reboot your PC, a database file can become corrupted.

This ominous-sounding problem is often pretty easy to fix. In the Access opening screen, *before* you have any database loaded, the File menu includes Repair Database. By selecting this option and telling Access which database you want to repair, you can often fix any so-called corruption. After you do so, you shouldn't have any trouble.

And as usual, your safest course of action is to back up your database once a day. Access can fix many kinds of corruption that happen to database files, *but not all*. If Access can't repair a database, the only surefire way to get it back is to restore it from a backup copy.

When Something Won't Print At All

When a report, form letter, or datasheet won't print *at all*, the problem usually isn't with Access. More likely, there's a problem with the printer. Here are the things to check:

- ✓ **Is the printer plugged in and turned on?** Strange but true, this is the most common reason why things won't print. (If your printer is plugged in but won't turn on, make sure that you paid your electric bill this month. If you didn't, pay it.)

- ✓ **Is the printer on-line?** Most printers have a little button labeled "Online". Next to this button is a little light. If the printer is on-line, this light should be on. If it's off, press the button and see if the light comes on. If it does, you're all set.

- ✓ **Is the printer out of paper?** If the printer's out of paper, put some in. We're not talking rocket science, here.

- ✓ **Is the printer cable tightly connected at both ends?** Shut down Access, shut down Windows, and turn off both your PC and printer. And just to be extra safe, unplug both your PC and printer. Look at the back of your PC and locate the cable that goes to your printer. Then make sure that the cable is tightly connected to the port at the back of your PC and the similar port on the back of your printer.

When Something Won't Print Right

By "not printing right," I mean anything ranging from crummy printing to incomprehensible garbage. Here are several things to check:

- ✓ **If a report or other document is printing sideways**, Access is printing in Landscape mode. Stop printing and try again. This time, when the Print dialog box appears, click on the Setup button to open a dialog box that lets you change from Landscape to Portrait orientation.

- ✓ **If you're getting garbage on the printed page**, go into the Windows Control Panel and make sure that Windows is using the right printer driver for your printer.

> ✔ **If you're printing some kind of report**, did you make some minor error in the report design? Double-check.
>
> Turn the printer off, wait a moment, and then turn it back on. Sometimes, this is all that's needed. You may never know what went wrong, but as long as it got fixed, who cares?

A few words of wisdom: It's usually not the really hard stuff that trips you up because you're careful with that stuff. It's usually something so simple that when you find it, you want to kick yourself. (But don't kick yourself. At your age, you could sprain your knee.)

When You Finish Your Work And There's Nothing Good on TV

When you finish your work, it's time to kick back and relax for a little while. But what to do? All that's on CNN is a bunch of talking heads jabbering about the latest international crisis. All that's on the local channels are infomercials that boast a cure for baldness and hawk the Psychic Friends Network.

Don't despair! Here are some things you can do to occupy your time away from Access:

> ✔ **Read your Access manuals.** *Naah.*
>
> ✔ **Play the neat games in Windows.** Solitaire and Minesweeper.
>
> ✔ **If you have a CompuServe account, you can type GO WINFUN to get to the Windows Fun Forum**, where you can download both shareware and freeware games that run under Windows. (Remember: if the game is shareware and you keep it, you should send some money to the author!)
>
> ✔ **Learn a foreign language.** Spanish is a good choice. It's becoming more and more common in the United States, particularly in the Southwest.
>
> ✔ *As a last resort*, **try talking to your spouse or significant other.** He or she will probably be glad to see you.

Chapter 24

Ten Secret Things Only Geniuses Do with Access

....

In This Chapter

▶ Secrets with macros
▶ Secrets with forms
▶ Secrets with queries
▶ Secrets about freeing up disk space

....

*E*very area of life has its little secrets. Access is no different. There are literally hundreds or thousands of things you can learn about using Access. In this chapter, you get to glimpse some of the secrets that only geniuses know about Access. You'll only get a taste of what's possible. If you want more than a taste — who can eat just one? — the rest is up to you.

Of course, because only geniuses know about these secrets, after you read this chapter. . . Well, you were a genius already.

You knew it. You were just too modest to say so.

To understand the ideas in this chapter, you should know the concepts of a database (Chapter 2), a table (Chapter 3), a form (Chapter 10), and queries (Chapters 11 and 12). To do the exercises, you need to have created the Customer Records table (Chapter 3), the Sales table (Chapter 12), and the Caveat Customers form (Chapter 10). To create the subform, you also need to have linked the Customer Records and Sales tables (Chapter 18).

Macro Secrets Are Not Macadamia Nuts

The first secret of macros is, "What the heck is a macro?" It sounds like something you'd get stuck between your teeth.

Macro just means abbreviation. Of course, computer people couldn't just *say* abbreviation — they had to make up a special word for it. Starting way back in the 1960s, computer people used macros as names for things that involved a whole bunch of steps. Rather than perform each step separately, they just "called" the macro, which took care of everything.

Suppose, for example, that you want to perform the following actions:

- Rob a liquor store
- Walk the dog
- Shave the cat
- Eat dinner (but not the cat)

You can give the name *HoHum* to a macro that's designed to accomplish all these actions. Then whenever you say *HoHum*, the macro does the actions automatically for you. And you can go to an awful movie at the mall.

In other words, a macro is a named sequence of actions. Rather than do each action separately, you just run the macro.

Typically, you will want to create a macro in Access when you find yourself repeating the same series of actions. If you abbreviate those actions with a macro, you never have to do them separately again. You just run the macro.

Creating a simple macro, or, We are easily entertained

Here's how to create and run a simple macro to open the Sales table in the book's example database. You can use these same basic techniques to create macros to do lots of other things, though you can't exceed the speed of light, predict the Super Bowl point spread, or understand the federal budget.

From the Caveat database window, click on the Macro tab. Then click on the New button. After the Macro window appears, follow these steps:

1. **In the Window menu, select Tile.**

   The Macro window and the Database window appear side by side on-screen.

2. **In the Database window, click on the Table tab.**

   The Customer Records and Sales tables are listed in the window.

3. **Using the mouse, drag the Sales table from the Database window to the top left cell of the Macro window.**

   As soon as you release the mouse button, the command *OpenTable* appears where you dragged the Sales table. If you look in the bottom half of the Macro window, the Sales table is listed on the line marked Table Name. That means that the *OpenTable* command will be applied to the Sales table — in other words, Access will open the Sales table.

4. **Open the File menu, select Save, and save the macro under the name *Open Sales Table*.**

And it's done! That's how to create an Access macro. This macro only has one action, but the Macro window has plenty of empty lines for more. In fact, a macro usually does more than one thing, but this example was deliberately kept simple.

As a housekeeping detail, close the Macro window. Then take out the trash and do the dishes. Sit up straight. Clean up your room. (Your mother would be proud.)

Running a macro, a marathon, or a gin joint

Running a macro is even easier than creating it. In the Database window, click on the Macro tab to display the available macros. Highlight the desired macro, click on the Run button (at the top of the Database window).

Imagine how much time you can save if you create a macro that incorporates 20 separate steps. You can do so by using the same basic techniques described in the preceding section.

Adding a macro push button to a form

This section explains how to do something *really* fancy: add a macro push button to a form. Though a specific example appears here, you can use the same basic steps to create a button for any macro on any form.

Suppose that you use the Customer Records form a great deal, and when you do, you often need to look at the Sales table. After you create a macro that opens the Sales table, you can put a button on the Caveat Customers form that runs the macro (automatically opening the table on-screen). Follow these steps:

1. **In the Database window, click on the Form tab.**

   Access displays a list of the available forms.

2. **With the Caveat Customers form highlighted, click on the Design button.**

   The Design window appears on your screen.

3. **If the Toolbox isn't visible, open the View menu and select Toolbox.**

   The Toolbox appears on the screen.

4. **Click on the Command Button tool.**

   The Command Button tool is the second tool from the bottom on the right side of the Toolbox. If you're in doubt, just hold the mouse pointer on the tool for a few seconds and Access will tell you which one it is.

5. **Move the mouse pointer just under the Notes field and click the left mouse button.**

   The Command Button Wizard dialog box appears.

6. **In the Categories list, click on Miscellaneous.**

7. **In the *When button is pressed* list, click on Run Access Macro.**

8. **Click on the Next button. Another dialog box appears. Click again on the Next button.**

9. **In the dialog box, click in the circle (called a *radio button*) next to the word Text.**

10. **In the blank to the right of Text, delete the original text (Run Macro) and type Open Sales Table.**

11. **Click on the Finish button.**

And that's it! The Caveat Customers form now has a button on it. Save the form and switch from Design to Form view by clicking on the Form button in the toolbar (it's the second button from the left). When you click on this button, the Sales table opens automatically. And you get a food pellet.

Psst ... The Secret of Subforms!

One of the most useful secrets you can learn about forms is the *subform*, which is a form that's inside another form. Putting forms inside forms inside forms is a technique pioneered by some government agencies and insurance companies. But Access subforms are much easier than the average tax form.

What the heck good is a subform? Suppose that you have a form to show customer records, and that you want the form to show all books purchased by each customer as his or her record is shown on the screen. To do so, you can put a subform inside the Customer Records form.

 In order for a subform to work, the two tables involved must be linked, as described in Chapter 18. For example, in order for Access to know which Sales records go with which Customer Records, the tables must be linked on the Cust ID field.

Follow these steps:

1. **In the Database window, click on the Form tab and then on the New button.**

   The New Form dialog box appears.

2. **Select Customer Records as the table and then click on the Form Wizards button.**

   Access asks which Wizard you want.

3. **Select the Wizard for Main/Subform.**

   Access asks, *Which table or query contains the data for the subform?*

4. **Click on the Sales table. Then click on the Next button.**

   Access asks which fields you want to use from the Customer Records table on your form.

5. **From the Available Fields list, select the fields Cust ID, First Name, Last Name, City, and State.**

   Access lists the selected fields in the Fields on main form blank.

6. **Click on the Next button.**

   Access asks which fields you want on your subform.

7. **Select the fields Sale Date, Title, and Price for the subform. Then click on the Finish button.**

   Access displays a message saying that you have to save the subform.

8. **Click on OK and then save the subform under the name Sales Subform.**

Access now displays the new form. As you go from one customer record to the next, the subform shows you the books purchased by each customer. Save the new form as Customer/Sales Form. Then close the Form window and return to the Database window.

Creating Queries That Talk to the User

As if your database users didn't have enough problems, now you can create queries that *talk* to them! It's not as goofy and pointless as it sounds. A talking query (like a talking dog) can ask the user for information. And that can make life much easier. A talking query is called a *parameter query*.

For instance, think about the queries described earlier in this book. If you want to search the example Sales table for all the books sold between August 21 and August 26, you can do so. You just use the Between operator in your query.

The trouble with that approach is that it's inflexible: for each range of dates, you must create a separate query. A parameter query, however, asks users which starting and ending dates they want to use. (Some other possibilities for parameter queries include searching for particular author names, price ranges, and so on. The only limit is your imagination.)

In this section, you learn how to create a parameter query that searches the Sales table for all books sold between two dates. These dates aren't included in the query; they're entered by the user when the query is run.

Follow these steps:

1. **In the Database window, click on the Query tab and then on the New button.**

    The New Query dialog box appears.

2. **Click on the New Query button.**

    The Query Design window appears, with the Add Table dialog box in front of it.

3. **In the Add Table dialog box, double-click on the Sales table. Then click on the Close button.**

4. **Double-click on the title bar of the Sales field list.**

    All the fields in the list are highlighted.

5. **Drag the fields to the top left cell of the Query grid.**

6. **Click in the Sort row of the Sale Date column. Open the list box and select Ascending sort order.**

7. **Click in the Criteria row of the Sale Date column.**

8. **In the Criteria/Sale Date cell, type the following, making sure that you use square brackets:**

   Between [Enter first date:] And [Enter last date:]

9. **Press Enter.**

10. **Save the query as Sales by Date.**

Shhh! How to run a talking query

To run the query, click on the Run button in the toolbar (the button with an exclamation point). Access displays a dialog box that asks for the first date. Remember, that's the prompt that's written into the query!

In the blank, type **26-Aug-94**. (Don't type the period.) As soon as you press Enter or click on OK, a new dialog box appears, asking for the last date. Type **31-Aug-94** and press Enter. Access runs the query, displaying only the records in the specified date range.

Close the query answer window and return to the Caveat Database window. Do not talk. Unless you feel like it.

Wild times, or, Searching for wildcard characters

The asterisk (*) and the question mark (?) are *wildcard characters*. You can use them in queries to search for data when you're not quite sure what you want but think that you'll know it when you see it. You can also use them as wildcards in poker, but only if you're playing with *real gullible people.* In Access (but not in poker), the asterisk stands in for any number of letters or digits; the question mark stands for a single letter or digit.

For example, suppose you're searching a 5,000-record Customer Records table for a customer's last name. If you use *W** in the query, Access finds all records where the last name begins with the letter *W*. If you use *W?s?*, Access find all records where the last name has four letters, begins with a *W* and has an *s* in the third slot. In other words, Access would find *Wass* and *West* but not *Walters*.

But if Access knows that the asterisk and question mark are wildcards, what do you do when you want to search for some text that actually contains an asterisk or question mark? What if the singer Prince (or whatever) changes his name again, this time to *P?* How can you search for his name in a query?

To search for wildcard characters in a query, put them in square brackets. To search for *P?*, for example, type **P[?]** in the query. You can use the same trick to search for text containing asterisks.

Freeing Up Disk Space

Access, like most programs these days, takes up a lot of disk space. Even a large hard disk can fill up very fast. And if you need the extra disk space, you can delete certain files after you don't need them anymore.

In particular, once you're familiar with Access, you can free up 2.5 MB of disk space by deleting the sample application files in the C:\ACCESS\SAMPAPPS directory.

If your PC isn't hooked up to a network, you can also delete any files that have the same name as your database files but end in the extension *.LDB*. Files whose names end in the .LDB extension (such as the *CAVEAT.LDB* file that goes with the book's CAVEAT.MDB database file) are only needed if more than one person might use the database simultaneously — such as on a PC network. But make *sure* not to delete any file ending in an .MDB extension!

Chapter 25

Ten Awful Database Terms (And Suggested Penalties for Using Them)

*I*n this chapter, you learn ten of the awfulest, dumbest database terms in the world, and that means the *entire universe*, not just the planet Earth, although Earth people do seem to be very good at coming up with awful words that confuse everyone and Earth people are good at writing long run-on sentences that seem to go on forever like did you ever try to read Hegel in the original German or make your way through a *New Yorker* article about just about anything geez what a bore and when you think about how much money those people make it's really incredible, well, it's time for me to take a breath now so I have to stop.

Application

Application just means *program*, so the term is redundant because there's already a word for program, which is — guess what? — *program*. Sometimes the word *application* is used to describe a program that's written in a database language, such as Access BASIC, and that works only inside a database program, in which case the program is called a *database application*. But that's just more clutter in the language.

Penalty: Application of three coats of wax to the offender's tongue, using the celebrated "wax on, wax off" method.

Dynaset

A *dynaset* is the part of a database that Access displays as the answer to a query. Why Microsoft couldn't just say that is a mystery. *Dynaset* sounds like a term that was cooked up by an overstressed advertising executive who was drinking too much coffee and smoking too many cigarettes. Access dynasets are great, but the word bites.

Penalty: Three weeks eating nothing but Dynatrim and building "huge, manly muscles" with Dynaflex.

Easy

The term means nothing. Zip. Nada. Every database program ever created is supposed to be *easy*. And if you got an 800 (a perfect score) on the math portion of the SAT, all databases probably *are* easy.

Penalty: Take the math portion of the SAT every day until you achieve an 800.

Fourth-Generation Language (4GL)

A *4GL* is a computer programming language that is *easy* (see preceding definition) and *powerful* (defined later in this chapter). Because *easy* and *powerful* don't mean anything, *fourth-generation language* doesn't either. Access BASIC, which you used some in this book, is a fourth-generation language, or maybe it isn't — who knows?

Penalty: Learn the PC's *machine language*, a first-generation language that is neither easy nor powerful.

Key

Key means either the main field by which a table is sorted or what you're looking for when you search a database. More often, *key* is what you're looking for when you can't get into your house.

Penalty: Watch all of the next "Green Acres" marathon on *Nick at Nite*. Even if it lasts a week.

Normalize

Normalize means get rid of redundant data — though what getting rid of redundant data has to do with a word like *normalize* is a complete mystery. The idea is that you shouldn't store the same data in several different places because doing so wastes disk space and increases the chance of error. In other words, each piece of data should be in a database only once. This is a very simple concept. People who use the word *normalize* just want to be sure you know that they graduated from M.I.T. or Stanford.

Penalty: Attend a monster truck show and make friends with three people who are definitely *not* normal.

Post

When you have one table that holds data about sales transactions and two other tables that hold inventory and customer balance data, you update the latter two tables by *posting* the data from the transactions table. This term comes from accountants — which explains a lot.

Penalty: Think of at least one anagram of the word *post* that begins with the letters *s* and *t*. Then do so.

Powerful

The term means nothing. Zip. Nada. Every database program ever created is supposed to be *powerful*. If people call a program *powerful*, they mean that the program does what it's supposed to do. Arnold Schwarzenegger is powerful; database programs either work or they don't. In that sense, Access really *is* powerful.

Penalty: Go to a discount store and buy a really *powerful* cologne. Then wear it to the office all week.

Relational

Relational has three meanings. First, it can mean that a database "conforms to the relational model" — one of those heavy-duty computer science things that's long on theory but doesn't make much difference in practice. Second, it can mean that a database has linked tables, in which case the word is being used incorrectly because nonrelational databases can have linked tables, too. Third, it can mean "Good! Buy this!" — its most common meaning.

Penalty: Attend this year's family reunion and get reacquainted with all those relations you've tried so hard to forget.

Structured Query Language (SQL)

SQL is a database language that's used to find and manipulate data. More often, *SQL* simply means good. People tend to look for database managers that support SQL, even though they have no idea what SQL is or what they'd do with it if they knew.

Penalty: Learn what SQL is. Then figure out what to do with it.

Part VI

Appendixes

EXCUSE ME MA'AM-ROYAL CANADIAN MOUNTED PROGRAMMERS-SOMEONE HERE REPORT A MISSING FILE?

In this part...

You can't do much with a database until you've put some data in it. In this part, Appendix A gives you sample data for the Customer Records and Sales tables that are used in the book's example database.

Likewise, you can't do much with Access until you've got it installed on your PC. Appendix B shows you how to set up the program on your PC's hard disk so that you can use Access from Microsoft Windows.

Appendix A
Database Data for This Book

● ●

*T*o work through the chapters in this book, you have to enter some data into the Access database. You could hire a high school kid to do the work, of course. But what if your hard-working student is distracted by something on MTV, *then where will you be?* Out of data and out of luck, thank you. So you should probably enter this data yourself.

On the bright side, you can enter as many or as few of these data records as you like. On the down side, if something really great comes on MTV, you must restrain yourself and keep typing.

The "Customer Records" Table

1
Prof. James West
Jimbo
Mythic University
Martinsville, CA 98035
415-555-4678

2
Ms. Harriett Stowe
Ms. Stowe
14 Parakeet Lane
New York, NY 10087
212-555-2345

3
Mr. Jules Twombly
Jules
The ABC Hotel
Las Vegas, NV 34567
201-555-6213

4
Mr. Arnold Harris
Arnie
101 Fifth Avenue
Boise, ID 23413
321-555-9876

5
Ms. Teri Lane
Ms. Lane
5678 15th Street, #5-A
Santa Barbara, CA 93101
805-555-1234

6
Ms. Susan Brown
Ms. Brown
World-Wide Import
5541 LaBrea
Los Angeles, CA 90069
310-555-8617

7
Dr. Thomas Baker
Tom
342 Gallifrey Street
Shreveport, LA 14325
205-555-7681

8
Ms. Janet White
Janet
Gates Office Supply
745 Microsoft Way
Redmond, WA 98052
206-555-3111

9
Mr. Harris Harrison
Mr. Harrison
21 El Embarcadero
Goleta, CA 93105
805-555-9026

10
Ms. Tracy Dancer
Tracy
11 Waterside Place
Zuma Beach, CA 90078
213-555-7741

11
Ms. Diane Walker
Ms. Walker
Walker-Townsend PR
551 Second Street
San Francisco, CA 94107
415-555-1079

12
Ms. Shirley Edison
Ms. Edison
Dept. of Electricity
Bloomington University
Bloomington, IN 47401
812-555-5873

13
Mr. Don Wilds
Don
Vintage Phoenix
114 E. 6th Street
Bloomington, IN 47408
812-555-9770

14
Mr. Jack Stein
Jack
Majorland Oil & Gas Corp.
113 E. 6th Street
Bloomington, IN 47408
812-555-1299

15
Prof. Irwin Jones
Shirley
Dept. of Prognostication
Bloomington University
Bloomington, IN 40401
812-555-1191

The "Sales" Table

Although there are 15 customers in the Customer Records table, the sales are only for account numbers 1 to 5 — just in case you didn't enter all 15 customer records. The fields are listed in the following order: Cust ID, Sale Date, Title, Author, and Price.

4
8/21/94
How to Write a Computer Book
Obscurantis, Jargun
2.95

1
8/25/94
In Praise of Idleness
Russell, Bertrand
12.95

2
8/26/94
Getting Your Husband Off His Lazy Butt
Russell, Mrs. Bertrand
12.95

5
8/27/94
How I Turned $25 Cash into a Successful Business
Fleiss, Heidi
24.95

5
8/28/94
Access 2 For Dummies
Palmer, Scott
14799.95

5
8/26/94
Fershlugginers I Have Known
Smith, Joe
11.66

1
8/27/94
Atlas Shrugged
Rand, Ayn
12.95

2
8/28/94
Love in the Time of Cholera
Garcia-Marquez, Gabriel
12.00

4
8/30/94
Deep Thoughts
Clinton & Quayle
1.95

3
8/31/94
"Supertrain" Forever!
Silverman, Fred
1.95

Appendix B
Installing Access

• •

*I*nstalling Access is easy. But before you install Access on your PC — in fact, before you even *buy* Access — make sure that your PC is capable of running it.

What You Need to Install and Run Access

Like most Windows applications, Access requires a lot of PC horsepower and disk space to work properly. You don't need to understand what all these things are, but you should make sure that your PC has at least

✔ **An 80386 processor**

An 80486 or Pentium (80586) processor is better. Processor speeds are rated in megahertz (MHz), so a 33-MHz 80386 processor is faster than a 20-MHz 80386 processor. However, higher-numbered processors are faster, so a 33-MHz 80486 processor is faster than a 33-MHz 80386 processor.

✔ **A hard disk with at least 15MB of free disk space**

More free space is better. You can get by with less than 15 megabytes, but trust me, you don't want to.

✔ **At least 4MB of RAM**

Six MB of RAM (electronic memory) is better, 8MB is even better, and 16MB is *spectacular*. The more RAM you have, the faster Access is likely to run.

✔ **A mouse or other pointing device, such as a trackball**

✔ **MS-DOS version 3.1 or later**

✔ **Windows 3.1 or later**

Installing Access on Your PC

To install Access on your PC, follow these steps:

1. Put the first Access disk into the appropriate floppy disk drive. Usually, this drive is drive A, but it can be drive B.

2. If Windows isn't already running, start it up.

3. From the Windows Program Manager, open the File menu and choose Run.

4. In the dialog box that appears, type **a:setup** if the first Access disk is in drive A; type **b:setup** if the disk is in drive B.

5. Click on the OK button. The Access Setup program starts.

6. Follow the instructions that appear on-screen.

By the way, you can choose among three types of installation:

- **Typical**, which installs the parts of Access needed by most people
- **Complete/Custom**, which lets you choose the parts of Access you want to install
- **Minimum**, which only installs the *absolutely essential* things you need to run Access (good of laptops and other PCs with limited hard disk space)

Index

• *U* •

• *V* •

• *W* •

• *Y* •

• *Z* •

The Fun & Easy Way™ to learn about computers and more!

Windows® 3.11 For Dummies, 3rd Edition
by Andy Rathbone

ISBN: 1-56884-370-4
$16.95 USA/
$22.95 Canada

Mutual Funds For Dummies™
by Eric Tyson

ISBN: 1-56884-226-0
$16.99 USA/
$22.99 Canada

DOS For Dummies, 2nd Edition
by Dan Gookin

ISBN: 1-878058-75-4
$16.95 USA/
$22.95 Canada

The Internet For Dummies, 2nd Edition
by John Levine & Carol Baroudi

ISBN: 1-56884-222-8
$19.99 USA/
$26.99 Canada

Personal Finance For Dummies™
by Eric Tyson

ISBN: 1-56884-150-7
$16.95 USA/
$22.95 Canada

PCs For Dummies, 3rd Edition
by Dan Gookin & Andy Rathbone

ISBN: 1-56884-904-4
$16.99 USA/
$22.99 Canada

Macs® For Dummies, 3rd Edition
by David Pogue

ISBN: 1-56884-239-2
$19.99 USA/
$26.99 Canada

The SAT® I For Dummies™
by Suzee Vlk

ISBN: 1-56884-213-9
$14.99 USA/
$20.99 Canada

Here's a complete listing of IDG Books' ...For Dummies® titles

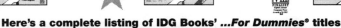

Title	Author	ISBN	Price
DATABASE			
Access 2 For Dummies®	by Scott Palmer	ISBN: 1-56884-090-X	$19.95 USA/$26.95 Canada
Access Programming For Dummies®	by Rob Krumm	ISBN: 1-56884-091-8	$19.95 USA/$26.95 Canada
Approach 3 For Windows® For Dummies®	by Doug Lowe	ISBN: 1-56884-233-3	$19.99 USA/$26.99 Canada
dBASE For DOS For Dummies®	by Scott Palmer & Michael Stabler	ISBN: 1-56884-188-4	$19.95 USA/$26.95 Canada
dBASE For Windows® For Dummies®	by Scott Palmer	ISBN: 1-56884-179-5	$19.95 USA/$26.95 Canada
dBASE 5 For Windows® Programming For Dummies®	by Ted Coombs & Jason Coombs	ISBN: 1-56884-215-5	$19.99 USA/$26.99 Canada
FoxPro 2.6 For Windows® For Dummies®	by John Kaufeld	ISBN: 1-56884-187-6	$19.95 USA/$26.95 Canada
Paradox 5 For Windows® For Dummies®	by John Kaufeld	ISBN: 1-56884-185-X	$19.95 USA/$26.95 Canada
DESKTOP PUBLISHING/ILLUSTRATION/GRAPHICS			
CorelDRAW! 5 For Dummies®	by Deke McClelland	ISBN: 1-56884-157-4	$19.95 USA/$26.95 Canada
CorelDRAW! For Dummies®	by Deke McClelland	ISBN: 1-56884-042-X	$19.95 USA/$26.95 Canada
Desktop Publishing & Design For Dummies®	by Roger C. Parker	ISBN: 1-56884-234-1	$19.99 USA/$26.99 Canada
Harvard Graphics 2 For Windows® For Dummies®	by Roger C. Parker	ISBN: 1-56884-092-6	$19.95 USA/$26.95 Canada
PageMaker 5 For Macs® For Dummies®	by Galen Gruman & Deke McClelland	ISBN: 1-56884-178-7	$19.95 USA/$26.95 Canada
PageMaker 5 For Windows® For Dummies®	by Deke McClelland & Galen Gruman	ISBN: 1-56884-160-4	$19.95 USA/$26.95 Canada
Photoshop 3 For Macs® For Dummies®	by Deke McClelland	ISBN: 1-56884-208-2	$19.99 USA/$26.99 Canada
QuarkXPress 3.3 For Dummies®	by Galen Gruman & Barbara Assadi	ISBN: 1-56884-217-1	$19.99 USA/$26.99 Canada
FINANCE/PERSONAL FINANCE/TEST TAKING REFERENCE			
Everyday Math For Dummies™	by Charles Seiter	ISBN: 1-56884-248-1	$14.99 USA/$22.99 Canada
Personal Finance For Dummies™ For Canadians	by Eric Tyson & Tony Martin	ISBN: 1-56884-378-X	$18.99 USA/$24.99 Canada
QuickBooks 3 For Dummies®	by Stephen L. Nelson	ISBN: 1-56884-227-9	$19.99 USA/$26.99 Canada
Quicken 8 For DOS For Dummies, 2nd Edition	by Stephen L. Nelson	ISBN: 1-56884-210-4	$19.95 USA/$26.95 Canada
Quicken 5 For Macs® For Dummies®	by Stephen L. Nelson	ISBN: 1-56884-211-2	$19.95 USA/$26.95 Canada
Quicken 4 For Windows® For Dummies, 2nd Edition	by Stephen L. Nelson	ISBN: 1-56884-209-0	$19.95 USA/$26.95 Canada
Taxes For Dummies,™ 1995 Edition	by Eric Tyson & David J. Silverman	ISBN: 1-56884-220-1	$14.99 USA/$20.99 Canada
The GMAT® For Dummies™	by Suzee Vlk, Series Editor	ISBN: 1-56884-376-3	$14.99 USA/$20.99 Canada
The GRE® For Dummies™	by Suzee Vlk, Series Editor	ISBN: 1-56884-375-5	$14.99 USA/$20.99 Canada
Time Management For Dummies™	by Jeffrey J. Mayer	ISBN: 1-56884-360-7	$16.99 USA/$22.99 Canada
TurboTax For Windows® For Dummies®	by Gail A. Helsel, CPA	ISBN: 1-56884-228-7	$19.99 USA/$26.99 Canada
GROUPWARE/INTEGRATED			
ClarisWorks For Macs® For Dummies®	by Frank Higgins	ISBN: 1-56884-363-1	$19.99 USA/$26.99 Canada
Lotus Notes For Dummies®	by Pat Freeland & Stephen Londergan	ISBN: 1-56884-212-0	$19.95 USA/$26.95 Canada
Microsoft® Office 4 For Windows® For Dummies®	by Roger C. Parker	ISBN: 1-56884-183-3	$19.95 USA/$26.95 Canada
Microsoft® Works 3 For Windows® For Dummies®	by David C. Kay	ISBN: 1-56884-214-7	$19.99 USA/$26.99 Canada
SmartSuite 3 For Dummies®	by Jan Weingarten & John Weingarten	ISBN: 1-56884-367-4	$19.99 USA/$26.99 Canada
INTERNET/COMMUNICATIONS/NETWORKING			
America Online® For Dummies, 2nd Edition	by John Kaufeld	ISBN: 1-56884-933-8	$19.99 USA/$26.99 Canada
CompuServe For Dummies, 2nd Edition	by Wallace Wang	ISBN: 1-56884-937-0	$19.99 USA/$26.99 Canada
Modems For Dummies, 2nd Edition	by Tina Rathbone	ISBN: 1-56884-223-6	$19.99 USA/$26.99 Canada
MORE Internet For Dummies®	by John R. Levine & Margaret Levine Young	ISBN: 1-56884-164-7	$19.95 USA/$26.95 Canada
MORE Modems & On-line Services For Dummies®	by Tina Rathbone	ISBN: 1-56884-365-8	$19.99 USA/$26.99 Canada
Mosaic For Dummies, Windows Edition	by David Angell & Brent Heslop	ISBN: 1-56884-242-2	$19.99 USA/$26.99 Canada
NetWare For Dummies, 2nd Edition	by Ed Tittel, Deni Connor & Earl Follis	ISBN: 1-56884-369-0	$19.99 USA/$26.99 Canada
Networking For Dummies®	by Doug Lowe	ISBN: 1-56884-079-9	$19.95 USA/$26.95 Canada
PROCOMM PLUS 2 For Windows® For Dummies®	by Wallace Wang	ISBN: 1-56884-219-8	$19.99 USA/$26.99 Canada
TCP/IP For Dummies®	by Marshall Wilensky & Candace Leiden	ISBN: 1-56884-241-4	$19.99 USA/$26.99 Canada

For scholastic requests & educational orders please call Educational Sales at 1. 800. 434. 2086

FOR MORE INFO OR TO ORDER, PLEASE CALL ▶ 800 . 762 . 2974

For volume discounts & special orders please call Tony Real, Special Sales, at 415. 655. 3048

The Internet For Macs® For Dummies® 2nd Edition	by Charles Seiter	ISBN: 1-56884-371-2	$19.99 USA/$26.99 Canada
The Internet For Macs® For Dummies® Starter Kit	by Charles Seiter	ISBN: 1-56884-244-9	$29.99 USA/$39.99 Canada
The Internet For Macs® For Dummies® Starter Kit Bestseller Edition	by Charles Seiter	ISBN: 1-56884-245-7	$39.99 USA/$54.99 Canada
The Internet For Windows® For Dummies® Starter Kit	by John R. Levine & Margaret Levine Young	ISBN: 1-56884-237-6	$34.99 USA/$44.99 Canada
The Internet For Windows® For Dummies® Starter Kit, Bestseller Edition	by John R. Levine & Margaret Levine Young	ISBN: 1-56884-246-5	$39.99 USA/$54.99 Canada

MACINTOSH

Mac® Programming For Dummies®	by Dan Parks Sydow	ISBN: 1-56884-173-6	$19.95 USA/$26.95 Canada
Macintosh® System 7.5 For Dummies®	by Bob LeVitus	ISBN: 1-56884-197-3	$19.95 USA/$26.95 Canada
MORE Macs® For Dummies®	by David Pogue	ISBN: 1-56884-087-X	$19.95 USA/$26.95 Canada
PageMaker 5 For Macs® For Dummies®	by Galen Gruman & Deke McClelland	ISBN: 1-56884-178-7	$19.95 USA/$26.95 Canada
QuarkXPress 3.3 For Dummies®	by Galen Gruman & Barbara Assadi	ISBN: 1-56884-217-1	$19.99 USA/$26.99 Canada
Upgrading and Fixing Macs® For Dummies®	by Kearney Rietmann & Frank Higgins	ISBN: 1-56884-189-2	$19.95 USA/$26.95 Canada

MULTIMEDIA

| Multimedia & CD-ROMs For Dummies® 2nd Edition | by Andy Rathbone | ISBN: 1-56884-907-9 | $19.99 USA/$26.99 Canada |
| Multimedia & CD-ROMs For Dummies® Interactive Multimedia Value Pack, 2nd Edition | by Andy Rathbone | ISBN: 1-56884-909-5 | $29.99 USA/$39.99 Canada |

OPERATING SYSTEMS:

DOS

| MORE DOS For Dummies® | by Dan Gookin | ISBN: 1-56884-046-2 | $19.95 USA/$26.95 Canada |
| OS/2® Warp For Dummies® 2nd Edition | by Andy Rathbone | ISBN: 1-56884-205-8 | $19.99 USA/$26.99 Canada |

UNIX

| MORE UNIX® For Dummies® | by John R. Levine & Margaret Levine Young | ISBN: 1-56884-361-5 | $19.99 USA/$26.99 Canada |
| UNIX® For Dummies® | by John R. Levine & Margaret Levine Young | ISBN: 1-878058-58-4 | $19.95 USA/$26.95 Canada |

WINDOWS

| MORE Windows® For Dummies® 2nd Edition | by Andy Rathbone | ISBN: 1-56884-048-9 | $19.95 USA/$26.95 Canada |
| Windows® 95 For Dummies® | by Andy Rathbone | ISBN: 1-56884-240-6 | $19.99 USA/$26.99 Canada |

PCS/HARDWARE

| Illustrated Computer Dictionary For Dummies® 2nd Edition | by Dan Gookin & Wallace Wang | ISBN: 1-56884-218-X | $12.95 USA/$16.95 Canada |
| Upgrading and Fixing PCs For Dummies® 2nd Edition | by Andy Rathbone | ISBN: 1-56884-903-6 | $19.99 USA/$26.99 Canada |

PRESENTATION/AUTOCAD

| AutoCAD For Dummies® | by Bud Smith | ISBN: 1-56884-191-4 | $19.95 USA/$26.95 Canada |
| PowerPoint 4 For Windows® For Dummies® | by Doug Lowe | ISBN: 1-56884-161-2 | $16.99 USA/$22.99 Canada |

PROGRAMMING

Borland C++ For Dummies®	by Michael Hyman	ISBN: 1-56884-162-0	$19.95 USA/$26.95 Canada
C For Dummies® Volume 1	by Dan Gookin	ISBN: 1-878058-78-9	$19.95 USA/$26.95 Canada
C++ For Dummies®	by Stephen R. Davis	ISBN: 1-56884-163-9	$19.95 USA/$26.95 Canada
Delphi Programming For Dummies®	by Neil Rubenking	ISBN: 1-56884-200-7	$19.99 USA/$26.99 Canada
Mac® Programming For Dummies®	by Dan Parks Sydow	ISBN: 1-56884-173-6	$19.95 USA/$26.95 Canada
PowerBuilder 4 Programming For Dummies®	by Ted Coombs & Jason Coombs	ISBN: 1-56884-325-9	$19.99 USA/$26.99 Canada
QBasic Programming For Dummies®	by Douglas Hergert	ISBN: 1-56884-093-4	$19.95 USA/$26.95 Canada
Visual Basic 3 For Dummies®	by Wallace Wang	ISBN: 1-56884-076-4	$19.95 USA/$26.95 Canada
Visual Basic "X" For Dummies®	by Wallace Wang	ISBN: 1-56884-230-9	$19.99 USA/$26.99 Canada
Visual C++ 2 For Dummies®	by Michael Hyman & Bob Arnson	ISBN: 1-56884-328-3	$19.99 USA/$26.99 Canada
Windows® 95 Programming For Dummies®	by S. Randy Davis	ISBN: 1-56884-327-5	$19.99 USA/$26.99 Canada

SPREADSHEET

1-2-3 For Dummies®	by Greg Harvey	ISBN: 1-878058-60-6	$16.95 USA/$22.95 Canada
1-2-3 For Windows® 5 For Dummies® 2nd Edition	by John Walkenbach	ISBN: 1-56884-216-3	$16.95 USA/$22.95 Canada
Excel 5 For Macs® For Dummies®	by Greg Harvey	ISBN: 1-56884-186-8	$19.95 USA/$26.95 Canada
Excel For Dummies® 2nd Edition	by Greg Harvey	ISBN: 1-56884-050-0	$16.95 USA/$22.95 Canada
MORE 1-2-3 For DOS For Dummies®	by John Weingarten	ISBN: 1-56884-224-4	$19.99 USA/$26.99 Canada
MORE Excel 5 For Windows® For Dummies®	by Greg Harvey	ISBN: 1-56884-207-4	$19.95 USA/$26.95 Canada
Quattro Pro 6 For Windows® For Dummies®	by John Walkenbach	ISBN: 1-56884-174-4	$19.95 USA/$26.95 Canada
Quattro Pro For DOS For Dummies®	by John Walkenbach	ISBN: 1-56884-023-3	$16.95 USA/$22.95 Canada

UTILITIES

| Norton Utilities 8 For Dummies® | by Beth Slick | ISBN: 1-56884-166-3 | $19.95 USA/$26.95 Canada |

VCRS/CAMCORDERS

| VCRs & Camcorders For Dummies™ | by Gordon McComb & Andy Rathbone | ISBN: 1-56884-229-5 | $14.99 USA/$20.99 Canada |

WORD PROCESSING

Ami Pro For Dummies®	by Jim Meade	ISBN: 1-56884-049-7	$19.95 USA/$26.95 Canada
MORE Word For Windows® 6 For Dummies®	by Doug Lowe	ISBN: 1-56884-165-5	$19.95 USA/$26.95 Canada
MORE WordPerfect® 6 For Windows® For Dummies®	by Margaret Levine Young & David C. Kay	ISBN: 1-56884-206-6	$19.95 USA/$26.95 Canada
MORE WordPerfect® 6 For DOS For Dummies®	by Wallace Wang, edited by Dan Gookin	ISBN: 1-56884-047-0	$19.95 USA/$26.95 Canada
Word 6 For Macs® For Dummies®	by Dan Gookin	ISBN: 1-56884-190-6	$19.95 USA/$26.95 Canada
Word For Windows® 6 For Dummies®	by Dan Gookin	ISBN: 1-56884-075-6	$16.95 USA/$22.95 Canada
Word For Windows® For Dummies®	by Dan Gookin & Ray Werner	ISBN: 1-878058-86-X	$16.95 USA/$22.95 Canada
WordPerfect® 6 For DOS For Dummies®	by Dan Gookin	ISBN: 1-878058-77-0	$16.95 USA/$22.95 Canada
WordPerfect® 6.1 For Windows® For Dummies® 2nd Edition	by Margaret Levine Young & David Kay	ISBN: 1-56884-243-0	$16.95 USA/$22.95 Canada
WordPerfect® For Dummies®	by Dan Gookin	ISBN: 1-878058-52-5	$16.95 USA/$22.95 Canada

For scholastic requests & educational orders please call Educational Sales at 1. 800. 434. 2086

FOR MORE INFO OR TO ORDER, PLEASE CALL ▶ 800 762 2974

For volume discounts & special orders please call Tony Real, Special Sales, at 415. 655. 3048

Fun, Fast, & Cheap!™

10/31/95

NEW!

NEW!

SUPER STAR

SUPER STAR

The Internet For Macs® For Dummies® Quick Reference
by Charles Seiter

ISBN:1-56884-967-2
$9.99 USA/$12.99 Canada

Windows® 95 For Dummies® Quick Reference
by Greg Harvey

ISBN: 1-56884-964-8
$9.99 USA/$12.99 Canada

Photoshop 3 For Macs® For Dummies® Quick Reference
by Deke McClelland

ISBN: 1-56884-968-0
$9.99 USA/$12.99 Canada

WordPerfect® For DOS For Dummies® Quick Reference
by Greg Harvey

ISBN: 1-56884-009-8
$8.95 USA/$12.95 Canada

Title	Author	ISBN	Price
DATABASE			
Access 2 For Dummies® Quick Reference	by Stuart J. Stuple	ISBN: 1-56884-167-1	$8.95 USA/$11.95 Canada
dBASE 5 For DOS For Dummies® Quick Reference	by Barrie Sosinsky	ISBN: 1-56884-954-0	$9.99 USA/$12.99 Canada
dBASE 5 For Windows® For Dummies® Quick Reference	by Stuart J. Stuple	ISBN: 1-56884-953-2	$9.99 USA/$12.99 Canada
Paradox 5 For Windows® For Dummies® Quick Reference	by Scott Palmer	ISBN: 1-56884-960-5	$9.99 USA/$12.99 Canada
DESKTOP PUBLISHING/ILLUSTRATION/GRAPHICS			
CorelDRAW! 5 For Dummies® Quick Reference	by Raymond E. Werner	ISBN: 1-56884-952-4	$9.99 USA/$12.99 Canada
Harvard Graphics For Windows® For Dummies® Quick Reference	by Raymond E. Werner	ISBN: 1-56884-962-1	$9.99 USA/$12.99 Canada
Photoshop 3 For Macs® For Dummies® Quick Reference	by Deke McClelland	ISBN: 1-56884-968-0	$9.99 USA/$12.99 Canada
FINANCE/PERSONAL FINANCE			
Quicken 4 For Windows® For Dummies® Quick Reference	by Stephen L. Nelson	ISBN: 1-56884-950-8	$9.95 USA/$12.95 Canada
GROUPWARE/INTEGRATED			
Microsoft® Office 4 For Windows® For Dummies® Quick Reference	by Doug Lowe	ISBN: 1-56884-958-3	$9.99 USA/$12.99 Canada
Microsoft® Works 3 For Windows® For Dummies® Quick Reference	by Michael Partington	ISBN: 1-56884-959-1	$9.99 USA/$12.99 Canada
INTERNET/COMMUNICATIONS/NETWORKING			
The Internet For Dummies® Quick Reference	by John R. Levine & Margaret Levine Young	ISBN: 1-56884-168-X	$8.95 USA/$11.95 Canada
MACINTOSH			
Macintosh® System 7.5 For Dummies® Quick Reference	by Stuart J. Stuple	ISBN: 1-56884-956-7	$9.99 USA/$12.99 Canada
OPERATING SYSTEMS:			
DOS			
DOS For Dummies® Quick Reference	by Greg Harvey	ISBN: 1-56884-007-1	$8.95 USA/$11.95 Canada
UNIX			
UNIX® For Dummies® Quick Reference	by John R. Levine & Margaret Levine Young	ISBN: 1-56884-094-2	$8.95 USA/$11.95 Canada
WINDOWS			
Windows® 3.1 For Dummies® Quick Reference, 2nd Edition	by Greg Harvey	ISBN: 1-56884-951-6	$8.95 USA/$11.95 Canada
PCs/HARDWARE			
Memory Management For Dummies® Quick Reference	by Doug Lowe	ISBN: 1-56884-362-3	$9.99 USA/$12.99 Canada
PRESENTATION/AUTOCAD			
AutoCAD For Dummies® Quick Reference	by Ellen Finkelstein	ISBN: 1-56884-198-1	$9.95 USA/$12.95 Canada
SPREADSHEET			
1-2-3 For Dummies® Quick Reference	by John Walkenbach	ISBN: 1-56884-027-6	$8.95 USA/$11.95 Canada
1-2-3 For Windows® 5 For Dummies® Quick Reference	by John Walkenbach	ISBN: 1-56884-957-5	$9.95 USA/$12.95 Canada
Excel For Windows® For Dummies® Quick Reference, 2nd Edition	by John Walkenbach	ISBN: 1-56884-096-9	$8.95 USA/$11.95 Canada
Quattro Pro 6 For Windows® For Dummies® Quick Reference	by Stuart J. Stuple	ISBN: 1-56884-172-8	$9.95 USA/$12.95 Canada
WORD PROCESSING			
Word For Windows® 6 For Dummies® Quick Reference	by George Lynch	ISBN: 1-56884-095-0	$8.95 USA/$11.95 Canada
Word For Windows® For Dummies® Quick Reference	by George Lynch	ISBN: 1-56884-029-2	$8.95 USA/$11.95 Canada
WordPerfect® 6.1 For Windows® For Dummies® Quick Reference, 2nd Edition	by Greg Harvey	ISBN: 1-56884-966-4	$9.99 USA/$12.99/Canada

For scholastic requests & educational orders please call Educational Sales at 1. 800. 434. 2086

FOR MORE INFO OR TO ORDER, PLEASE CALL ▶ 800. 762. 2974

For volume discounts & special orders please call Tony Real, Special Sales, at 415. 655. 3048

"Macworld Complete Mac Handbook Plus CD covered everything I could think of and more!"

Peter Tsakiris, New York, NY

"Very useful for PageMaker beginners and veterans alike— contains a wealth of tips and tricks to make you a faster, more powerful PageMaker user."

Paul Brainerd, President and founder, Aldus Corporation

"Thanks for the best computer book I've ever read—Photoshop 2.5 Bible. Best $30 I ever spent. I love the detailed index....Yours blows them all out of the water. This is a great book. We must enlighten the masses!"

Kevin Lisankie, Chicago, Illinois

"Macworld Guide to ClarisWorks 2 is the easiest computer book to read that I have ever found!"

Steven Hanson, Lutz, FL

"...thanks to the Macworld Excel 5 Companion, 2nd Edition occupying a permanent position next to my computer, I'll be able to tap more of Excel's power."

Lauren Black, Lab Director, Macworld Magazine

Macworld® QuarkXPress 3.2/3.3 Bible
by Barbara Assadi & Galen Gruman
ISBN: 1-878058-85-1
$39.95 USA/$52.95 Canada
Includes disk with QuarkXPress XTensions and scripts.

Macworld® PageMaker 5 Bible
by Craig Danuloff
ISBN: 1-878058-84-3
$39.95 USA/$52.95 Canada
Includes 2 disks with PageMaker utilities, clip art, and more.

Macworld® FileMaker Pro 2.0/2.1 Bible
by Steven A. Schwartz
ISBN: 1-56884-201-5
$34.95 USA/$46.95 Canada
Includes disk with ready-to-run data bases.

Macworld® Word 6 Companion, 2nd Edition
by Jim Heid
ISBN: 1-56884-082-9
$24.95 USA/$34.95 Canada

NEWBRIDGE BOOK CLUB SELECTION

Macworld® Guide To Microsoft® Word 5/5.1
by Jim Heid
ISBN: 1-878058-39-8
$22.95 USA/$29.95 Canada

Macworld® ClarisWorks 2.0/2.1 Companion, 2nd Edition
by Steven A. Schwartz
ISBN: 1-56884-180-9
$24.95 USA/$34.95 Canada

Macworld® Guide To Microsoft® Works 3
by Barrie Sosinsky
ISBN: 1-878058-42-8
$22.95 USA/$29.95 Canada

Macworld® Excel 5 Companion, 2nd Edition
by Chris Van Buren & David Maguiness
ISBN: 1-56884-081-0
$24.95 USA/$34.95 Canada

NEWBRIDGE BOOK CLUB SELECTION

Macworld® Guide To Microsoft® Excel 4
by David Maguiness
ISBN: 1-878058-40-1
$22.95 USA/$29.95 Canada

Microsoft is a registered trademark of Microsoft Corporation. Macworld is a registered trademark of International Data Group, Inc.

For scholastic requests & educational orders please call Educational Sales, at 1. 800. 434. 2086

FOR MORE INFO OR TO ORDER, PLEASE CALL ▶ 800 762 2974

For volume discounts & special orders please call Tony Real, Special Sales, at 415. 655. 3048

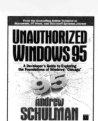

Unauthorized Windows® 95: A Developer's Guide to Exploring the Foundations of Windows "Chicago"
by Andrew Schulman

ISBN: 1-56884-169-8
$29.99 USA/$39.99 Canada

Unauthorized Windows® 95 Developer's Resource Kit
by Andrew Schulman

ISBN: 1-56884-305-4
$39.99 USA/$54.99 Canada

Best of the Net
by Seth Godin

ISBN: 1-56884-313-5
$22.99 USA/$32.99 Canada

Detour: The Truth About the Information Superhighway
by Michael Sullivan-Trainor

ISBN: 1-56884-307-0
$22.99 USA/$32.99 Canada

PowerPC Programming For Intel Programmers
by Kip McClanahan

ISBN: 1-56884-306-2
$49.99 USA/$64.99 Canada

Foundations™ of Visual C++ Programming For Windows® 95
by Paul Yao & Joseph Yao

ISBN: 1-56884-321-6
$39.99 USA/$54.99 Canada

Heavy Metal™ Visual C++ Programming
by Steve Holzner

ISBN: 1-56884-196-5
$39.95 USA/$54.95 Canada

Heavy Metal™ OLE 2.0 Programming
by Steve Holzner

ISBN: 1-56884-301-1
$39.95 USA/$54.95 Canada

Lotus Notes Application Development Handbook
by Erica Kerwien

ISBN: 1-56884-308-9
$39.99 USA/$54.99 Canada

The Internet Direct Connect Kit
by Peter John Harrison

ISBN: 1-56884-135-3
$29.95 USA/$39.95 Canada

Macworld® Ultimate Mac® Programming
by Dave Mark

ISBN: 1-56884-195-7
$39.95 USA/$54.95 Canada

The UNIX®-Haters Handbook
by Simson Garfinkel, Daniel Weise, & Steven Strassmann

ISBN: 1-56884-203-1
$16.95 USA/$22.95 Canada

Learn C++ Today!
by Martin Rinehart

ISBN: 1-56884-310-0
34.99 USA/$44.99 Canada

Type & Learn™ C
by Tom Swan

ISBN: 1-56884-073-X
34.95 USA/$44.95 Canada

Type & Learn™ Windows® Programming
by Tom Swan

ISBN: 1-56884-071-3
34.95 USA/$44.95 Canada

For scholastic requests & educational orders please call Educational Sales, at 1. 800. 434. 2086

FOR MORE INFO OR TO ORDER, PLEASE CALL ▶ 800 762 2974

For volume discounts & special orders please call Tony Real, Special Sales, at 415. 655. 3048